Chesapeake Bay Cooking
with John Shields

CHESAPEAKE BAY COOKING
with JOHN SHIELDS

The Companion Cookbook to the Public Television Series

John Shields

Broadway Books / New York

BROADWAY

Broadway Books titles may be purchased for business or promotional use
or for special sales. For information, please write to: Special Markets Department, Bantam Doubleday Dell Publishing Group, Inc., 1540 Broadway,
New York, NY 10036.

BROADWAY BOOKS and its logo, a letter B bisected on the diagonal,
are trademarks of Broadway Books, a division of Bantam Doubleday Dell
Publishing Group, Inc.

Library of Congress Cataloging-in-Publication Data
Shields, John (John Edward)
Chesapeake Bay cooking with John Shields : the companion cookbook to
the public television series / John Shields. — 1st ed.
p.   cm.
Includes index.
ISBN 0-7679-0028-6 (hardcover)
1. Cookery—Chesapeake Bay Region (Md. and Va.)   2. Chesapeake Bay
Region (Md. and Va.)—Description and travel.   I. Title.
TX714.S534   1998
641.59755′18—dc21   97-655   CIP

FIRST EDITION

Designed by Richard Oriolo
Photographs by Jed Kirschbaum
Map by Jackie Aher

98 99 00 01 02 10 9 8 7 6 5 4 3 2

This book is dedicated with love to my kitchen and life teachers, who gave me the joy and passion for the food of the Chesapeake Bay: Gertie, Mom-Mom, and Mealy. And to John Francis for his encouragement, support, and insight.

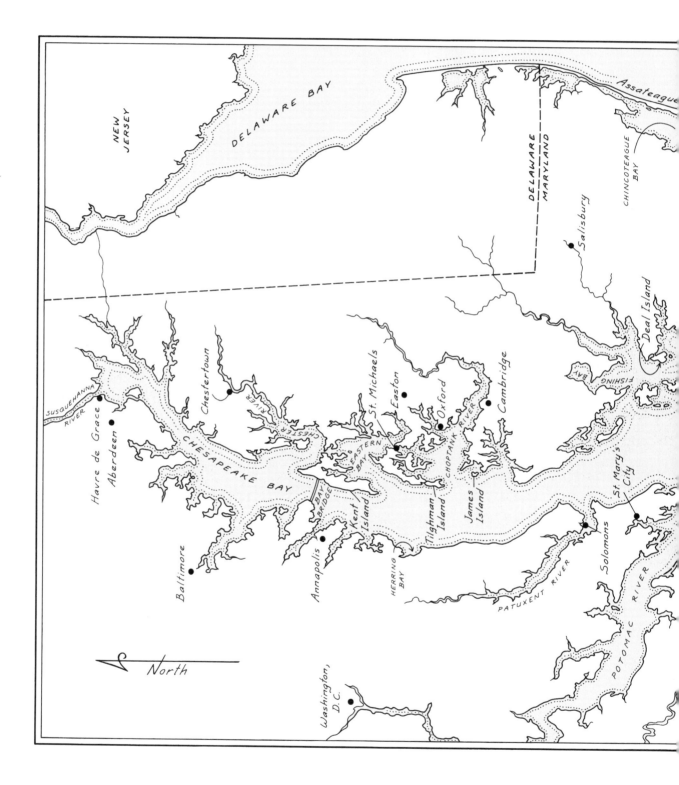

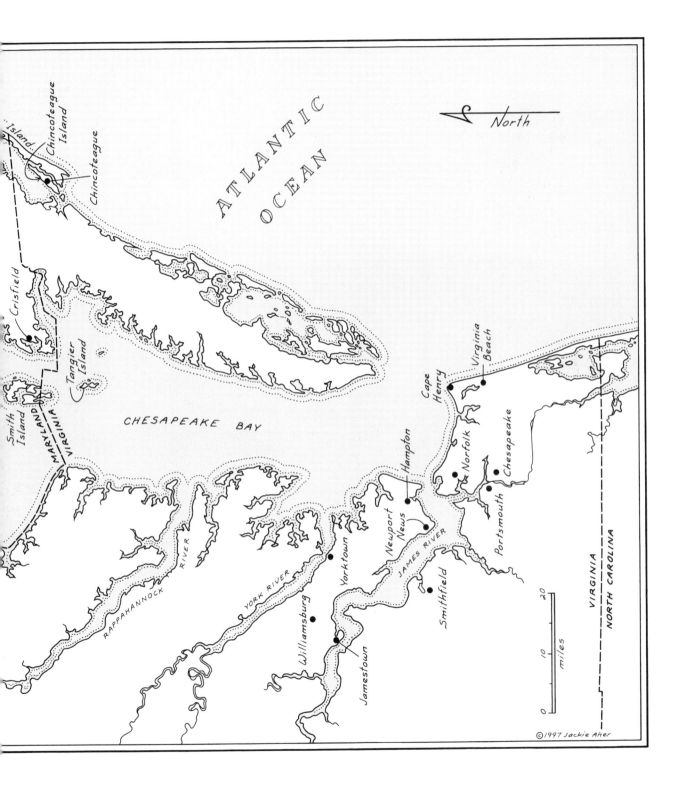

Contents

Acknowledgments

Mickey Rooney and Judy Garland made it look so easy. However, from my experience I have found that putting on a show—in this case, a television series coupled with a companion cookbook—requires the skill, talent, encouragement, and friendship of many, many individuals. It was seemingly eons ago and during a promotional tour for one of my cookbooks that Baltimore radio host Elane Stein suggested I speak with Mike Styer, then an executive at Maryland Public Television. Mike turned me over to producer Donald Thoms, who gave me an on-camera tryout. Thanks to these three people for planting the seed and helping me to bring *Chesapeake Bay Cooking* to life.

When it was time to literally "get the show on the road," and I began conversations in earnest with John Potthast, Maryland Public Television's Vice President of National Productions, whose support and guidance have been instrumental in bringing the series and the book to fruition. The crew and support staff at MPT have been incredible—hugs and crabs to Melissa Martin, Abbie Kealy, and Don Barto for our initial episodes and series development. More hugs and crabs go to my fantastic producer Beth Nardone and brilliant director Natalie Seltz for breathing new life into the series. Cooking on the road isn't quite as easy as it looks on a TV set at home, but our *Chesapeake Bay Cooking* crew made it seem effortless—thanks to Marlene Rodman, Terry Williams, John Miyagawa, Gordon Masters, and the rest of the MPT production crew. Others at MPT without whom I could not have successfully completed this project and who deserve much recognition include Lisa Delaney, Mary Helford, Mike Fevang, Susan Noonan, and Rich "Inside Scoop on Camden Yards" Dubroff.

While all this television production was taking place, a book had to be produced as well. God love Angela Miller, my agent, who listens to me with great patience yet keeps me on track, and who brought me into partnership with the remarkable staff at Broadway Books. Thanks to Bill Shinker, Broadway's publisher, who has assembled a talented group of people as will ever be found in the publishing business. My editor, Harriet Bell, has a reputation for being one of the best food editors in the country, and that reputation is well founded—thanks Harriet, you know your stuff and I'm glad to be working with you! Of course Harriet has assistance to complete her task, and all her team members have helped me greatly: Daisy Alpert and Lisa De Mairo kept me moving when I started to lag a little behind; Janice Race acted as the book's production editor extraordinaire; Roberto de Vicq de Cumptich created the splendid cover of this book; Richard Oriolo brought Chesapeake Bay cooking to life with his interior design; and Catlin Connelly and Trigg Robinson are making sure the rest of the world knows about my book and series. To them, and all the other people at Broadway who have worked on this project, my heartfelt thanks.

I have provided the recipes and text, but what would a book featuring the marvelous Chesapeake Bay region be without photographs? It was my lucky day nine years ago when I first met my now good friend and photographer, Jed Kirschbaum. This is our third book together, and Jed's dazzling photos never cease to amaze me. My appreciation also extends to Jeffery Bill, Assistant Director of Photography at the *Baltimore Sun*, for his zip drive wizardry. During our sessions photographing the food we were ably assisted by Jed's wife, Thelma, a food lover and exceptional cook, and by Jed's best friend, the late Dick Mayo. Dick, with his wicked sense of humor, was a real trouper during the long hours of arranging and rearranging the food shots; he died in a boating accident soon after we had finished the photography—Dick, you are sorely missed by us all.

I feel tremendously fortunate to be partnered with the State of Maryland's Department of Tourism in my Chesapeake Bay endeavors.

Dean Kenderdine, George Williams, and Liz Fitzsimmons of the Maryland Department of Tourism, along with the directors of tourism of each of Maryland's counties, share my passion for the Chesapeake and its people. They have been instrumental in making the series a reality. Thank you all.

In my hometown of Baltimore I have many thanks to convey. To my mentor and "Godmother from the West Side," Rikki Spector, who has kept me going through the long process of putting this series together, I send my love. When my spirits would sag my dear, sweet Rikki would perk me up, ever reminding me to stay focused and not to worry. Dave and Marla Oros, my good friends and business partners, have been there to see me through every trial and tribulation, keeping the faith in our projects even when mine would sometimes falter. Tony Sartori, my buddy since childhood, has been, still is, and forever will be the best cheerleader and PR man for which a guy could ask. Without Tony, his wife, Mary Garlington, and their son (my godson), Lil' A, I do not know how I would have made it through. After living a decade on the West Coast it has been wonderful to be back at home with my family. Mom-Mom (who started it all), my sister, Patricia, and her sons (my nephews), Joey and Tommy, Kathleen and Ralphie, Patrick, and Lynn and Priscilla—much love for all your support and strength. I am very grateful to Rich Ashley, my brother-in-law and business manager, who has been my confidante, adviser, and great friend for many years. Thanks also to Vaughn Milby for his friendship and the use of his gorgeous kitchen. Bonnie North has been a great help in scouting locations for the series—but Bons, next time we'll have to procure maps with larger print size or have our eyeglass prescriptions changed!

Last, but certainly not least, I must eternally thank John Gilligan, who gave up his career on the West Coast, packed his bags, and headed east to help create our production company. Typist, Web-page designer, cookbook editor, graphic artist, recipe-testing guinea pig, food stylist, personal trainer, research assistant, and associate producer of the *Chesapeake Bay Cooking* series are just a few of the hats this man wears, and wears quite well. I am blessed to have such a partner, traveling companion, and best friend.

These thanks are just the tip of the iceberg. My gratitude to Dolly LaViolette, Susan King, Susan Stiles Dowell, Mona Alves and Noreen McKeon, Jim Bruce, Alma Blackman, John and Gail Gilligan, Maggie McIntosh, the staff of Williams-Sonoma in Cross Keys, Elizabeth

Carduff, John Harris, Arlene Gillis, Glen Jordan, Linda Gerson, Robbie Fabian, Joanne Sutro, and the countless others I am undoubtedly forgetting at this moment. There have been so many fantastic people involved in every facet of both this cookbook and the cooking series that I could go on forever. My heartfelt thanks and appreciation goes out to you all for helping me bring the spectacular food and people of the Chesapeake Bay to the rest of the world.

Introduction

～～～

Welcome to the Chesapeake Bay. Tucked away in the middle of the Mid-Atlantic coast lies the Chesapeake Bay. While most of its eastern seaboard neighbors have become vast urban areas, transforming themselves into cosmopolitan centers, the Chesapeake region has quietly continued its more genteel way of life with a self-sufficient lifestyle and time-honored cooking traditions. Recently the Chesapeake has enjoyed a rediscovery by the rest of the country. Visitors from all parts are making the Bay a destination, perhaps seeking out an environment still relatively unspoiled that has a culture and way of life that recall simpler times, a style of living that is rapidly disappearing elsewhere.

For generations the Chesapeake and its inhabitants have kept a relatively low profile on the food scene, with many of their classic recipes and cooking preparations locked away in family recipe boxes or orally handed down from one generation to the next. For those who have not had the pleasure of sitting down to a hearty Chesapeake meal of blue crab, rockfish, fresh clams and oysters, chicken, waterfowl, country hams, and tangy barbecued meats—complete with all the trimmings—it is my pleasure to introduce this glorious region and its outstanding cuisine.

I grew up on the shores of the Chesapeake, feasting on the bounties of the Bay, enjoying the sweet meat of blue crab, briny Chincoteague oysters, and panfried wild rockfish. I delighted in eating freshly picked Silver Queen corn, vine-ripened red tomatoes, homemade country sausages, and salty, smoked Smithfield hams. I took pleasure in every bite of savory roasted wild goose, crisp fried chicken, and pies filled to nearly overflowing with fresh peaches, apples, blackberries, or strawberries laced with simmered rhubarb. Looking back I now realize that I was blessed to have grown up in a region rich with the best foods that land and water have to offer. As is often the case with locals, I took many of these culinary joys for granted. It's true about the best things in life being right under your nose: I traveled around the world in search of fine cuisine only to learn that some of the finest eating to be found was in my Chesapeake homeland.

Many people I speak to know of the Chesapeake Bay and its wealth of seafood—primarily crab and oysters—but are at a loss when asked about the Chesapeake's precise whereabouts. New York, Rhode Island, and Massachusetts are the most popular "possible" locations for the Bay. This inability to place the Chesapeake is ironic given its size. The Bay is the largest estuary in North America and spans across Maryland, Delaware, and Virginia, some two hundred miles in length. Its watershed reaches into four more states. Its forty-six hundred miles of shoreline and myriad of rivers and creeks, and thousands of acres of lush wetlands and marshes has made the Chesapeake a destination for boaters, hunters, and fishermen from all over the country.

The Chesapeake region is often referred to as "America in miniature" because of its wide diversity of terrain. On the western shores, rolling hills are thickly covered by forests that shade rippling streams, and along the middle of the western shoreline is an enormous expanse of sheer cliffs that dramatically drop to the Bay. Dotting the western reaches of the Bay are the great metropolitan cities of Baltimore, Norfolk, Virginia, and Washington, D.C. To the west the Chesapeake is vitalized by the streams and rivers springing forth from the Allegheny mountains (part of the Appalachian range) with their small self-sufficient towns seemingly trapped in time, tucked deeply into the mountains' hollers. On the Eastern Shore, the terrain is wide open and flat as far as the eye can see, with acres of farmland and orchards interspersed with groves of oak, maple, hickory, and pine trees, while the picturesque fishing villages on the shoreline are nestled into the Bay's inlets. The southern reaches of the Chesapeake are home to some of the most impressive marshes and wetlands still in existence in North America, breeding grounds for an extraordinary variety of wildlife: waterfowl, blue crab, muskrat, mink, and otter, to name but a few.

Starting at the mighty Susquehanna River to the north, the Chesapeake Bay extends the length of Maryland, the Delmarva (Delaware-Maryland–Virginia) Peninsula, and Tidewater Virginia, where its southern reaches merge with the Atlantic Ocean. Several rivers on the Bay's western shores are integral parts of America's rich history. The James River is the site of Jamestown, the first settlement in the New World; the Potomac is the flowing body of water most closely connected with Revolutionary American history and home to the nation's capital, Washington, D.C.; and the Patapsco River is where Francis Scott Key wrote "The Star-Spangled Banner" during the War of 1812.

Chesapeake cooking began in 1608 when, story has it, Captain John Smith guided his ship into the mouth of the Chesapeake Bay and landed in what was to become Jamestown, Virginia. From his writings it's clear that it did not take him long to discover that he and his crew had happened upon a veritable Garden of Eden. "The fish were so thick, we attempted to catch them with frying pans," Captain John wrote.

In a sense, John Smith's arrival was the first step in the development of today's Chesapeake Bay cuisine. By no means was Captain Smith's party the first to discover the biologically rich Bay, abundant with crabs, oysters, and clams. The original Keepers of the Waters were Indian tribes, and they called it as they saw it: "Chesapeake" in Susquehannock Indian language means Great Shellfish Bay. Judging from the amount of oyster shells found at former Indian village sites, it seems these early Chesapeake inhabitants had quite a taste for shellfish.

After John Smith's exploration of the Bay, the region would never again be the same. The colonists built towns and ports along the shores of the Chesapeake, and the Bay became the only convenient way to travel between Annapolis, Baltimore, Washington, Norfolk, Williamsburg, and Richmond. Great ports blossomed along its shore, and the Chesapeake Bay was soon teeming with ships bringing goods from Europe and carrying away New World riches such as tobacco, smoked hams, and cotton.

The new residents of the Chesapeake developed a cooking style that remains with us today. Early Chesapeake Bay kitchen duty was not an easy task given the crude, sometimes cumbersome kitchen facilities of the times, resulting in a provincial cooking style in which one pot contains all the ingredients for the meal, such as a savory venison or chicken stew or a Smithfield ham and potato casserole. Seafood soups and chowders were made very simply with the freshest possible ingredients, resulting in dishes like clam chowder and oyster stew. These dishes necessitated the development of excellent timing skills: Each ingredient must be added at just the right moment so that one meal emerges from the pot, yet each food must retain its individual characteristics.

What exactly is Chesapeake Bay cooking? Blue crabs, oysters, clams, finfish, terrapins, ducks, geese, wild turkeys, pheasants, rabbits, chickens, deer, muskrats, squirrels, beef, pork, lamb. However, if a visitor is asked what Chesapeake Bay food is all about, the likely reply will be "Chesapeake Bay blue crab." The locals have had a culinary love affair with the feisty crustaceans for a long time—but to sum up Chesapeake Bay cooking as simply crabs does a great injustice to the true variety of this regional cuisine.

A large amount of land lies adjacent to the Bay and its tributaries, and Chesapeake cuisine has distinctly local characteristics. The plantation flavors of the southern reaches of the Bay are fashioned into the famous St. Mary's County Stuffed Ham and Smithfield Crab Imperial. On the Eastern Shore, where you "catch the fish in frying pans," cooking is quick and simple as in Crisfield Crab Cakes, Chincoteague Single-Fried Oysters, and a smoked bacon–wrapped Baked Stuffed Rockfish. There are the dishes of Baltimore's European ethnic enclaves, such as the Italian-influenced Chicken Breasts with Crabmeat and Mozzarella, the German-inspired Grandma Wissman's Sour Beef and Dumplings, and the Polish-styled East Baltimore Herring Salad with apples, beets, and black walnuts. The Chesapeake also lies south of the Mason-Dixon Line. The ingredients and cooking techniques of the South are ingrained in its culinary heritage, witnessed by African-American cooking traditions in the seafood-rich Pauleen's Seafood Gumbo, Johnnycake enriched with stoneground yellow cornmeal, and pieces of crisp Maryland Panfried Chicken smothered in pan gravy.

Chesapeake cookery is one of the oldest and simplest of North America's regional cuisines with certain traits that shape its preparation, flavor, and presentation. The classic crab cake calls for lumps of blue crabmeat, lightly bound and spiced, producing a mound of crab that can be lightly fried or broiled. Chesapeake oysters are served on the half shell, or bathed in hot milk and enriched with butter in a sublimely elegant stew. Pots of manninose, or soft-shell clams, are carefully cooked with wine and aromatic vegetables until the fragile shells open and release their briny juices, producing a delicious dipping broth. Pork is slowly transformed into hams, sausages, and bacon in the legendary smokehouses that dot the shores of the Bay. And in Chesapeake kitchens, crab pots handed down from generation to generation hold steaming baskets of jumbo blue crabs for boisterous feasts.

The people who live around the Chesapeake Bay introduce many of the recipes in this book through their words and images. The finest examples of Chesapeake cuisine are found in the kitchens of watermen, farmers, proprietors of small back-road inns and taverns, and most especially at community events where locals come together to celebrate the seasonal holidays, rites of passage, and their common love for the Chesapeake Bay.

The people of the Chesapeake are fun-loving, warm, and welcoming. They respect the ways and forces of nature and its impact on the Bay and their lives, and they live with a hopeful trust in the future. They accept life on life's terms. This simplicity and honesty spills over into the cuisine with an intense pride in the quality of the food.

I remember as a small boy in Baltimore my grandmother Gertie's excitement as each season approached, promising new treasures for the table. We would marvel at the first asparagus of spring, breathe in the sweet fragrance of ripe Eastern Shore melons, and laugh at the antics of blue crabs as they escaped from overflowing bushel baskets. When my grandmother prepared the food, be it vine-ripened tomatoes or fresh-from-

the-Bay rockfish, I was always aware of the quiet reverence she felt for those gifts of the land and sea.

This reverence is still felt by those of us who know the Chesapeake Bay as a source of culinary abundance and pleasure. Now, however, we must be more careful than ever with how we treat this precious resource. It is a national treasure; we must not take it for granted; we have been entrusted with keeping its waters life-giving. Traveling around the Bay while researching this book gave me new hope as I watched everyday people performing great deeds to help keep the Chesapeake alive and well, not just for themselves but for future generations.

A new vision for the Chesapeake kitchen becomes necessary as we enter the twenty-first century. Here on the shores of the Chesapeake Bay and its far-reaching tributaries, it seems appropriate to sit back and reflect on what has happened during the past century in our communities, families, and homes. Where are we now in our relationship with the Chesapeake, and how can we modify our lifestyles to make changes that will improve the quality of our lives and of the surrounding environment? It is apparent that some of these changes are crucial for the Chesapeake Bay and mankind's survival. When we begin to think about the many issues involved in the sustainability of man on this planet, it can become overwhelming. But as we have seen in recent times, sometimes the most effective change is a small action, on the grassroots level. And it often happens right in our own homes.

A new eating trend that has recently become popular is really the oldest method for recipe planning: using seasonal foods. Simply put, it means using fresh foods grown in your region during the season in which they are grown. If there is too much of one crop being harvested, you preserve the surplus and by doing so, you supplement your recipes during the winter months. Studies have found that using seasonal foods in your diet helps your body obtain maximum nutritional benefits. And purchasing seasonal foods is not only good for you, it is good for the local economy and local communities. Small farmers begin to thrive. A climate is created for people who want to continue or return to farming, and for those who want to begin, thus reducing acres available to urban sprawl. And by shopping locally you begin to reconnect with others in your community and thus the daily task of purchasing food becomes more social and enjoyable.

How does this kind of thinking and behavior affect our environment? When we take time to prepare our meals with care and understand how our food nurtures us, we cannot help but develop a heightened awareness of our natural environment. It's all connected. Let's look at the spectacular Chesapeake Bay. For us locals, it is our lifeline—we are blessed with a region rich in seafood, game, waterfowl, and an exceptional array of produce. Just by using these wonderful, local, seasonal treasures, we become constantly aware of the Chesapeake and our common link to it.

I regard the Chesapeake as our communal soup pot. When creating a delicious meal for loved ones, what kind of cook would pour dirty motor oil into the soup pot? Would you throw in a cup and a half of battery acid, or a touch of oven cleaner? I hope not, but when we put blinders on and believe our day-to-day actions are not the same as mixing these type of toxins into our soup pots, we are sadly mistaken. Again, this awareness is paramount, and we can begin in our own kitchens, stores, local farmers' markets, or right in our own backyard vegetable gardens.

All around the Chesapeake Bay and the United States, communities and organizations are forming as people come together, join hands, hearts, and minds, and say, "No more. We will not allow monetary interests to destroy our precious natural treasures, and ultimately the fabric of our lives." One such organization is the Chesapeake Bay Foundation (CBF), the largest environmental group on the Chesapeake.

CBF is involved in all matters affecting the health of the Bay and its watershed, which encompasses six states. It has been highly successful initiating both state and federal legislation which has positively affected the Chesapeake, including land use, wetlands protection, and the reduction of chemical pollutant runoff. CBF also facilitates extensive educational outreach programs, giving thousands of children and young adults firsthand knowledge of the ecology of the Bay, and the foundation has helped set up and organize community groups to reduce pollution through various stream, river, and creek adoption programs, giving citizens hands-on experience to help save the Bay.

To quote William Baker, president of the Chesapeake Bay Foundation: "Restoring the Bay is possible only if we do not limit ourselves to pursuing that which can be easily achieved. Success will come if we set our sights high and work cooperatively. Anything less will be overwhelmed by the crush of population growth. History may record that a well-meaning, but ultimately timid society, lost the Chesapeake Bay in the last decade of the twentieth century. Or it can be written that the Bay was saved. The choice is ours." And many of those choices begin in our Chesapeake kitchens.

Now let's do some cooking, Chesapeake-style. Sit back and relax while I take you off the highways and onto the byways and backroads of the Chesapeake. Listen to some local folk, hear a few tall tales, and sample the recipes of my friends, family, and fellow chefs. Some are fancy recipes and some are "just the way God intended it to be cooked." Try out those that sound good to you and get the saliva glands working. My bet is that you'll be spending a good number of hours in your own kitchen sampling these Chesapeake delights.

Captain John Smith, the Chesapeake's first press agent, wrote, "Heaven and earth never agreed better to frame a place for man's habitation." And Captain John was quite right. Welcome to what we natives call the "land of pleasant living."

Ingredients of the Chesapeake Region

Regional cuisines around the country and the world have distinctive ingredients, spices, and herbs, and these ingredients are used in certain ways or combinations that give a cuisine its unique characteristics. Pungent curries flavor the recipes of India and Southeast Asia, while hot chilies and pots of long-simmered, cumin-scented frijoles are trademarks of Mexican and Southwestern dishes. The same is certainly true of Chesapeake

Bay fare: This regional cuisine assimilates the Chesapeake's wealth of culinary resources, time-honored cooking traditions, and rich variety of cultures to form a New World flavor all its own.

As would be expected, one of the Chesapeake cuisine's premier ingredients is a reflection of the Bay's local harvests: An abundance of apple orchards has made apple flavorings prominent through ciders, applejack, and cider vinegars. Old and New World cooking techniques and processes were integrated to create extraordinary "new" products, such as smoked country hams that are salt-cured and wood-smoked hickory-cured bacon. And as an important shipping and trade center, the Baltimore harbor was scented with spices from all over the world, which resulted in a seasoning concoction that came to be synonymous with Chesapeake cooking: the ubiquitous Chesapeake seasoning blend.

I have compiled a list of the most influential ingredients that bring flavor to the Chesapeake Bay's rich culinary heritage. Many of the star ingredients and products such as crabs, oysters, and poultry have received more individual attention in their respective chapters, so I did not mention them in this section. While many of the ingredients listed here are available throughout the country, I have provided a resource list for some of the more specialized ones at the end of the book (see pages 274–276).

Apple Cider is a flavoring that has been used by Chesapeake cooks for generations—not surprisingly, since plentiful amounts of apples have always grown here. In addition to the commercial growers, many folks have an apple tree or two of their own. Local orchards make their own cider and applejack. *Applejack* is a ciderlike product that has been allowed to ferment. It has a tart apple flavor and packs a wallop due to its alcohol content. Apple cider products may be used in marinades, sauces, and dressings, but are more widely used as braising liquids with pork roasts, chops, sauerkraut, and baked apples.

Beer and the Chesapeake go together like bread and butter. Beer is used for drinking, of course: It is the time-honored companion drink to go with steamed crabs, crab cakes, soft-shell crabs, oysters, fried fish, and barbecued foods; come to think of it, just about anything washes down well with beer. Locals also cook with beer in a variety of ways. It is an absolute must for steamed crabs and steamed shrimp, as well as for marinades and batters for poultry and fish, such as beer-battered soft-shell crabs and seafood and poultry fritters. Beer is also often used as a braising agent for meats, cabbage, sausages, and sauerkraut.

Black Walnuts are to Chesapeake cooking what pecans are to the cuisine of the Deep South. Black walnut trees are common around the Chesapeake and their slightly bitter meats often become integrated into cakes, pies, and cookies. When toasted, the strong-flavored nuts may be used in leaf lettuce or composed salads. If you are purchasing black walnuts, buy only the quantity you will use over a short period of time; due to their high fat content, they tend to go rancid if stored for too long. The more common English walnut may be substituted in Chesapeake recipes, although its flavor is more subtle and less distinct than that of the black walnut.

Country Bacon is not only a Bay breakfast staple but it is also used as a seasoning in all styles of soups, stews, and casseroles. It is used for larding meats and seafood and often is cut into pieces and added uncooked to foods that require long periods of simmering, such as greens, soups, and stews. Its by-product, bacon fat or drippings, is used for sautéing vegetables, frying meats and seafood, and in corn bread and muffin batters.

Country Hams were smoked in Early America by hanging them in chimneys. But with the arrival of certain spices to the New World, other smoking and curing techniques came into use. Eventually every self-respecting plantation or manor house possessed its own smokehouse, and distinctive regional flavors emerged from these structures. Today, Maryland's country ham and Virginia's Smithfield country ham predominate in the Chesapeake Bay area, and they have become synonymous with fine dining throughout the nation as well.

Country ham is quite different from simple cured ham; country ham is the product of a much more complicated and lengthy curing, smoking, and aging process. Most country hams are dry cured, that is, they are rubbed with a mixture of salt and spice that is absorbed into the skin; other country-style hams are brined in a sugar-and-spice solution in barrels. Afterward, both types are smoked and later hung in paper bags to age from six months to three years. Hams that are aged over one year become quite dry and salty, as is the case with the Smithfield ham. As a country ham ages, its taste becomes rich, full, and complex; the process is not unlike the aging of fine wine. Simple cured hams, that is, mass-produced

hams, have a less full, almost neutral taste, and are very lightly smoked, if at all, with little to no aging.

Maryland country hams are aged from two to three years and possess a rich, smoky flavor due to a curing process that has been handed down from one generation of smokehouse operators to the next. These hams complement the Bay's seafood, and the two have been paired to create numerous dishes. Southern Maryland is famous for its stuffed ham, which is not only a feast but also a culinary feat.

Smithfield hams, produced in Smithfield, Virginia, are highly salted aged hams possessing a distinctive flavor and texture that has gained them worldwide acclaim. These hams were the New World's first export and they graced the tables of European nobility. The hogs that are raised for these hams are strictly peanut fed. The Smithfield process to cure and age the hams has not changed since colonial times. In fact, the method is so precise that it is protected by law—only a ham cured within the Smithfield town limits can bear the name.

The Chesapeake region's country hams are not only served up on their own, but the bones, skin, and meat are used to flavor vegetables, soups, stews, and many one-pot dishes. The flavor imparted by country hams to other foods is a major element of the unique Chesapeake Bay taste.

Hominy is one of the original staples of the Chesapeake Bay kitchen, predating Western European–style kitchens by quite some time. Indians living in what is now known as Tidewater Virginia knew how to make hominy from corn. The Chesapeake-style hominy, pearl hominy, is different from its Southwestern cousin, posole. Posole is a whole grain hominy that still contains the germ and is much more coarse in texture than the Chesapeake variety. Posole is also soaked in an alkali, or lye solution, and needs to be rinsed before using. In contrast, pearl hominy is much more tender than posole. It is processed with steamed water in a reverse osmosis process, and when it is canned, it congeals, producing a texture similar in appearance to canned cranberry sauce. When cooking pearl hominy, there is no need to rinse it; simply break apart the lumps with a fork before using.

Pearl hominy is quite versatile, working well with, and in, many dishes. It is processed under the label of Manning's Hominy by the Lake Packing Company. Mrs. Manning created her unique brand of pearl hominy in Baltimore during the late 1800s, when Baltimore was the center of the nation's canning industry. She and her husband started a backyard cannery near the Patapsco River, and they sold her hominy door-to-door by horsedrawn cart.

Horseradish permeates Baltimore, which is known as one of the horseradish centers of the country because of the number of local companies that prepare and bottle it, rather than because of per capita consumption. Around the Bay it is used to jazz up cocktail sauces, oysters, clams on the half shell, seafood sauces, and all manner of edibles, plain and fancy.

Mace is made from the ground outer covering of the nutmeg seed. It has traditionally been used in Chesapeake cooking to season everything from seafood, stews, meats, poultry, and game to desserts. In eighteenth-century Chesapeake cookery, before mace was sold ground, recipes for seafood soups or stews called for a blade of mace, which referred to a single strand.

Molasses is a by-product of the refining of cane sugar. At each stage of the refining process a different type of molasses is formed. The final and darkest stage is what is known as blackstrap molasses, which was widely used in Early American recipes. Nowadays, molasses is found in many Chesapeake cakes, pies, and breads. I prefer the type of molasses one step up from blackstrap, simply called dark molasses. It has a more agreeable taste that is not quite as heavy and intense as that of blackstrap.

Chesapeake Seasoning is a blend of herbs and spices that is typically used around the Bay to flavor seafood, poultry, and meat. Given the amount of crab and other seafood that is prepared in Chesapeake kitchens, the distinctive aroma of this seasoning scents the air on many a humid day. Several local companies prepare this salt-based blend, which contains a slew of tastes, such as dry mustard, mace, ginger, paprika, cardamom, cloves, bay leaves, thyme, and cayenne pepper.

A staple in every Bay kitchen, the Chesapeake seasoning's fragrance and unique taste bring back memories to us locals of glorious Chesapeake meals. There are many brands on the market.

Oyster Liquor is the name given to the juices surrounding the oyster meat inside the shell. When shucking oysters, always save this liquid. If the oysters are purchased already shucked, pour the oysters and their liquor into a sieve or strainer over a bowl to catch the juice. This reserved liquor, with its concentrated briny taste, is invaluable for use in oyster or seafood soups, stews, and casseroles.

Tabasco Sauce is a hot sauce of Southern origins dating back to the Civil War. It is made from red hot chilies that have been ground and aged with salt in oak barrels for three years, then mixed with vinegar. It is used in many Chesapeake sauces, and is often drizzled onto freshly shucked raw oysters on the half shell. It's quite hot, so go easy with it.

Worcestershire Sauce, judging from the amount of it used in Bay cooking, would appear to have been invented and manufactured on the shores of the Chesapeake. This is not the case, however. It originally comes from England and is made from vinegar, molasses, garlic, anchovies, and other spices. The locals use it liberally in soups, crab cakes, sauces, meat loaf, and various casserole recipes.

Crabs

Out of the Bay, Baltimore ate divinely," Baltimore sage H. L. Mencken once wrote. "Any poor man could go down to the banks of the river, armed with no more than a length of stout cord, a home-made net on a pole, and a chunk of cat's meat, and come home in a couple of hours with enough crabs to feed his family."

While I'm unsure about "cat's meat," I do know generations of locals have been using eel, chicken necks, and other unusual foods for bait to catch plenty of crabs, piling the steamed crustaceans sky-high on picnic tables for family and friends.

Folks around the Chesapeake Bay not only steam crabs, they use crab to make moist and flavorful crab cakes. Sometimes they just eat the crabs simply prepared on white bread—when the crabs are soft-shells, of course. And crab is often used as an ingredient, as in a cheesy Crabmeat Omelet Filling (page 209), when locals prepare an entree.

The influence of the blue crab on Chesapeake cuisine is quite extensive, so I've broken down this chapter into five parts:

Crabformation

Blue crab is perhaps the most famous denizen of the Chesapeake Bay. To seafood lovers around the world, the Chesapeake is synonymous with this amazing crustacean. The Latin name for the blue crab is *Callinectes sapidus,* which translates to "savory beautiful swimmer." And that it is. These crabs are emblematic of Chesapeake Bay cuisine, and have become a local icon, emblazoned on signs, billboards, trucks, flags, and T-shirts all along the Bay's thousands of shoreline miles. The crabs are also quick, alert, feisty little scrappers, so handle with care. I've seen many a bitten finger.

As each Memorial Day approaches, we Chesapeake Bay folk emerge from our winter hibernation filled with a sense of excitement that is almost unbearable. Oak trees are full of newly formed leaves, azaleas are in bloom, people perched precariously on ladders are hanging screen windows, and warming breezes are blowing away the evening chill—all sure signs that summer is coming. And summer means no school, carefree lazy days and, most importantly, blue crab!

Although we may claim the blue crab as our own, to be perfectly honest its true range stretches from Rhode Island to Florida and the Gulf of Mexico. Statistics indicate that 50 percent of the weight of the total crab catch in the United States is blue crab; of that amount, 60 percent comes from the Chesapeake Bay. We feel reasonably sure that this means the blue crab enjoys its Chesapeake home, and a better neighborhood it could not ask for. The Chesapeake's many tributaries, coves, and lush marsh grasses provide perfect conditions for the blue's propagation and thriving numbers.

With the arrival of spring, the watermen have put up their dredges and tongs from the oyster season and baited their crab pots for the opening of crabbing season on the Bay. For these rugged watermen, the blue crab is the most reliable catch of the yearly fishing season. It is the basis for a prosperous seafood industry.

Chesapeake watermen, it seems, have an inherent knowledge of the blue crab's behavior and sometimes unreliable habits. During their ten-to-fifteen-hour workdays, the watermen can tell what the crabs are up to by the wind direction, the phases of the moon, and, sometimes, by just plain sniffing them out. They have conjured up countless names for the crustaceans over the last hundred years: jimmies, sooks, peelers, softs, she-crabs, buckrams, doublers. The list goes on and on.

Jimmies are male crabs. They are the best to use for steaming and can be distinguished from the females by an inverted T-shape on their underside. Sooks, immature females, have a fuller, rounded apron. The females mostly end up in the picking plants where their meat is removed from the shells to be sold as crabmeat.

There's also the matter of hard-shell and soft-shell crabs. Blue crabs are in the hard-shell stage most of their lives; however, as they grow they molt, or shed their shells, up to twenty-three times in their three-year life span. Each molting results in a 25 to 40 percent increase in shell size. So, to make a long story short, a soft-shell crab is a blue crab that has just molted and backed out of its shell.

The harvesting of soft-shell crabs is a painstaking task. Watermen can discern when a crab is ready to molt by markings on the body and legs. These crabs, which are dubbed "peelers," are moved to holding floats where they are constantly checked to see when they have shed their shells. Once the crabs have backed out of their shells they are considered "softs," and they are taken out of the water; this stops the rehardening of the shell. The crabs are then graded according to size, packed, and shipped. What started out as a small cottage industry less than a hundred years ago is now one of the biggest seafood businesses of the Chesapeake Bay.

The blue crab, along with the oyster, has been a major culinary influence on Chesapeake regional fare. The crab cakes of the Baltimore & Ohio Railroad dining cars are legendary. During the 1920s, deviled crab was all the rage on the eastern seaboard, keeping the Chesapeake's crab pickers working around the clock.

The ethnic heritages of the locals helped shape the crab dishes of the Chesapeake, such as English and French-style soups, bisques, and soufflés. There are also African-American–inspired gumbos and Creole-based dishes, and many pasta dishes and crab-laden sauces from Italy and the Mediterranean.

The blue crab has been and always will be a key element in the cooking and eating lives of Chesapeake Bay locals. We steam them, fry them, fritter them, in the shell, out of the shell, or soft-shell. To put it mildly, if you can't already tell, we love them!

Blue crab season on the Chesapeake runs from the beginning of May through early October, depending on the weather. There are almost as many methods and strategies for luring the blue crabs from the Bay waters as there are crabbers. The commercial fishermen generally use trotlines, which are long lines baited at intervals that run along the bottom of the water and are anchored at both ends. Or they use crab pots: baited, mazelike traps that are quite easy for the crabs to get into, but nearly impossible from which to escape.

Seasoned sport crabbers usually employ the crabbing procedures used by commercial fishermen; however, "weekend crabbers" are a different story. These carefree crabbers will try almost anything to seduce the blues from the Bay. They crab from bridges, off piers and docks, and on the edge of the water. "Chicken neckers" they are called, and they are responsible for a large percentage of the crabs caught for backyard crab feasts.

Grandpap Rabuck's "Crab-Cough" Cough Syrup

Buck Rabuck, a steel mill worker at Bethlehem Steel in Sparrows Point, and his son Ty are a veteran crabbing team who have spent many a year on the Chesapeake pursuing their crabbing endeavors, to the delight of their neighbors in Dundalk, Maryland, who reap the fruits of the guys' toil at huge crab feasts Buck hosts in his backyard.

Buck says the best crabbing is in the very early morning, the evenings, or in rainy weather, and that sometimes after spending long hours on the water "it gets you in the chest," producing wheezing coughs. No big problem for the Rabucks. They are a crabbing family from way back, and Buck's got the cure: his grandpap's homestyle cough syrup.

2 ounces glycerine
2 ounces rock candy

1 pint rye whiskey (Pikesville brand works real good)

"The rock candy cuts the phlegm in your throat, the glycerine is a healing agent, and the rye whiskey makes it drinkable. For medicinal purposes only: Take one shot a day, sometimes two if you're feeling real poorly."

The Meat of the Matter

For the weak of heart or not so nimble of finger, blue crabmeat is available cooked, picked, and packed in containers, ready to use. (To order blue crabmeat by mail, see pages 274 and 275.) Crabmeat is graded according to the part of the crab it came from. Crabmeat may be sold fresh, which is the best; pasteurized, which is the next best; and frozen, which will do nicely, although some of the flavor is lost when it is defrosted. There are four grades:

Jumbo Lump is the very best crabmeat money can buy: big, clean pieces with absolutely no shell or cartilage—all crab. Jumbo lump is the type I use in crab cake recipes when I want to really impress.

Backfin, as the name implies, is meat taken from the backfin section of the crab. These are large pieces of lump and some broken body meat with a low shell content. This is an excellent product for crab cakes and most other crab recipes.

Special identifies meat from the entire body of the crab, which includes both jumbo lump (a very small amount) and flaky pieces which are picked from the center chambers of the crab. Higher in shell content than lump and backfin, this type requires careful picking over to remove small bits of cartilage. I use this type in soups and as a filler to blend with jumbo lump or backfin for a more economical crab cake.

Claw is the dark, sweet meat from the claws. Excellent for soups and chowders, it also makes a very good, lower-cost crab cake. Claw meat tends to have a higher moisture content, which requires a touch more binding to hold the cakes together. There is also a cocktail claw available. This is the large claw of the crab with the shell removed and the meat intact—the tip of the shell is left on to accommodate dipping the claw meat in sauces.

The Other White Meat

Although many connoisseurs regard the blue crab as the best on the market, this is a matter of taste dictated by individual preference and geographic location. Other excellent crab varieties harvested and available in North America may be used as an ounce-for-ounce or pound-for-pound substitute for blue crabmeat. The moisture content generally is higher in these other types of crabmeat, however, so I suggest draining the excess moisture from them as much as possible. To drain, spread out the crabmeat in a colander with a plate under it and gently press on the meat so the moisture drains through the holes. If you feel more draining is warranted, place the colander with the plate and crabmeat in the refrigerator for an hour to continue draining. When making crab cakes, a bit of additional binding (cracker crumbs, bread crumbs, or mayonnaise) may be necessary to hold the cakes together when the crabmeat is on the damp side.

Although I'm a stickler for using only blue crab, keep in mind that I'm a Chesapeake Bay boy and that's where my loyalties lie. Many of my friends whose culinary skills I greatly respect swear by the crab of their respective regions. Do try other crab varieties if blue crab is not available in your area. The resulting dishes will be tasty and satisfying.

Dungeness Crab is much larger than blue crab. It weighs anywhere from 1½ pounds to 4 pounds or more, with a succulent, sweet meat that is a bit stringy. From the Pacific Coast, it is sold live, boiled, or as picked meat.

Alaskan King Crab is a crustacean of mammoth proportions, often measuring 10 feet across claw-to-claw and weighing 10 to 15 pounds. Luckily this crab with snowy-white meat is not sold live, only frozen, or previously frozen, in the form of legs and claws.

Stone Crab is caught in waters from North Carolina to Texas, but it is most abundant in Florida. Only the claw meat, which is sold frozen, is eaten.

Imitation Crab is just that—a bit of pressed, tinted, and flavored fish. It is of lesser quality than the other crabmeats and is best utilized in casseroles and dips.

Canned Crab is the canned tuna of the crab world and is similar in quality to imitation crabmeat. Different varieties are canned in many parts of the world and sold in the United States.

It's August on the Chesapeake Bay and so incredibly hot and humid that it is a challenge just to get from the hammock to the iced tea pitcher. As locals prop themselves up in backyard chaise longues and watch their children run through sprinklers, a Chesapeake spirit comes wisping through the neighborhood, taking possession of heretofore rational souls. Crabs. Hot steamed crabs. Big ole heavy jimmy crabs full of meat and encrusted with spices. Once the spirit has taken hold, you just have to have your fill of those succulent creatures, no ifs, ands, or buts. A person who just moments before was laid low with near heat prostration leaps from the lounge chair and begins the preparations. Phone wires burn as the crab-alert is sounded to friends and family. There is going to be a crustacean revival meeting and plans must be made. Whether it be the home crab pot fired up or everyone meeting at a Chesapeake crab house, there's going to be a crab feast tonight.

    The crab feast of the Chesapeake Bay is a traditional gathering, much like clambakes in New England or barbecues in Texas. Folks get together to feast on and celebrate the most prized gift of the Chesapeake, the blue crab. During the summer months there's always a party going on, with steamed crabs piled high, beer flowing freely, and the smell of spicy crab seasonings wafting through the humid summer air.

    To an outsider the backyard crab feast may seem like an all-hell-has-broken-loose occasion. Several generations gather—aunts, uncles, cousins, brothers, sisters, in-laws, outlaws—all jumping madly about while bushel baskets of live crabs are loaded into the family crab pot. Children run screaming down the lawn, pursued by renegade crabs that have escaped

The Chesapeake Bay Crab Feast

A Chesapeake Crab Feast Tale

Talking and spinning tales are the main ingredients of a successful feast, and one favorite subject is former crab feasts, especially tales of heroism and adventure. "Back in '48 all the crabs were at least ten inches across and heavy as horses . . . Your uncle Elmer could pick a crab clean as a whistle with one hand, while drinking down a mug of beer with the other without taking a breath . . . Remember the time when that crab got hold of Sis's toe, and she ran round the backyard, crab clamped onto her toe, like a bat outta hell?"

I was always particularly intrigued by Aunt Marge's tale of dearly departed Aunt Seal.

"Now, your aunt Seal loved a good crab feast almost as much as she loved her pink Catawba wine.

"That last crab feast over at Uncle Elmer's, she was laughing and singing, 'I'm Gonna Wash That Man Right Outta My Hair.' In fact, Elmer had to get her down off the table.

"Anyhow, I seen her polish off at least two dozen crabs and two bottles of pink Catawba. And she said that was just for starters. Thing that always got me was how she'd pile Uncle Elmer's secret seasonings on the crabs and then suck it off her fingers. She just kept going, eating about two, three more dozen crabs, piled with seasoning, and two more bottles of pink Catawba.

"Round then, Seal said she needed to run inside and take off her girdle. She didn't come back for quite some time, so Aunt Treasie went looking for her. Next thing I know, I heard Treasie screaming like a banshee. She found that poor dear Seal dead as a doornail on the powder room floor, and I thought my heart would break!"

After this tale was told, the next hour would inevitably bring the great family debate: What killed Aunt Seal, Uncle Elmer's seasonings or the pink Catawba?

---

from overflowing crab baskets. Hot steamed crabs are dumped onto picnic tables covered with newspapers. Then, in a flash, the crabs are being devoured by the entire clan—mallets tapping, shells flying, and pitchers of cold beer flowing.

However, backyards are not the only locales where these feasts take place. When not wanting to go through all the rigmarole and cleanup involved in putting on one's own crab feast, many Chesapeake locals opt to head on over to one of their favorite crab houses. Out-of-town visitors who have heard of these world-famous temples of crab often insist that they be taken to one on their first night's stay.

A few of these crab hackeries are fancy dinner spots, but nine out of ten have the look of a club basement moved one floor up. They are lined with tables covered with heavy brown paper or out-of-date newspapers. These crab joints are teeming with boisterous patrons, ready to party. They are staffed with a tribe of professional "girls," hair piled high, wing-tipped glasses, orthopedic shoes. The waitresses, their daughters, and their mothers have all been slinging crab since the dawn of crustacean creation. The girls mean business and can handle the roughest, rowdiest customers by sliding their glasses to the ends of their noses and staring the trouble-makers down. They also provide lightning-fast, table-side, crab-picking demonstrations for novices.

In Baltimore, at a Gunning's Crab House Veteran Waitresses Symposium and Confab, Sharon Willis, Vickie Leonard, and Renée Kline talk of the ins-and-outs of picking, slinging, and other blue crab matters. Waitress Vickie, after discussing countless crab-picking techniques, leaned over to me and asked in dead earnest, "Can you even remember anybody teaching you *how* to eat crabs? You just figure you're born knowing how!" No, Vickie, I don't remember. And I believe that if you put that question to just about any Chesapeake native, you'd get the same answer. We accept it as a skill genetically bestowed upon Chesapeakans.

New to this crazy let-your-hair-down world of crab feasts? Don't worry. Take yourself on down to the crab house, where the girls, those seasoned experts and crab slingers, will be your personal tutors in the art of crab picking.

If you're a businessman, or a bit refined looking, you will be instructed to first remove your coat and tie. Next, roll up those sleeves or you'll look like a rookie. Okay, now you're dressed properly. Take a deep breath and let it out slowly. Let go of your inhibitions. The idea here is to make a big mess. "Go to town, hon. The dirtier you get, the better you'll like them crabs!"

Crabs are steamed with spicy seasonings that coat the shell. Do not ask for these spices to be washed off. Your ignorance will show. "That's the good stuff on there, hon. It tastes great."

Out-of-towners sometimes complain that these feasts are too much work for too little crabmeat. Developing crab-picking skills does take time, and even after one learns how to pick a crab clean, the quantity of crabmeat is not the point. The crab feast is a delightful and fun-filled Chesapeake social ritual. Grab some friends, a bushel of crabs, and plenty of beer and enjoy.

Official Chesapeake Bay Crab House Picking Instructions

H ere is an official set of instructions, but remember: You'll find as many methods for crab picking as you'll find waitresses. Each crab house (and waitress) has its favorite technique.

Have the crabs unceremoniously dumped on the newspaper or brown paper.

Flip the crab over.

Flip open the apron.

Flip off the top shell.

You'll notice a bunch of stuff hanging out, the spongy gills and the devil.

Pull the gills and devil out; throw them on the newspaper. That's what the paper's for.

The yellow stuff in the middle is the "mustard." Actually it's fat and quite delicious. Eat it.

Break the body in half, leaving the legs and claws on.

Squish down the backfin end (flippers) and twist it around. You'll get a big piece of backfin meat.

Pull the swimming legs and claws off of the body, one by one. There will be a little piece of meat at the end of each. Suck it. Save the claws.

Take a paring knife and split each half of the crab through horizontally, exposing chambers of crabmeat. Use the paring knife to pick out the meat.

Now here comes the mallet. Take a big claw and break it apart at the joint. Break each half in two by using the mallet to drive the paring knife through the claw, and gently pull out a whole piece of claw meat. This takes practice.

Keep repeating the above steps until you've eaten your fill. Remember that practice makes perfect. Before you know it you'll be picking crabs like one of the gals down at the picking plants.

Ginger Beer Fruit Punch   Serves 10 to 15

Ginger beer, a nonalcoholic beverage, has been a favorite at Chesapeake crab feasts for generations. While similar in taste to ginger ale, ginger beer has a stronger, more prominent flavor of ginger than ginger ale does. This recipe continues that tradition, making an effervescent fruity punch with a zesty ginger bite.

2 cups cranberry juice	Sugar, to taste
2 cups pineapple juice	Ice cubes
2 cups grapefruit juice	3 bottles (12 ounces each) ginger beer

Mix the juices together in a pitcher. Check to see if the mixture is too tart for your taste. If so, sweeten with a bit of sugar. Pour into a punch bowl over ice. Add the ginger beer just as the company's coming in the door.

Cold Beer is the crab pickers' all-time favorite beverage. I can't smell one without thinking of the other.

Dead Man is a one-step-beyond synonym of guts and devil, denoting the legendary end result.

Devil is another term for the innards and guts. This is also the entity you may meet face-to-face if you insist on eating this part of the crab.

Flippers are the rear propellers of the crabs. When the flippers are gently twisted and pulled from the body of the crab, big beautiful lumps of backfin meat will come with them. Fantastic eating at a crab feast.

Guts is a self-explanatory, graphically accurate description of a crab's intestinal area. See also devil.

Ice Cold Ginger Ale is the drink for beer abstainers, kids, and designated drivers, as is Ginger Beer Fruit Punch.

Lungs are the gills, or spongy mass, exposed when the top shell is removed.

Mallets are for gently cracking the crabs' claws so that full pieces of meat will emerge, not for smashing up the crabs into little bits with the hope of getting to the meat.

Feast Equipment and Lingo

Growing Up on the Bay

Being a child at a Chesapeake Bay crab feast is not an easy thing, to which I can personally attest. The memories of certain events still haunt me, such as the anatomy lessons from great-aunts and -uncles. "Now this here's the 'devil.' Look at it. It'll kill you! Don't you ever eat it, you hear me?" Of course I wouldn't eat it! Hell, I didn't even want to touch it.

Or late in the evening, when the backyard feasts were over, kids would be busy chasing lightning bugs and the bells of the ice cream man could be heard in the distance. That's when Aunt Treasie would perk up and grab the nearest child by the elastic waistband of his Bermuda shorts, pull him over to her lawn chair, and declare, "Do you know that if you eat ice cream right after you eat crabs, you'll get sick as a dog? Yeah! Them crabs will turn to rock, right in your stomach! Yes siree, sick as a dog!" All the other elders would nod their heads in silent agreement. Now where did they come up with that one? You got me, but it stuck. To this day, I don't know even one of my young crab-picking compatriots who actually ever dared to put the ice cream theory to the test.

Mustard is the yellowish matter in the center of the crab body. It is the crab's fat. This is some good eating.

Newspapers are the ritualistic covering for the feast table. They are practical because during the meal you throw everything right onto the paper, and when the feast is complete, you just roll up the whole shebang. A little hint in case the trashman's not coming around for a day or two: Sprinkle some soap powder (Tide is good) over the top of all the crab shells before rolling up the paper. It keeps the odor down.

Paring Knives are handy for cutting the crab body in half to expose the chambers of meat and for picking the meat out with the tip of the knife.

Swimming Legs are the small legs of the crab. I do not advise trying to pick the meat out of these. Just suck out the meat from the end of the leg that was pulled from the body of the crab.

Crabs

2 cans (12 ounces each) flat beer
    (see below)
2 cups distilled white vinegar
Ice water (optional)

24 live large male blue crabs
    (jimmies)
³/₄ cup Chesapeake seasoning
6 tablespoons kosher salt

Pour the beer and vinegar into a steamer pot or a large heavy pot with a tight-fitting lid. Put a round raised rack that is tall enough to clear the liquid into the pot. Bring the liquid to a boil.

While the pot is coming to a boil, fill a tub with ice water, if desired, and put the crabs in it for 3 minutes or so.

Mix the Chesapeake seasoning and salt together in a small bowl. Place a layer of crabs on the rack in the pot. Sprinkle with a generous coating of the seasoning. Working quickly, continue layering and seasoning the crabs until all the blues are in the pot and you have used up all the seasoning. Put on the lid and steam over medium-high heat until the crabs are bright red, about 25 to 30 minutes. Remove the crabs with tongs.

Serve hot. Leftover crabs may be refrigerated and either eaten cold the next day or picked for crabmeat to use in your favorite recipe.

Every Chesapeake family has its own recipe for steamed crabs—actually "recipe" is a misnomer, as it is more a process rather than an exact recipe. Some insist on washing the crabs before steaming, but others claim that washing takes away the brininess of the crab. Another method is to place the live crabs in an ice water bath before cooking. This icing process numbs the crabs, making them easier to handle, keeps the crabs from losing their claws during the steaming process, and helps the seasonings stick to the shells.

Serves 4 novice pickers or 2 pros

Flat Beer

Locals insist on flat beer whenever steaming crabs or shrimp. They feel flat beer does not impart the harsh, almost metallic taste that fresh beer does. To flatten beer, simply pour it into a bowl and leave it at room temperature for an hour or two. A trick the natives use to hasten the flattening process is to sprinkle a little salt into the beer—they swear it flattens the beer quicker than who-struck-John.

Crab Feast Side Dishes

At a crab feast, many people eat crabs and nothing else, but each clan has its own traditions. Here are some Chesapeake favorites for accompaniments. Keep in mind that crab feasting is a messy affair—it's not a time when you want to use a knife or fork—as you eat crabs with your *hands*. The vegetable side dishes mentioned below—tomatoes, corn, and assorted salads—are not actually eaten with the crabs, but are placed on a buffet table and left for crab revelers to enjoy between rounds of crab picking. We call it time-out food.

Bowls of vinegar (cider or red wine) for dipping the picked crabmeat.

Melted butter for dipping. Lobster fans and out-of-towners are quite fond of this pairing. It's not the traditional Chesapeake way, but it is tasty.

Platters of sliced tomatoes.

Mounds of sweet corn on the cob.

Assorted salads such as coleslaw, potato salad, macaroni salad, or marinated vegetables.

Desserts are not traditionally served but could include strawberry shortcake, lemon meringue pie, peach cake, watermelon, or pickled watermelon rind. Remember, no ice cream!

Crab Cakes

Paris may have its foie gras, New Orleans its gumbo, and Spain its paella, but the folks living along the shores and far-reaching tributaries of the Chesapeake Bay have their own signature dish: the crab cake. No dish is more closely associated with the Chesapeake and the blue crab than the mighty crab cake.

When asked to describe their aquatic culinary prize, locals are hard-pressed to come up with a concise description. "Well, hon, it ain't a confection, and you don't normally bake them, and sure ain't a dee-sert . . . naa . . . it's not exactly made in a cake pan either . . . well . . . oh hell, it's more like a ball of crab all spiced up and fried."

Now the crab cake may well be a unifying source of fierce regional pride, but its many recipes produce more squabbling, feuding, and heated family debates than either the local ball club or politics. Tucked away in each family's archives is The Crab Cake Recipe. It is the only one; it is the best; and all the others are wrong. Period. I've witnessed barroom brawls over which restaurant or tavern serves the best crab cake. Research on the ubiquitous cake provides tremendous pleasure for the stomach, but is, all in all, a dangerous business.

The Chesapeake crab cake has been a staple of the local diet dating back to at least the sixteenth century. Crab cakes were made by local Indian women who mixed the crabmeat with herbs, vegetables, and cornmeal, forming them into small cakes that were fried in sizzling hot bear fat. They were called "cakes of crab." The preparation technique has changed only slightly over the centuries, with the exception that bear fat is not used for frying these days.

What remains true of Bay crab cakes today is that different regions of the Chesapeake have their own style of cakes. On the Eastern Shore folks prefer their crab cakes prepared simply so that the flavor of the crab is allowed to shine through. This happens by moistening the crab just slightly with lemon butter and adding virtually no filler, or what locals sometimes refer to as "sawdust." Since there is little binding to hold the cakes together they must be broiled and handled with great care. The end result for a crab purist is sheer bliss: an absolutely pure, unadulterated crab cake. Folks from other parts of the Bay, particularly near the big cities, scoff at this notion and find these cakes bland. They prefer the style of cake that is flavored by a spicy, mayonnaise-enriched batter with a bread or cracker binding. The cake is then either fried or broiled. A third version of a crab cake, which is common in the southern parts of the Bay, is made by using a lightly seasoned cream sauce to hold the crabmeat together. The cakes are then chilled to firm them up and later lightly coated in bread crumbs and lightly fried. There are crab cake recipes for a full spectrum of tastes, yet people continue to experiment and discover even more.

Now, what's all the fuss about? They're just little balls of crab all mushed together, right? Wrong. Here's a guide to the structural makeup of a crab cake.

Choosing Crabmeat for Crab Cakes

This is like choosing a pet. Should it have a fancy pedigree or be a mixed breed? This all depends on your tastes and, in some cases, your wallet. The crab cake dishes in this book list the crabmeat grade the recipe's originator believes works best, but feel free to substitute any type of crabmeat.

Jumbo Lump Crabmeat is what purists generally insist on. Crab cakes made with all jumbo lump are best sautéed or broiled rather than deep-fried.

Backfin Crabmeat makes a beautiful cake of large, delectable lumps of crab and a bit of body meat. Just a touch of binding holds the backfin cake together nicely. This meat is pefect for any style crab cake you may wish to prepare.

Special Crabmeat does not make a particularly nice crab cake on its own, but works quite well when mixed with jumbo lump or backfin.

Claw Meat provides a dark, sweet, and less expensive crab cake. These cakes, while not regarded as top of the line, are what are served in many coffee shops and neighborhood taverns, as well as at local fairs and carnivals. They are quite tasty and economical for large gatherings and parties.

Mixed Cakes are made from a blend of two or more types of crabmeat. My favorite mix is half jumbo lump and half special, but actually any combination will work. Try your own formulas to find what you like best.

Bindings

These are the ingredients used to hold together and season the crab cakes. The wet ingredients are mixed with various seasonings, tossed with the crabmeat, and held together with breading. The principle is to try to use the least amount of breading possible to get the cakes to hold together without exerting pressure to compact them. Some traditional binding ingredients are eggs, mayonnaise, cream, cream sauces, seasonings, bread crumbs, cracker crumbs, and bread soaked in milk.

Seasonings

The local seasoning concoctions—quantities, ratios, secret mixing methods—can enhance or mask the crab, and may or may not bring tears to the eyes. The following seasonings are the ones most commonly used in crab cakes, as well as in many other typical Chesapeake blue crab dishes.

Lemon Juice means juice from freshly squeezed lemons, not the bottled stuff.

Mustard, including dry and prepared (Dijon is especially popular), is often added to crab cake mixtures.

Chesapeake Seasoning is virtually synonymous with crabs. Can't have one without the other—not around the Chesapeake anyway. For years I have been a spice courier, traveling back and forth across the country delivering this concoction to homesick Chesapeake Bay natives. The seasoning is a must for steamed crabs and perfect for crab cakes, crab imperials, and the like.

Parsley is sometimes chopped and added by the tablespoonful.

Prepared Horseradish is the white kind found in jars in the grocer's dairy case.

Tabasco Sauce or any hot chili sauce is made from Tabasco peppers, or other small spicy chili peppers that have been fermented with vinegar.

Worcestershire Sauce is of English origin and is made from vinegar, molasses, garlic, anchovies, and other spices.

These are the most important steps in making successful crab cakes.

Picking Pick the crabmeat over carefully for shells. Be gentle: The lumps of crabmeat are the beauty of the crab cake and must not be torn apart while picking.

Batter Mix the batter (that is, the eggs, mayonnaise, seasonings) in a separate bowl from the one that holds the crabmeat. Sprinkle the breading (that is, the bread crumbs or cracker crumbs) over the crabmeat and then pour the batter on top of the breading. Gently toss or fold the ingredients together with a rubber spatula or your hands, again taking great care not to break up the lumps of crab.

Forming Form the crab cake mixture into slightly flattened, rounded masses. Some folks recommend gently packing the mixture into an ice cream scoop and then tapping it out. It can, of course, be formed by hand or molded into small, rounded cups. Again, *gently* is the key word when describing how to form a cake. Do not compact the crab cakes too much. They should be held together loosely. The size of the cake depends on the maker. Most cakes weigh about $2^{1}/_{2}$ to 3 ounces each. Recipes that call for 1 pound of crabmeat will yield eight cakes, enough to feed four people. Veteran crab cake makers feel it is best to refrigerate the cakes for at least an hour before cooking. This allows the binding to absorb some of the moisture so that the cakes hold together better.

Preparing and Forming Crab Cakes

Cooking

Frying is the most common cooking method for crab cakes. They can be panfried in hot cooking oil (usually vegetable or peanut oil), about $1/2$ inch deep, or deep-fried, with the oil heated to 375°F.

Sautéing is high-class crab cake cooking, generally using clarified butter, olive oil, or a combination of the two. When sautéing crab cakes it is best to form the cakes just a tad thinner so that they will heat all the way through, which will take about four minutes per side.

Broiling is one of the best ways to cook cakes, because the flavor of the crab does not have to compete with that of the cooking oil. All you need to do is brush the cakes with a little melted butter if desired and place them about three inches from the heat in a preheated broiler until nicely browned. Plan on broiling about eight to ten minutes per side.

Sauces

Locals are quite opinioned about what type of sauce, if any, should be served with crab cakes. Lemon wedges are always served with cakes, but here are some other favorites.

Tartar Sauce (page 34) is the most traditional accompaniment to crab cakes.

Mustard Either a prepared, horseradish-laden type or Dijon mustard will do.

Red Wine Vinegar or Cider Vinegar Just a dab will do.

Rémoulade Sauce (page 37) is a classic French-inspired sauce that is a nice change with cakes.

Chesapeake Hollandaise Sauce Chesapeake Hollandaise Sauce (page 48) and other sauces from the hollandaise family are impressive with a fancy crab cake dinner.

Accompaniments

At restaurants and taverns along the Bay, most crab cakes are served with french fries and mounds of fresh coleslaw. At home everyone has a favorite accompaniment. Try saltines—that's right, hon, sit a piece of cake on top of the cracker and go for it. Potato salad, sliced ripe tomatoes, fresh steamed asparagus, cucumber salad, corn on the cob, corn bread, and biscuits are other possibilities.

1 egg
2 tablespoons mayonnaise
1 teaspoon dry mustard
1/2 teaspoon freshly ground
   black pepper
1 teaspoon Chesapeake
   seasoning
2 teaspoons Worcestershire
   sauce
Dash of Tabasco Sauce

1 pound backfin crabmeat,
   picked over
1/3 cup saltine cracker crumbs
Vegetable oil, for frying
   (optional)
Clarified butter (see Note)
   and/or olive oil, for sautéing
   (optional)
Tartar Sauce (recipe follows)
   and lemon wedges, for
   accompaniment

Gertie's Crab Cakes

Gertie Cleary hailed from Baltimore's Greenmount Avenue and her cooking was legendary throughout St. Ann's parish and northeast Baltimore. Her crab cakes are my absolute favorite. I must, however, admit my bias. Gertie was my grandmother, and I grew up on these wonderful spiced morsels of crab. This recipe is in the most traditional style of Bay crab cakes. It uses a slightly spiced mixture of mayonnaise and egg, and is lightly bound together with cracker crumbs.

Serves 4

Mix the egg, mayonnaise, mustard, pepper, Chesapeake seasoning, Worcestershire, and Tabasco together in a blender or mixing bowl until frothy. Place the crabmeat in a bowl and sprinkle on the cracker crumbs. Pour the egg mixture over the top. Gently toss or fold the ingredients together, taking care not to break up the lumps of crabmeat. Form the cakes by hand or with an ice cream scoop into 8 mounds about 3 inches in diameter and 3/4 inch thick. Do not pack the mixture too firmly. The cakes should be as loose as possible, yet still hold their shape. Place the cakes on a tray or platter lined with wax paper, cover, and refrigerate for at least 1 hour before cooking.

Pour oil into a heavy skillet to a depth of about 1 1/2 inches. Heat the oil and fry the crab cakes, a few at a time, until golden brown, about 4 minutes on each side. Remove with a slotted utensil to paper towels to drain. Or broil the cakes: Slip them under a preheated broiler until nicely browned, turning to cook evenly, about 4 to 5 minutes on each side. Or sauté the cakes: Heat a small amount of clarified butter or olive oil, or a combination, in a skillet and sauté the cakes, turning several times, until golden brown, about 8 minutes total cooking time.

Serve at once, with Tartar Sauce and lemon wedges on the side.

Note: To clarify butter, place solid unsalted butter into a heavy-bottomed pot and slowly melt over a low heat. When the butter is completely melted, remove from the heat. There will be three distinct parts of the butter remaining: a foam on the top; a clear, golden-colored liquid in the center; and a milky liquid on the bottom. The trick is to separate the golden liquid from the foam and milky solids.

First, skim off the foamy topping and discard. Next, with a small ladle, carefully remove the golden liquid to a clean, dry container, being careful not to take up any of the milky solids from the bottom. The clear, golden butter is clarified butter and is excellent for most sautéing needs.

Tartar Sauce Makes 1¹/₂ cups

1 cup mayonnaise
¹/₂ cup finely chopped dill
pickle
¹/₄ cup minced onion

2 tablespoons chopped parsley
1 tablespoon dill pickle juice

Mix all the ingredients together in a bowl. Chill for at least 1 hour before serving.

Dirty Gertie Serves 1

This nasty-sounding drink will "put hair on your chest," a phrase my uncle Rob used as a selling point when persuading you to try something you wouldn't normally do. It is actually a "fishy" version of a Bloody Mary. For the ultimate in drink garnish, hang a peeled, deveined, and steamed jumbo shrimp on the glass.

1¹/₂ ounces vodka
1 tablespoon fresh lemon juice
1 tablespoon Worcestershire sauce
¹/₄ teaspoon Chesapeake seasoning
Dash of freshly ground black pepper

¹/₂ teaspoon prepared horseradish
3 dashes of Tabasco Sauce
2 parts tomato juice
1 part clam juice, fresh or bottled
Celery stick, for garnish

Fill a tall glass with ice. Pour in the vodka, lemon juice, Worcestershire, Chesapeake seasoning, black pepper, horseradish, and Tabasco. Stir. Fill the glass with a mixture of tomato and clam juice. Stir well. Garnish with the celery stick.

Note: To regulate chest hair growth, increase or decrease the amounts of horseradish and Tabasco accordingly.

1 pound jumbo lump crabmeat,
   picked over
1 cup crushed saltines
1/2 cup mayonnaise
1 egg
1 tablespoon Dijon mustard
1 tablespoon Worcestershire
   sauce

Dash of Tabasco Sauce
Vegetable oil, for frying
   (optional)
Clarified butter (see pages
   33–34) and/or olive oil, for
   sautéing (optional)
Tartar Sauce (page 34)

Spread the crabmeat out in a flat pan and sprinkle the crushed saltines over the top.

Mix together the mayonnaise, egg, mustard, Worcestershire, and Tabasco in a small bowl. Pour the mayonnaise over the crabmeat and gently toss or fold the ingredients together, taking care not to break up the lumps of crabmeat. Let the mixture sit for 2 to 3 minutes before forming the cakes.

Form the cakes by hand or with an ice cream scoop into 8 mounds about 3 inches in diameter and 3/4 inch thick. Do not pack the mixture too firmly. The cakes should be as loose as possible, yet still hold their shape. Place the cakes on a tray or platter lined with wax paper, cover, and refrigerate for at least 1 hour before cooking.

Pour oil into a heavy skillet to a depth of about 1 1/2 inches. Heat the oil and fry the crab cakes, a few at a time, until golden brown, about 4 minutes on each side. Remove with a slotted utensil to paper towels to drain. Or broil the cakes: Slip them under a preheated broiler until nicely browned, turning to cook evenly, about 4 to 5 minutes on each side. Or sauté the cakes: Heat a small amount of clarified butter or olive oil, or a combination, in a skillet and sauté the cakes, turning several times, until golden brown, about 8 minutes total cooking time.

Serve at once, with Tartar Sauce on the side.

Faidley's World Famous Crab Cakes

Faidley's Seafood stall, the Chesapeake seafood centerpiece of Baltimore's world-renowned Lexington Market, is the home of Charm City's most famous crab cake. Nancy and Bill Devine preside over the bustling family-run business. Nancy often serves as Maryland's Seafood Marketing Association's ambassador, dashing off to Europe with crabs and steaming equipment in tow, hosting Baltimore-style crab feasts held for food aficionados on the Continent. These cakes are light on seasoning with a slight infusion of Dijon mustard and a fair amount of cracker crumbs, a combination that produces a moist, yet light, almost airy crab cake.

Serves 4

Crab Cakes Rémoulade

These crab cakes become extraordinarily tasty with the addition of sautéed bell peppers, green onions, and a hot mustard infusion. The result is a refreshingly new kind of crab cake. Rémoulade Sauce, a classic French mayonnaise-based sauce infused with capers, mustard, and herbs, is a marvelous accompaniment for just about any crab cake recipe.

Serves 4

Rémoulade Sauce (recipe follows)
1 pound backfin or jumbo lump crabmeat, picked over
4 tablespoons ($^1/_2$ stick) butter
2 tablespoons finely diced yellow onion
$^1/_4$ cup minced green onion
$^1/_2$ small green bell pepper, seeded, deveined, and finely diced
$^1/_2$ small red bell pepper, seeded, deveined, and finely diced
1 egg
2 tablespoons mayonnaise
2 teaspoons Worcestershire sauce
1 tablespoon coarse-grain mustard or any prepared hot mustard
$^1/_2$ teaspoon salt
$^1/_4$ teaspoon freshly ground black pepper
$^1/_8$ teaspoon cayenne
$^1/_4$ cup fine dry bread crumbs

COATING
2 eggs
$^1/_2$ cup milk
$^1/_2$ cup all-purpose flour
1 cup fine dry bread crumbs

Vegetable oil, for frying

Prepare the Rémoulade Sauce and chill for several hours.

Place the crabmeat in a mixing bowl and set aside.

Melt the butter in a saucepan over medium-high heat. Add the yellow onion, green onion, and green and red bell peppers and sauté until soft, about 5 minutes. Set aside to cool to room temperature.

Combine the egg, mayonnaise, Worcestershire, mustard, salt, black pepper, and cayenne in a mixing bowl. Mix in the sautéed peppers. Sprinkle the $^1/_4$ cup bread crumbs over the crabmeat and pour the egg mixture over the top. Gently toss or fold the ingredients together, taking care not to break up the lumps of crabmeat. Form the mixture into 8 cakes about 1 inch thick. Do not pack the mixture too firmly. The cakes should be as loose as possible, but still hold their shape. Place the cakes on a tray or platter lined with wax paper, cover, and refrigerate for at least 30 minutes before coating.

To prepare the coating, combine the eggs and milk in a bowl and beat until well mixed. Place the flour and bread crumbs in separate bowls. Dust each cake lightly in flour, dip in the egg-milk mixture, and then coat well with bread crumbs. Chill the cakes for at least 1 hour before cooking.

Pour oil into a heavy skillet to a depth of about 1½ inches. Heat the oil and fry the crab cakes, a few at a time, until golden brown, about 4 minutes on each side. Remove to paper towels to drain briefly.

Serve at once, with the Rémoulade Sauce on the side.

Rémoulade Sauce Makes about 2½ cups

1 cup mayonnaise
6 tablespoons finely minced
    celery
2 tablespoons finely minced
    green onion
1 tablespoon chopped parsley
½ teaspoon minced garlic
2 tablespoons coarse-grain
    mustard

1 tablespoon chopped capers
2 tablespoons ketchup
2 tablespoons Worcestershire
    sauce
1 teaspoon Tabasco Sauce
1 teaspoon paprika
¼ teaspoon salt

Mix together all the ingredients in a bowl. Cover and chill for several hours before serving.

Black and Blue Crab Cakes

Susan Gunn, aka Susoise, vivacious chef extraordinaire and graduate of Baltimore's Culinary Institute, developed these mildly bruised, but-oh-so appealing crab cakes. The recipe is a truly fascinating blend of the traditional Chesapeake-style crab cake, the blackening method of New Orleans, and a fragrant haute cuisine butter sauce. These crab cakes may also be served as an appetizer: Simply form the mixture into sixteen cakes rather than eight.

Serves 4

1 pound jumbo lump crabmeat, picked over
²/₃ cup mayonnaise
¹/₄ cup sour cream
¹/₄ cup fresh lemon juice
¹/₄ cup Dijon mustard
1 tablespoon Chesapeake seasoning
¹/₂ teaspoon Worcestershire sauce
¹/₂ teaspoon Tabasco Sauce
2 tablespoons chopped parsley
¹/₂ cup fine dry bread crumbs
Blackening Spice (recipe follows)
Reddened Butter Sauce (recipe follows)
Clarified butter (see pages 33–34), for sautéing

Place the crabmeat in a large mixing bowl and set aside.

Combine the mayonnaise, sour cream, lemon juice, mustard, Chesapeake seasoning, Worcestershire, Tabasco, and parsley in a small bowl. Mix well. Sprinkle the bread crumbs over the crabmeat and pour the mayonnaise mixture over the top. Gently toss or fold the ingredients together, taking care not to break up the lumps of crabmeat. Form the mixture into 8 mounds about 3 inches in diameter and 1 inch thick. Do not pack the mixture too firmly. The cakes should be as loose as possible, yet still hold their shape. Place the cakes on a tray or platter lined with wax paper, cover, and refrigerate for at least 1 hour before cooking.

Prepare the Blackening Spice and the Reddened Butter Sauce. Keep the sauce warm over very low heat.

Heat a large cast-iron skillet over high heat until smoking hot (the hotter the better). Dip each cake in clarified butter and roll in the spice. Fry for 3 to 4 minutes on each side.

Serve at once with the Reddened Butter Sauce.

Note: Whenever using this blackening method, be sure you are working in a well-ventilated area. This process produces a lot of smoke, so put on the exhaust fan and open the windows or the smoke alarms will be wailing.

Blackening Spice Makes about 2²/₃ cups

½ cup paprika
½ cup Chesapeake seasoning
¼ cup cayenne
1 tablespoon dried oregano
1 tablespoon dried basil
1 tablespoon dried thyme leaves

1 tablespoon onion powder
1 tablespoon garlic powder
1 teaspoon ground cumin
1 teaspoon freshly ground black
   pepper

Combine all the ingredients in a small bowl and mix well.

Reddened Butter Sauce Makes about 1½ cups

1 tablespoon olive oil
1 tablespoon minced onion
1 teaspoon minced garlic
Juice of 1 lemon
½ cup dry white wine
1 tablespoon tomato paste
2 cups heavy (whipping) cream

1 teaspoon Blackening Spice
   (optional)
4 tablespoons (½ stick) butter,
   cut into small pieces
1 teaspoon chopped parsley
Salt and freshly ground black
   pepper, to taste

Warm the olive oil in a small saucepan over medium-high heat. Add the onion and garlic and sauté for 2 minutes. Add the lemon juice and wine. Bring to a boil and reduce slightly. Whisk in the tomato paste and cream. Continue cooking until reduced by half. Add the Blackening Spice, if using, reduce the heat to low, and slowly whisk in the butter, piece by piece. Remove from the heat. Add the parsley, salt, and pepper. Keep warm until ready to serve.

Crisfield Crab Cakes

I the waterfront town of Crisfield, Maryland— self-proclaimed Seafood Capital of the World—the locals can't see taking a sterling commodity such as crabmeat and covering it up with a lot of heavy sauces. True to form with the Eastern Shore cooking philosophy of using simple preparations to let the crabmeat "do the talking," these cakes are flavored with a lemon butter, bound with bread crumbs, and lightly fried. Pure, unadulterated, and mouth-watering crab cakes are the Eastern Shore trademark.

Serves 4

1 egg, beaten
8 tablespoons (1 stick) butter, melted
1 tablespoon fresh lemon juice
1 tablespoon Worcestershire sauce
2 tablespoons chopped parsley
1 pound backfin crabmeat, picked over
1 cup dry bread crumbs
Vegetable oil, for frying (optional)
Clarified butter (see pages 33–34) and/or olive oil, for sautéing (optional)
Tartar Sauce (page 34) and lemon wedges, for accompaniment

Mix together the egg, butter, lemon juice, Worcestershire, and parsley in a small bowl. Place the crabmeat in a bowl and pour the egg mixture over the top. Mix gently, sprinkle with bread crumbs, and toss. Form the cakes by hand into 8 mounds about 3 inches in diameter and ³/₄ inch thick. Do not pack the mixture too firmly. The cakes should be as loose as possible, yet still hold their shape. Place the cakes on a tray or platter covered with wax paper, cover, and refrigerate for at least 1 hour before cooking.

Pour oil into a heavy skillet to a depth of about 1¹/₂ inches. Heat the oil and fry the crab cakes, a few at a time, until golden brown, about 4 minutes on each side. Remove with a slotted utensil to paper towels to drain. Or broil the cakes: Slip them under a preheated broiler until nicely browned, turning to cook evenly, about 4 to 5 minutes on each side. Or sauté: Heat a small amount of clarified butter or olive oil, or a combination, in a skillet and sauté the cakes, turning several times, until golden brown, about 8 minutes total cooking time.

Serve at once, with Tartar Sauce and lemon wedges on the side.

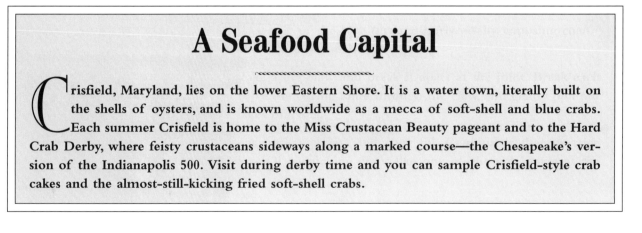

A Seafood Capital

Crisfield, Maryland, lies on the lower Eastern Shore. It is a water town, literally built on the shells of oysters, and is known worldwide as a mecca of soft-shell and blue crabs. Each summer Crisfield is home to the Miss Crustacean Beauty pageant and to the Hard Crab Derby, where feisty crustaceans sideways along a marked course—the Chesapeake's version of the Indianapolis 500. Visit during derby time and you can sample Crisfield-style crab cakes and the almost-still-kicking fried soft-shell crabs.

1 egg
3 slices of white bread
1 tablespoon mayonnaise
1 tablespoon Dijon mustard
2 teaspoons Chesapeake
   seasoning
1 tablespoon snipped parsley
   (optional)

1 pound jumbo lump or backfin
   crabmeat, picked over
Vegetable oil, for frying
   (optional)
Clarified butter (see pages
   33–34) and/or olive oil, for
   sautéing (optional)
Tartar Sauce (page 34)

Beat the egg in a bowl. Remove the crusts from the bread and break the slices into small pieces. Add to the egg. Mix in the mayonnaise, mustard, Chesapeake seasoning, and parsley, if using, and beat well. Place the crabmeat in a bowl and pour the egg mixture over the top. Gently toss or fold the ingredients together, taking care not to break up the lumps of crabmeat. Form the cakes by hand or with an ice-cream scoop into 8 mounded rounds about 3 inches in diameter and ³/₄ inch thick. Do not pack the mixture too firmly. The cakes should be as loose as possible, yet still hold their shape. Place the cakes on a tray or platter covered with wax paper, cover, and refrigerate for at least 1 hour before cooking.

Pour oil into a heavy skillet to a depth of about 1¹/₂ inches. Heat the oil and fry the crab cakes, a few at a time, until golden brown, about 4 minutes on each side. Remove with a slotted utensil to paper towels to drain. Or broil the cakes: Slip them under a preheated broiler until nicely browned, turning to cook evenly, about 4 to 5 minutes on each side. Or sauté the cakes: Heat a small amount of clarified butter or olive oil, or a combination, in a skillet and sauté the cakes, turning several times, until golden brown, about 8 minutes total cooking time.

Serve at once, with Tartar Sauce on the side.

Senator Barb's Spicy Bay Crab Cakes

The honorable Senator Barbara Mikulski is an east Baltimore gal through and through. Her Capitol Hill style is legendary, and so are her crab cakes. They may be one of the reasons she keeps getting reelected. Instead of a cracker or bread crumb binding, Barbara prefers to use soft, crustless bread to hold the cakes together and adds a dollop of sharp Dijon mustard to liven up her mix.

Serves 4

Crabettes

These little devils, whose name sounds suspiciously like a follies review over to the Steelworkers Hall, were created as miniature crab cakes. A spicy mayonnaise base infused with fresh ginger and black soy sauce binds these crabby morsels. They pack a zesty punch, and are perfect cocktail party pass-arounds or an unusual first course appetizer. Serve with lime wedges or with Skipjack Salsa (page 118).

Serves 6 to 8

1 egg, beaten
3 tablespoons mayonnaise
1 teaspoon Tabasco Sauce
1 teaspoon black soy sauce (see Note) or soy sauce
$^1/_2$ teaspoon Chesapeake seasoning
$^1/_2$ teaspoon freshly ground black pepper
1 teaspoon finely chopped fresh ginger
1 teaspoon chopped garlic
2 to 3 serranos or other hot chilies, finely chopped
2 tablespoons chopped cilantro
1 pound claw crabmeat, picked over
Dry bread crumbs, as needed
Vegetable oil, for frying

Mix together the egg, mayonnaise, Tabasco, soy sauce, Chesapeake seasoning, pepper, ginger, garlic, chilies, and cilantro. Whip by hand or in a blender until well mixed and frothy. Place the crabmeat in a bowl and pour the egg mixture over it. Add the bread crumbs, a little at a time, tossing gently, until the mixture holds together and can be formed into patties. Mold into round patties $1^1/_2$ inches in diameter and $^1/_2$ inch thick.

Pour oil into a heavy skillet to a depth of about $1^1/_2$ inches. Fry the crab cakes in hot oil, a few at a time, until golden brown, about 2 minutes on each side. Remove with a slotted utensil to paper towels to drain, then serve.

Note: Black soy sauce, which is very dark, thick, and sweetened with molasses, is a special variety of soy sauce. It can be found in most Asian markets and in specialty food shops. If it is not available, regular soy sauce may be substituted.

From the first full moon of May throughout the summer and into the fall in the brackish waters of the Chesapeake's marsh grasses, the blue crab goes through its remarkable growth process of molting. It is at this stage, when the crab has just backed out of its shell, that the soft-shell emerges. During a blue crab's average three-year life span, it may shed its shell up to twenty-three times. These moltings are the basis of the soft-shell crab industry, which is centered in Crisfield, Maryland.

The Chesapeake Bay accounts for 90 percent of the soft-shell crab production in the United States. This traditional crustacean of the South, the Chesapeake's most precious culinary emissary, is shipped around the globe to all the great gastronomic centers. Soft-shells are now on the menus of the finest restaurants in the country, with preparation techniques ranging from authentically simple styles to trendy pan-Pacific variations executed with Euro-Asian flavorings.

Soft-shell crabs are sold fresh (live) and frozen. Fresh soft-shells are far superior to the frozen, which are fine for frying or adding to a soup or chowder but do not retain the delicate flavor of the fresh.

Soft-shells are referred to by a number of terms, including softs, peelers, red signs, ranks, busters, buckrams, paper shells, Sally crabs, and snots. Most of these names come from the Chesapeake's watermen, who use the monikers to denote the various stages of the crab's molting.

Thought of as opulent dining in the rest of the world, soft-shells are just as "common as crabs" to the locals. During the summer months, fried softs can be found on virtually every menu, from fancy dinnerhouses to plain-jane coffee shops. Neighborhood kids sit on front stoops munching soft-shell sandwiches, with crab legs dangling over the edges of white bread. If it's summer, it's soft-shell time, and that's just about as good as eating gets.

Soft-Shell Crab Moutarde

Mustard and crab work beautifully together in crab cakes and casseroles, so it comes as no surprise that pairing mustard with soft-shells results in a felicitous splendid dish. These mustard-encrusted soft-shells have a slightly pungent taste, a crisp exterior, and are topped with a garlicky lemon butter sauce. The key to success with this recipe: Chill the softs after they have been coated with mustard.

Serves 4

8 prime soft-shell crabs, cleaned (see page 45)
$^1/_4$ cup Dijon mustard
All-purpose flour seasoned with salt and freshly ground black pepper
3 eggs, beaten
Fine dry bread crumbs
Clarified butter (see pages 33–34) or olive oil, for sautéing
Juice of 1 lemon
1 teaspoon minced garlic
8 tablespoons (1 stick) butter, cut into small pieces
2 tablespoons chopped parsley

Coat both sides of the softs with the mustard and refrigerate for 1 hour.

Lightly dust the crabs with the seasoned flour, shaking off any excess. Dip them in the eggs and then roll them in the bread crumbs. Heat the clarified butter or oil in a sauté pan. Add the softs and cook over medium heat for about 3 minutes on each side. Remove to paper towels to drain and keep warm.

Discard the fat from the pan and return it to medium heat. Add the lemon juice and deglaze the pan, scraping up all the browned bits. Add the garlic and reduce the heat to low. Whisk in the butter, bit by bit. Stir in the parsley. Spoon the sauce over the crabs and serve hot.

Grading and Cleaning Soft-Shells

Grading Soft-Shell Crabs

Soft-shells are graded by the size of the shell span:

Hotels 4 to $4^1/_2$ inches

Primes $4^1/_2$ to 5 inches

Jumbos 5 to $5^1/_2$ inches

Whales $5^1/_2$ inches and up

Cleaning Soft-Shell Crabs

Use soft-shell crabs that are alive.

Rinse the crabs with cold water.

Cut off the eyes and mouth with scissors. (Cut straight across the face, about $^1/_4$ inch behind the eyes.)

After making the cut described above, pull out the stomach, a small jellylike sac, also known as the "sand bag."

Remove the apron from the underside of the crab by pulling it away from the body, similar to pulling up a pop tab on a can of soda. The male crab apron is "T" shaped, and in females, round or triangular.

Lift the pointed ends of the shell upward, and pull or snip out the spongy gills.

Dry the crabs with paper towels and prepare as desired.

Alva's "No Bullhocky" Fried Soft-Shells

Tangier Island waterman Alva Crockett is a down-to-earth guy who doesn't take kindly to fancy soft-shell preparations. Just thinking about sautéed crabs with this and that on them sends his nerves all to hell. Here's a no-muss, no-fuss recipe he uses. He figures that if you fry them up like this, you'll never eat them any other way.

Serves 4

8 prime soft-shell crabs, cleaned (see page 45)
All-purpose flour seasoned with salt, freshly ground black pepper, and cayenne

Vegetable shortening, for frying
Tartar Sauce (page 34) and lemon wedges (optional), for accompaniment

Give the softs a good dose of seasoned flour. Melt shortening in a cast-iron or other heavy skillet to a depth of about 1 inch, then get it good and hot. Fry the crabs until golden brown, 3 minutes on each side. Remove with tongs or a slotted spoon to paper towels to drain.

Serve with Tartar Sauce and lemon wedges if you're so inclined.

Alva Crockett of Tangier Island, Virginia

Tangier Island is, to put it mildly, a hard-to-get-to kind of place. It breeds a hardy citizenry and one of the finest examples of Tangier stock is Alva Crockett, whose great uncle was Davy Crockett. Now how's that for hardy? A three-term former mayor of Tangier Island, Alva was born and raised here, and he is an outspoken champion of the attributes of Chesapeake Bay cooking, watermen's style. He possesses a gift for calling things as he sees them. He believes in simplicity: the simplicity of cooking and the simplicity of nature. He figures, "Why mess up nature by loading the cooking process with lots of spices?" Makes no sense to him, and after sampling his cooking I get his drift.

A Dockside Feed with Alva Crockett

Tangier Island Fifty Clam Chowder (page 120)
Alva's "No Bullhocky" Fried Soft-Shells
Kale and Country Ham (page 197)

4 jumbo or whale soft-shell
   crabs, cleaned (see page 45)
8 slices of white bread
Mayonnaise or Tartar Sauce
   (page 34)

4 large slices ripe tomato
Salt and freshly ground black
   pepper
4 leaves lettuce

First, fry the soft-shells. The method used in Alva's "No Bullhocky" Fried Soft-Shells (page 46) will do nicely. Then drain them on paper towels.

Lather the bread slices with mayonnaise or Tartar Sauce. Place a crab on each of 4 slices of the bread. Top each crab with a tomato slice, sprinkle with salt and pepper to taste, and then crown with a lettuce leaf. Put on the top bread slices and enjoy.

Soft-Shell Crab Sandwich

Oh, my God! There's little legs dangling out the sides of that sandwich." Outside of Chesapeake country you generally don't find soft-shell crab sandwiches. These culinary oddities contain a whole, lightly fried soft-shell crab nestled between two slices of fresh white bread and topped with vine-ripened tomatoes and crisp leaves of lettuce. If large soft-shells are not available, use two smaller crabs per sandwich.

Serves 4

Soft-Shells Stuffed with Crab Imperial

For those insatiable crab aficionados always wanting more crab, who feel they are not getting enough of a satisfyingly rich crab experience with just a pair of soft-shell crabs, this recipe will take the crab sensation one culinary step further. What a palate-pleasing thrill it is to bite into the slightly crunchy exterior of these soft-shells, followed by a burst of rich imperial stuffing. When broiling the soft-shells do not attempt to turn them, as the crabmeat stuffing will not stay in place. A somewhat longer broiling time than usual will cook the crabs completely through.

Serves 4

½ batch of your favorite imperial recipe (pages 63–64)
Chesapeake Hollandaise Sauce (recipe follows), optional

8 prime or jumbo soft-shell crabs, cleaned (see page 45)
3 tablespoons clarified butter (see pages 33–34)
Lemon wedges

Prepare the imperial and set aside. Prepare the sauce, if using, and keep warm. Preheat the broiler.

Stuff some of the imperial mixture under the sides and center of the top shell of each soft. Lightly grease a broiler pan with the butter and place the crabs on the pan, top shell up. Brush the crabs liberally with the butter. Slip the pan into the broiler, about 4 inches from the heat, and broil until done, 6 to 8 minutes.

Top with the sauce, if using, and lemon wedges and serve at once.

Chesapeake Hollandaise Sauce Makes about 2 cups

8 egg yolks
½ teaspoon Chesapeake seasoning
2 dashes of Tabasco Sauce
2 dashes of Worcestershire sauce

Juice of 1 lemon
½ pound (2 sticks) butter, melted and kept warm
Hot water, if needed

Place the egg yolks, Chesapeake seasoning, Tabasco, Worcestershire, and lemon juice in a blender. Blend until well mixed. With motor running, pour in the hot butter in a fine, steady stream, blending until thick. If the sauce is too thick, thin with a little hot water.

1½ cups all-purpose flour plus extra for dusting crabs
½ teaspoon baking powder
2 teaspoons salt
½ teaspoon freshly ground black pepper
¾ cup ice water
½ cup finely chopped toasted pecans

Vegetable oil, for frying
8 soft-shell crabs, cleaned (see page 45)
½ cup bourbon whiskey
Juice of 1 lemon
8 tablespoons (1 stick) lightly salted butter, cut into small pieces
2 tablespoons chopped parsley

Combine the 1½ cups flour, baking powder, salt, and pepper in a bowl. Slowly mix in the water to form a smooth batter. Refrigerate for 1 hour. When ready to use, fold in the pecans.

Pour oil into a skillet to reach a depth of about 1 inch and heat until very hot, about 375°F. Dust the softs in flour and lightly dip in the batter. Slip the crabs into the pan and fry until golden, about 3 minutes on each side. Remove to paper towels to drain. Keep warm.

Discard the cooking oil. Return the pan to high heat, add the whiskey, and deglaze the pan, scraping up all the browned bits. Pour in the lemon juice and reduce the heat to low. Whisk in the butter, bit by bit. Remove from the heat and stir in the parsley.

Arrange the soft-shells on a platter. Spoon the sauce over them and serve at once.

Pecan-Coated Soft-Shells with Whiskey-Lemon Butter

This recipe is a traditional crab fritter batter laden with toasted pecans and enhanced with a hootch-infused lemon-butter sauce. Our dear Miss Alma, my grandmother's boarder, who was, "God rest her soul," the originator of this concoction, would always confide to dinner guests that "I really don't like using the whiskey, but my mother told me it disinfects the crabs." So here it is, a medicinally pure and exceptionally tasty dish. Chilling the batter before adding the pecans ensures an even distribution of the nuts throughout the mixture.

Serves 4

Blackened Soft-Shells

The blackening technique of coating a piece of fish, meat, or poultry with a fragrant spice blend and searing it in an incredibly hot cast-iron pan has become extremely popular. Soft-shells lend themselves well to this blackening process because they require only a brief cooking time—the outer shell blackens perfectly while the meat inside remains moist and does not dry out. As the flavorful herb butter melts over the hot crabs, it embellishes the blackening spices by bathing the crabs in an outstanding butter sauce. (This recipe makes more mustard butter than is needed for the softs, but it is great to have on hand to top grilled fish fillets or grilled meats, such as steaks, chops, or chicken breasts.) This dish goes well with Lena's Spicy Rice (page 204) or a pilaf-style rice.

Serves 4

Herb Mustard Butter (recipe follows)
8 prime soft-shell crabs, cleaned (see page 45)
1 cup clarified butter (see pages 33–34), melted and cooled
$^1/_2$ cup Blackening Spice (page 39) or Chesapeake seasoning for blackening

Prepare the Herb Mustard Butter and refrigerate until firm.

Heat a large cast-iron skillet over high heat until smoking hot (the hotter the better). Dip the crabs in the clarified butter and then lightly coat them with the seasoning. Place each crab, top shell down, in the skillet. Fry for 2 to 3 minutes, then turn and cook on the second side for 2 to 3 minutes.

Place the crabs on warmed plates. Top each with a pat of Herb Mustard Butter. Serve at once.

Note: Whenever using this blackening method, be sure you are working in a well-ventilated area. This process produces a lot of smoke, so put on the exhaust fan and open the windows.

Herb Mustard Butter   Makes about 1 cup

$^1/_2$ pound (2 sticks) lightly salted butter, softened
3 tablespoons Dijon mustard
$^1/_4$ teaspoon minced garlic
$^1/_4$ teaspoon minced shallot
3 sage leaves, finely chopped
2 large basil leaves, finely chopped
3 chives, minced
3 tablespoons chopped parsley
Juice of 1 lemon
Freshly ground black pepper

Combine all the ingredients in a mixing bowl and whip together, either by hand or with an electric mixer, until well mixed. Spread the seasoned butter down the center of a length of wax paper. Roll the butter to form a log with a width the size of a quarter. Wrap in wax paper and refrigerate to firm up the butter before cutting.

8 prime or jumbo soft-shell
   crabs, cleaned (see page 45)
All-purpose flour seasoned with
   salt and freshly ground
   black pepper
8 tablespoons (1 stick) butter
$^1/_4$ cup olive oil
$^1/_4$ cup dry vermouth
$^1/_4$ cup Fish Stock (page 109),
   optional

1 teaspoon minced garlic
Juice of 1 lemon
2 tablespoons chopped drained
   capers
2 tablespoons chopped basil
Salt and freshly ground black
   pepper, to taste

Dust the soft-shells in the seasoned flour. Melt 2 tablespoons of the butter with the oil in a large skillet over medium heat. Add the crabs and cook, turning once, until golden, about 3 minutes on each side. Place the crabs on a platter and keep warm.

Discard the cooking oil. Return the pan to high heat, add the vermouth, and deglaze the pan, scraping up all the browned bits. Add the stock, garlic, and lemon juice. Cook until about $^1/_4$ cup liquid remains. Reduce the heat to low and add the capers and basil. Whisk in the remaining 6 tablespoons of butter, bit by bit. Season with salt and pepper.

Spoon the sauce over the crabs and serve at once.

Johnny's Sautéed Softs

This is my California-style, slightly frou-frou soft-shell preparation created for some persnickety Californians who were put off by the standard Chesapeake fried or panfried versions. It's just as well those Westerners balked at "fried" because they provided the impetus for the development of this recipe, which makes for an impressive meal. Tender springtime asparagus is the perfect vegetable accompaniment.

Serves 4

Handy's Beer-Battered Softs

This recipe employs a tempura-like batter to produce a very thin, crisp coating for the soft-shells. This cooking preparation is a favorite of the workers at the world's largest producer of soft-shell crabs, the John T. Handy Company in Crisfield, Maryland.

Serves 4

1¼ cups all-purpose flour, plus extra for dusting crabs
2 teaspoons salt
½ teaspoon baking powder
1 teaspoon paprika
1 bottle (12 ounces) flat beer (see page 27)

8 prime or jumbo soft-shell crabs, cleaned (see page 45)
Vegetable oil, for frying
Tartar Sauce (page 34) and lemon wedges, for accompaniment

Sift together the flour, salt, and baking powder in a mixing bowl. Mix in the paprika. Slowly mix in the beer to make a smooth batter. Let the batter stand at room temperature for 1 to 2 hours. It will thicken as it stands.

Lightly dust the softs with the flour, gently shaking off any excess. Pour oil into a deep skillet or deep-fat fryer to a depth of about 1 inch and heat until very hot, about 375°F. Dip each crab in the batter to coat evenly and then slip it into the hot oil. Do not crowd the pan. Fry until golden brown, 3 to 5 minutes. Remove to paper towels to drain briefly.

Serve at once with Tartar Sauce and lemon wedges on the side.

Crabs

Crab cakes and soft-shell crabs are the best known of Chesapeake crab dishes, but actually they are just the beginning. Crabmeat is used in a myriad of Chesapeake Bay meals. Spiced and herbed crabmeat is found in pie shells, tartlets, mushroom caps, salads, and Asian-style spring rolls. Casseroles are another popular choice for crabmeat as an ingredient, as Chesapeake cooks like to use crab in their mainstay dish, the one-pot meal.

Pastry Dough for a Single-Crust Pie (page 247)	8 ounces swiss cheese, finely shredded (2 cups)
3 eggs, lightly beaten	1/2 small onion, thinly sliced
1/2 cup mayonnaise	1 pound backfin or special crabmeat, picked over
2 tablespoons flour	Sprigs of thyme and sliced fresh fruit for garnish
1 teaspoon chopped thyme	
Freshly ground black pepper	

Prepare the pastry dough and line a 9-inch pan. Preheat the oven to 350°F.

Combine the eggs, mayonnaise, flour, thyme, and black pepper in a bowl. Mix well. Gently stir in the cheese, onion, and crabmeat. Pour the crab mixture into the pie shell.

Bake until a knife inserted in the center comes out clean, about 40 minutes.

Garnish each serving with a sprig of thyme and sliced fresh fruit.

Back Creek Inn's Crab Quiche

In southern Maryland near Solomons, where the Patuxent River joins the Chesapeake Bay, Carol Szkotnicki and Lin Cochran's charming Back Creek Inn sits on the tree-lined and tranquil banks of Back Creek.

This crab quiche is served to summer guests, who often help the proprietors catch crabs from the inn's pier.

Serves 6 to 8

Juan Kelly's Crabmeat Tapas

The late Señor Juan (John) Kelly, who was my best friend, a part-time resident of Seville, Spain, and a former Baltimore man-about-town, crafted this delightful Spanish-Chesapeake appetizer. If I'm in a hurry and don't have time to make the tartlet shells, I purchase miniature cream puff shells or frozen tartlet shells and fill them with the crab mixture. Another option is to arrange the entire crab mixture in a prebaked twelve-inch tart shell. The filling can also be turned into a salad by mounding it in butter lettuce leaves that have been lightly dressed with a vinaigrette.

Makes 12 tartlets

12 prebaked Flaky Pastry Tartlet Shells (recipe follows)
1/4 cup olive oil
1 red bell pepper, seeded, deveined, and finely diced
1/2 cup mayonnaise
2 tablespoons minced drained capers
2 hard-cooked eggs, finely chopped
2 tablespoons minced yellow onion
Juice of 1/2 lemon
1/4 cup chopped parsley
Freshly ground black pepper, to taste
1 pound backfin or special crabmeat, picked over
1/4 pound Smithfield ham or prosciutto, cut into small dice
Green Spanish olives, pitted, for garnish

Bake the tartlet shells and let cool completely. Warm the olive oil in a small skillet over medium-high heat. Add the bell pepper and sauté until soft, about 5 minutes. Set aside.

Mix together the mayonnaise, capers, eggs, onion, lemon juice, parsley, and black pepper in a large bowl. Gently fold the crabmeat, ham, and sautéed peppers into the mayonnaise mixture. Mound the mixture into the prebaked tartlet shells and garnish with olives. Place the tartlets on a serving platter and serve at once.

Flaky Pastry Tartlet Shells
Makes twelve 2 1/2-inch tartlet shells

2 cups all-purpose flour
1/2 teaspoon salt
8 tablespoons (1 stick) butter, cut into very small pieces
2 tablespoons vegetable shortening
1/4 cup ice water

Sift together the flour and salt into a mixing bowl. Work the butter and shortening into the flour with your fingertips or a pastry blender until the mixture is the consistency of coarse meal.

Add the water, 1 tablespoon at a time, mixing with a fork after each addition. Dough should be just moist enough to hold together. Form the dough into a ball. Wrap and refrigerate for at least 1 hour before using.

Preheat the oven to 425°F.

Divide the pastry into 4 equal portions. Work with 1 portion at a time and keep the others refrigerated.

On a lightly floured board, roll 1 portion of the dough into a round about $1/8$ inch thick. With a round cookie cutter measuring 3 inches in diameter, cut out dough rounds. Transfer each round to a tartlet pan about $2^1/2$ inches in diameter, pulling the dough gently to overlap the edges of the pan. Prick the bottoms with a fork. Line each pan with a small piece of aluminum foil pressed over the dough, or, better yet, stack another tartlet pan on top. Weight down with dried beans or raw rice.

Place the tartlets on sheet pans and bake for 8 to 10 minutes. Remove the foil or top pan and weights and bake, uncovered, until golden brown, about 1 minute.

Remove the tartlet pans from the oven and let cool completely. Carefully remove the pastry shells from the pans.

Thelma's Crab and Artichoke Dip

This rich and satisfying dip recipe is from Baltimore's Thelma Tunney. It teams blue crabmeat with tender artichoke hearts in a lightly spiced mayonnaise-based sauce and is actually prepared like a casserole. When guests find out Thelma has been invited to a potluck party they are also attending, their mouths start watering in anticipation of this dip. Thelma often serves this dish as an entree baked in individual ramekins accompanied by a fresh garden salad and a hot crusty baguette. When you serve it as a dip, provide plenty of baguette slices or crackers for dipping.

Serves 8 to 10

8 ounces sharp cheddar cheese, shredded
2 cups mayonnaise
1 tablespoon Dijon mustard
2 teaspoons Worcestershire sauce
Juice of 1 lemon
1/8 teaspoon cayenne
Freshly ground black pepper
1 jar (16 ounces) artichoke hearts, drained and cut into small pieces
1 pound backfin or special crabmeat, picked over
1/2 cup chopped parsley

Preheat the oven to 350°F. Butter a 6-cup casserole dish.

Combine the cheese, mayonnaise, mustard, Worcestershire, lemon juice, cayenne, and black pepper in a large bowl. Stir until well mixed. Gently fold in the artichoke hearts, crabmeat, and parsley. Pour the mixture into the casserole dish.

Bake for 20 to 25 minutes. Serve at once.

In Crabs They Trust

Baltimoreans love their food and don't hesitate to say so. The city is the melting pot of the Chesapeake Bay and ethnic communities still thrive here, each adapting the region's natural resources to their traditional cuisines.

The blue crab has become the common denominator uniting all these various groups. They all steam the crabs, dump them on newspapers spread on backyard tables, and whack them with mallets in the same manner as generations of Baltimore crab pickers have before them. Every neighborhood block has a tavern or two where locals meet to debate the merits of the Baltimore Orioles or Ravens ball clubs and to have a few cold ones with a plateful of crab cakes. These perfectly spiced crab dishes are the centerpiece of virtually every menu at the taverns and restaurants that call "Charm City" their home.

7 tablespoons butter

1 small onion, finely diced

1/2 medium green bell pepper, finely diced

3 teaspoons cornstarch

1 cup milk

2 eggs, lightly beaten

3 tablespoons mayonnaise

1 tablespoon prepared mustard

2 teaspoons Chesapeake seasoning

2 pounds backfin or special crabmeat, picked over

8 slices bread, crust removed, cubed

Cherry tomatoes, for garnish

Preheat the oven to 350°F.

Melt 3 tablespoons of the butter in a sauté pan. Add the onion and bell pepper and sauté over medium heat until slightly soft, about 3 minutes; set aside. Dissolve the cornstarch with the milk in a small saucepan. Whisk over low heat until a smooth paste is formed. Remove from the heat. Mix together the eggs, mayonnaise, mustard, Chesapeake seasoning, and cornstarch mixture in a bowl. Stir in the sautéed onion and bell pepper. Place the crabmeat in a separate mixing bowl and pour the wet mixture over the top. Add half of the cubed bread and mix gently.

Lightly butter a 10 × 14-inch baking dish. Add the crab mixture and spread evenly without packing down. Place the remaining cubed bread on top of the mixture. Melt the remaining 4 tablespoons of butter and spoon over the bread cubes. Bake for 35 minutes. Remove the casserole from the oven and let it stand 5 minutes before serving. Cut into 3-inch squares and serve on a platter garnished with cherry tomatoes.

Mrs. Kitching's Crab Loaf

Frances Kitching, culinary first lady of Maryland's Smith Island and coauthor of **Mrs. Kitching's Smith Island Cookbook,** *has served this crab loaf appetizer to countless visitors— including governors, senators, and famous celebrities—at her off-the-beaten-path restaurant located on the island. Baked in a casserole dish, the crab loaf is slightly cooled and cut into small squares, which may then be served as a first course or a pass-around with drinks.*

Serves 10 to 12 as an appetizer

Miss Alice's Crab Fluffs

The Harrisons of Tilghman Island are one of the Chesapeake's first families of seafood. The late matriarch Alice Harrison presided over their landmark Eastern Shore hotel and restaurant on Tilghman Island, Maryland, where part of the Chesapeake's legendary skipjack fleet is docked. Miss Alice's light-as-air crab fluffs, mounds of delicately spiced crab lumps coated with an aromatic batter, are Eastern Shore cookery at its finest.

Serves 8 to 10

1 pound backfin or claw
    crabmeat, picked over
1 egg
$^1/_3$ cup mayonnaise
1 teaspoon Worcestershire sauce
1 teaspoon dry mustard
$^1/_2$ teaspoon salt
$^1/_4$ teaspoon freshly ground
    black pepper
$^1/_2$ cup fine dry Italian bread
    crumbs

BATTER
$1^1/_2$ cups all-purpose flour
2 teaspoons baking powder
1 teaspoon Chesapeake
    seasoning
$^1/_2$ teaspoon salt
$^1/_4$ teaspoon celery seed
$^1/_4$ teaspoon lemon-pepper
    seasoning
2 eggs, beaten
2 tablespoons mayonnaise
$^1/_2$ teaspoon prepared mustard
1 cup milk

Vegetable oil, for frying
Tartar Sauce (page 34) or
    Rémoulade Sauce (page 37)

Place the crabmeat in a bowl and set aside.

Combine the egg, mayonnaise, Worcestershire, dry mustard, salt, and pepper in a mixing bowl. Mix well. Pour the egg mixture over the crabmeat and sprinkle the bread crumbs over all. Gently mix or fold the ingredients together. Form into balls about $1^1/_2$ inches in diameter. Refrigerate until ready to cook.

To prepare the batter, sift the flour and baking powder together into a mixing bowl. Combine all of the remaining batter ingredients and whisk together to make a smooth batter.

Pour oil into a deep skillet or a deep-fat fryer to a depth of 1 inch and heat until very hot, 375°F. Coat the balls with the batter and fry, a few at a time, until golden brown. Remove to paper towels to drain briefly.

Serve at once with Tartar Sauce or Rémoulade Sauce.

6 tablespoons (³/₄ stick) butter
16 to 20 medium-size
   mushrooms, stemmed
¹/₄ cup dry sherry
Salt and freshly ground black
   pepper, to taste
¹/₄ cup minced onion
¹/₄ cup chopped chives

2 tablespoons chopped parsley
2 tablespoons chopped fresh dill
   or basil
4 tablespoons (¹/₂ stick) butter,
   melted
¹/₂ cup sour cream
1 pound special or backfin
   crabmeat, picked over

Preheat the oven to 350°F.

Melt the 6 tablespoons butter in a skillet and sauté the mushroom caps for 5 minutes, or until barely tender. Pour in the sherry, turn up the heat, and reduce the liquid by half. Season with salt and pepper. Remove from the heat and let cool.

Mix the onion, chives, parsley, dill, melted butter, and sour cream in a bowl. Season with salt and pepper. Gently fold in the crabmeat. Stuff the caps with the mixture and arrange in a lightly buttered or oiled baking dish.

Cover with wax paper and bake about 20 minutes. Serve hot or warm.

Stuffed Mushroom Caps

This traditional Chesapeake recipe is normally prepared with domestic mushrooms, but I have tried it with lightly sautéed shiitake, portobello, and chanterelle mushrooms with excellent results.

Serves 4 to 6

Crab Spring Roll

East meets east—that is, the East meets the Eastern Shore. Crabmeat teams up with the Asian accents of pickled ginger and fresh vegetables in these spring rolls designed by chef Mark Salter of the Inn at Perry Cabin in St. Michaels, Maryland. During a stint as guest chef aboard the luxury cruise liner the **Queen Elizabeth II,** *Mark prepared these spring rolls to treat the ship's guests to a taste of Chesapeake crabmeat.*

Serves 4

Citrus Salad Dressing (recipe follows)
1/4 head bok choy, coarsely shredded
4 green onions, cut into small pieces
2 slices Japanese pickled ginger, chopped (see Note)
1/2 teaspoon chopped cilantro
Salt and freshly ground black pepper
4 ounces jumbo crabmeat, picked over
4 sheets spring roll wrappers (see Note)

1 egg, beaten
Vegetable oil, for frying
4 cups mesclun salad or assorted leaf lettuce
1 avocado, peeled, pitted, and sliced
1 pink grapefruit, peeled and sectioned
1/2 cup toasted sliced almonds
2 tomatoes, peeled, seeded, and diced
Chives, for garnish

Prepare the Citrus Salad Dressing and set aside.

Briefly blanch the bok choy in a pot of boiling salted water. Drain, using a skimmer or slotted spoon, and place in a bowl. In the same pot of water, briefly blanch the scallions. Drain and dry with a paper towel. Add to the bowl of bok choy. Add the ginger, cilantro, salt, and pepper. Mix well. Gently fold in the crabmeat taking care not to break up the lumps of crab.

Lay out the spring roll wrappers and brush the edges lightly with the beaten egg to help seal. Divide the crabmeat mixture among the wrappers, placing it in the center of the egg roll and roll each one tightly.

Pour the oil into a deep heavy frying pan to a depth of 1 1/2 inches and heat until very hot, about 400°F. Deep-fry the rolls until golden brown. Remove and drain on paper towels. Cut each in half.

Place a bed of lettuce lightly dressed with the Citrus Salad Dressing on each of 4 plates. Top with 2 halves of a spring roll. Garnish around the plate with avocado, grapefruit, almonds, tomato, and chives.

Note: Pickled ginger and spring roll wrappers can be found in Asian markets and specialty food stores.

Citrus Salad Dressing   Makes 1 1/2 cups

1 teaspoon sugar
Juice of 2 pink grapefruit,
    strained for seeds
Juice of 1 lime, strained for
    seeds

1/2 cup olive oil
1/2 cup vegetable oil
Salt and freshly ground black
    pepper

Dissolve the sugar in a little water in a small saucepan. Add the grapefruit juice. Reduce by half over medium heat, then remove the pan from the heat. Pour into a small mixing bowl. Whisk in the lime juice, olive oil, and vegetable oil. Lightly season with salt and pepper.

R and R: Rest in Refinement

On the northern end of the Tilghman Peninsula nesting on the Miles River is St. Michaels, Maryland, a destination for people in search of a peaceful, scenic, and sophisticated getaway. When visiting this picture-perfect little hamlet with Victorian architecture, it is not difficult to understand why this once out-of-the-way Eastern Shore town is now a popular tourist attraction for discerning visitors. St. Michaels is also home to many fine dining establishments and the Chesapeake Bay Maritime Museum.

A short ferry ride from St. Michaels is the waterside town of Oxford. Established in the mid-seventeenth century, the village is an off-the-beaten-path hideaway, ideal for a short, restful weekend excursion. Still primarily a fishing town, Oxford has seen some of its historic buildings carefully restored, with a number of them turned into bed and breakfast inns and restaurants featuring traditional Chesapeake fare.

Crabmeat Curry

Curry dishes were favorites of nineteenth-century Chesapeake genteel nobility and were served in the manor houses that lined the Bay's tributaries. English-style curries from that period were rather mildly spiced—not nearly as intense as the true curry dishes of India. This updated version of the classic ragout has a substantial kick to it. It works for shrimp as well as crab.

Serves 4

6 tablespoons (³/4 stick) butter
2 small onions, diced
1 cup finely diced celery
1 teaspoon chopped garlic
1¹/2 cups coconut milk (see Note)
2 large tomatoes, peeled, seeded, and chopped
1 large apple, peeled, cored, and diced
1 medium hot green chili, chopped
1 piece (1 inch) gingerroot, peeled and minced
1 tablespoon Madras curry powder
Pinch of ground cinnamon
Pinch of ground cloves
1 tablespoon sugar
1 tablespoon flour
1 pound backfin crabmeat, picked over
2 tablespoons fresh lemon juice
2 tablespoons chopped parsley
Salt and freshly ground black pepper, to taste
Cooked white rice, for accompaniment

Melt the butter in a saucepan. Sauté the onions, celery, and garlic until tender. Stir in the coconut milk, tomatoes, apple, chili, and ginger. Bring to a boil, reduce the heat, and simmer. Combine the curry powder, cinnamon, cloves, sugar, and flour in a small bowl. Stir in enough cold water to make a smooth paste. Slowly pour the mixture into the sauce, stirring constantly. Simmer, partially covered, for about 30 minutes, stirring often. Add the crabmeat, lemon juice, and parsley and heat through for about 5 minutes. Season with salt and pepper to taste.

Serve over white rice.

Note: Canned coconut milk can be found in Asian markets as well as in many grocery stores.

4 tablespoons (¹/₂ stick) butter

2 tablespoons diced green bell
pepper

2 tablespoons diced red bell
pepper or pimiento

¹/₂ cup chopped mushrooms

³/₄ cup mayonnaise

1 tablespoon Dijon mustard

1 tablespoon Worcestershire
sauce

¹/₄ teaspoon Tabasco Sauce

1 teaspoon capers, drained and
chopped

¹/₂ teaspoon freshly ground
black pepper

1 teaspoon Chesapeake
seasoning

1 pound jumbo lump crabmeat,
picked over

Imperial Topping (recipe
follows)

Preheat the oven to 350°F.

Melt the butter in a small skillet and sauté the bell peppers and mushrooms until soft. Set aside.

Combine the mayonnaise, mustard, Worcestershire, Tabasco, capers, pepper, and Chesapeake seasoning in a small bowl and mix well. Add the sautéed peppers and mushrooms.

Place the crabmeat in a mixing bowl and pour the mixture over it. Toss gently. Spoon the mixture into 4 individual gratin dishes or well-cleaned crab shells. (Place filled shells on a baking sheet.) Bake for 20 to 25 minutes.

Meanwhile, prepare the topping. Remove the casseroles from the oven. Preheat the broiler. Spoon the topping evenly over each casserole. Place under the broiler for 1 to 2 minutes, or until nicely browned. (If a broiler is unavailable, brown the top in the oven. It will take a bit longer.) Serve immediately.

Imperial Topping Makes ¹/₃ cup

1 egg, beaten

¹/₄ cup mayonnaise

Pinch of paprika

1 tablespoon chopped parsley

Combine all the ingredients in a small bowl and mix well.

Crab Imperial, Baltimore Style

Here is the pièce de résistance of Chesapeake Bay blue crab dishes. Basically, an imperial is a richly spiced crab casserole that is served in individual portions. It is reserved for the most special of family occasions and is the showpiece selection at fine Chesapeake dinnerhouses. Restaurant reputations are often made—and unmade—on the basis of their success with this dish.

Want to start a fight? Ask two or more Marylanders how to make the best crab imperial. The answer is a matter of fierce family pride and, in most cases, involves a recipe passed through countless generations. After several such scuffles, I arrived at this version of the fabled preparation. You can bake it in individual dishes or well-cleaned crab shells (see page 66).

Serves 4

Smithfield Crab Imperial

Crab imperial is one of the premier dishes of Chesapeake cookery, and this recipe, from Sting-Ray's Restaurant in Capeville, Virginia, does the dish proud. They use thin slices of Smithfield ham to give the crabmeat a distinctly smoky, Southern flair. Sting-Ray's is situated at an Exxon gas station truck stop on a lonely stretch of Route 13, where you might expect greasy-spoon fare. Nothing could be further from the truth—Sting-Ray's offers some of the best, honest-to-God Chesapeake cooking to be found.

Serves 4

1 egg
²/₃ cup mayonnaise
¹/₂ cup sour cream
2 tablespoons Dijon mustard
1 teaspoon Chesapeake seasoning
1 tablespoon chopped parsley
1 pound jumbo lump crabmeat, picked over
8 paper-thin slices Smithfield ham
4 tablespoons (¹/₂ stick) butter, melted

Preheat the oven to 400°F.

Beat the egg in a mixing bowl until fluffy. Add the mayonnaise, sour cream, mustard, Chesapeake seasoning, and parsley and mix well. Gently fold in the crabmeat. Butter 4 individual ramekins. Place 2 pieces of Smithfield ham in the bottom of each ramekin. Top the ham with the crab mixture. Drizzle the top of each with a little melted butter.

Bake for 15 to 18 minutes, or until golden brown. Serve at once.

6 tablespoons (³/₄ stick) butter
   or bacon drippings
¹/₄ cup minced onion
¹/₂ cup finely diced celery
1 cup chopped fresh
   mushrooms
¹/₂ cup finely diced green bell
   pepper
1 pound backfin crabmeat,
   picked over
8 slices of white bread, crusts
   removed, diced

4 eggs, lightly beaten
2 cups milk
2 cups heavy (whipping) cream
1 teaspoon salt
¹/₂ teaspoon freshly ground
   black pepper
1 teaspoon Worcestershire sauce
Dash of Tabasco Sauce
1 cup finely shredded sharp
   cheddar cheese

Bessie's Crab Pudding

My great-aunt Bessie, God love her, was a Southern spinster lady who did not spend a great deal of time in the kitchen. Fact of the matter is, she made only two things: chow mein and crab pudding. Back then, the family was never big on chow mein. But you couldn't keep them away from the table when they knew Bessie was baking up a pan of her savory crab pudding. This creamy casserole not only makes a fine dinner entree but is also a good change of pace for a Sunday brunch. Serve it with vine-ripened summer tomatoes, a steaming bowl of succotash, and hot biscuits.

Serves 6

Melt the butter in a skillet over medium-high heat. Add the onion, celery, mushrooms, and bell pepper and sauté until tender, about 5 minutes. Remove from the heat, fold in the crabmeat, and set aside.

Butter a 6-cup casserole or baking dish. Place half of the diced bread in the bottom of the dish. Spread the crabmeat-vegetable mixture over the top. Place the remaining diced bread on top of the crab mixture. Combine the eggs, milk, cream, salt, pepper, Worcestershire, and Tabasco in a mixing bowl. Mix well and pour over the casserole. Cover with aluminum foil and "tuck it in the Frigidaire for a few hours, so it'll set up."

Preheat the oven to 350°F.

Just before baking, remove the foil and sprinkle the casserole with the cheese. Bake for 15 minutes. Reduce the heat to 325°F. and continue baking until set, about 45 minutes. Serve hot.

Deviled Crab

Deviling, a cooking process that was popular at the turn of the century, takes a food product and cooks it with one or more hot ingredients such as hot sauce, chili peppers, or mustard. During the 1920s, this spicy crab casserole was all the culinary rage on the East Coast. Crab packers would include the crab's top shells along with the crabmeat so that the dish could be served in them. For this dramatic presentation, get your hands on some top shells from blue crabs if you can and clean them well. (See Note.)

Serves 4 to 6

4 tablespoons (¹/₂ stick) butter
2 tablespoons minced yellow onion
2 tablespoons minced green onion
2 tablespoons flour
1 teaspoon dry mustard
1 teaspoon Dijon mustard
1 cup heavy (whipping) cream
1 teaspoon Worcestershire sauce
1 teaspoon salt
¹/₄ teaspoon ground white pepper
¹/₈ teaspoon cayenne
Dash of Tabasco Sauce
1 pound backfin crabmeat, picked over
2 hard-cooked eggs, chopped
2 tablespoons chopped parsley
¹/₄ cup buttered fine dry bread crumbs, for topping

Preheat the oven to 375°F. Butter a 6-cup baking dish and set aside.

Melt the butter in a heavy-bottomed saucepan over medium-high heat. Add the yellow and green onions and sauté until soft, about 2 minutes. Whisk in the flour and dry mustard and cook for several minutes, stirring constantly. Remove from the heat and stir in the Dijon mustard, cream, Worcestershire, salt, white pepper, cayenne, and Tabasco. Return to medium heat and cook, stirring often, until thickened, about 10 minutes.

Place the crabmeat, eggs, and parsley in a large mixing bowl. Pour the cream mixture over the top and toss gently. Pour into the baking dish and top with the bread crumbs. Bake until nicely browned, 25 to 30 minutes. Serve at once.

Note: To clean crab shells, wash the shells well and place them in a pot of water with 1 teaspoon of baking soda. Bring the water to a boil for a few minutes. Rinse the shells and pat them dry. Mound the crab mixture in them, place the shells on a baking sheet, and bake as directed above.

Oysters

Shortly after Labor Day, as the brightly colored autumn leaves fall from the trees, the watermen of the Chesapeake put away their crab pots and stow the many yards of trotline used for the summer crabbing season and prepare to harvest the oyster beds, "the hardest, coldest job to be had." It is oyster season on the Chesapeake Bay, one of the few solaces that prepare me for the approaching

winter. Given my love of Chesapeake oysters, the old saying "one person's pain is another's gain" rings true.

The Chesapeake oyster industry is legendary. For over one hundred years the catches of oysters were seemingly endless; enormous fortunes were made, and prosperous bayside towns were built on the harvesting, processing, and shipping of oysters. An oyster craze gripped the nation in the late 1800s, and the Chesapeake oyster became an eagerly sought-after commodity by seafood distributors in the surrounding states. Demand was so strong that it resulted in the Chesapeake oyster wars of the 1860s, in which many watermen were killed over territorial disputes.

Oysters grow in natural beds in the Chesapeake Bay as well as in some of its tributaries. Two hundred years ago, more than twenty varieties of oysters could be found in the Bay—such as Choptank, Lynnhaven, and Rappahannock—and true oyster connoisseurs would know where an oyster had been harvested simply by its taste and texture. At the turn of this century, the oyster industry had reached its peak: Nearly twenty thousand Chesapeake residents and two thousand boats were working the water for oysters. By the 1960s, the number of skipjacks—the sail-powered workboats of the Chesapeake (see page 119)—had dropped to sixty-seven, and the oyster industry went into serious decline. During the past decade, harvests of oysters have yielded only 10 percent of the amount reaped only twenty to thirty years ago. This dramatic decrease is due to many factors, including overfishing, diminishing underwater bay grasses which filter the water, and the decimation of the oyster population by a parasite. Today, however, the catches are slowly on the rise again as new conservation efforts have taken effect. Innovative techniques of oyster farming are being developed, and it is hoped that in the next generation the oyster industry will rebound to acceptable levels.

Chesapeake watermen use two methods to harvest oysters: dredging and tonging. The famous Chesapeake skipjacks—the only fully sail-powered fishing fleet in the nation—employ the dredging technique. A large metal dredge, a giant iron claw hanging from a chain, is thrown from the deck of the ship into the water while the ship is sailing. The dredge drags along the oyster bed and is hauled in, and the captured oysters are deposited on the deck. The crew culls, or quickly sorts through and separates them according to size, throwing those that are too small or broken back into the water.

The hand-tonging method is an even more grueling task. The waterman lowers an oversized tong, which weighs 40 pounds and looks like two metal hands attached to a long pole, onto the oyster bed and closes the tong's hands. He then pulls the tong, now laden with oysters, from the water and back onto the deck, where the crew culls the oysters. Harvesting oysters is an arduous way to make a living, but the people who work the water on the Chesapeake are a hardy breed, many of them from families who have been on the water since the founding of this country.

Oyster season officially runs from late September through April, lending credence to the theory that oysters can only be eaten during the months with the letter *r* in their spelling. The *r* theory is a bit of lore that fishermen brought with them from the old country in Europe. In fact, oysters are available and are eaten year-round, although oysters harvested during the winter are of a higher quality. In the warmer months when the oysters are spawning, the meat is drier and slimmer and more perishable than in the winter.

Around the Bay, oysters are eaten fried, steamed, roasted, barbecued, or in stews and chowders as well as raw. Just about any variety of Chesapeake oyster will do nicely for the hearty oyster stews of the Eastern Shore or for platters of crisp panfried oysters. Real oyster lovers contend that the proper way to serve oysters is raw. Tangier and Chincoteague are the Chesapeake's best-known oysters. Both contain a high salt content due to the salinity of the surrounding waters, and connoisseurs of oysters on the half shell always gravitate to these brinier oysters. All you need to accompany a freshly shucked oyster is a squeeze of lemon or a dash of Tabasco Sauce. In a casserole, shucked oysters go perfectly with Chesapeake country hams.

When purchasing oysters in the shell, look for ones with tightly closed shells. Oysters can be refrigerated for several days, covered with a damp towel or burlap bag. When shucking oysters that are to be used in a recipe, be sure to reserve the oyster liquor to add it to the dish for heightened flavor. Previously shucked oysters are sold by the pint or quart; these save a tremendous amount of time and effort when preparing a recipe using a large quantity of oysters. When I am purchasing oysters I always make sure, as with any other seafood, that the establishment has a high turnover, which helps ensure a fresh product.

A Goiter-Free Populace

As its name suggests, Tilghman Peninsula has water just about everywhere. It is bordered by the Chesapeake Bay, the Miles and Tred Avon rivers, and Harris and Broad creeks, and around here that translates into seafood. The peninsula seafood philosophy, which comes from the now-defunct Tilghman Packing Plant, is "Eat seafood to ensure your good health—avoid goiter, prevent anemia, help your stomach, and keep a clear mind." It appears by the look of the rugged locals, the spring in their step, and the sparkle in their eyes, it must be true, for you'll be hard-pressed to find a dull-witted or iron-poor-blood one in the lot. A majority of the folk around here work on the water or in a related business, such as the seafood packing houses. They work long, hard hours to provide seafood to the rest of the country so that everyone may enjoy fish-filled, goiter-free lives. This is no small task, but the residents of St. Michaels, Claiborne, Bozman, McDaniel, Sherwood, Neauitt, and Tilghman Island do their best.

The peninsula is named for Colonel Tench Tilghman, George Washington's confidential secretary and right-hand man, who made a desperate ride on horseback à la Paul Revere during the Revolution. It appears the colonel was rather prolific, considering the number of Tilghman descendants up and down the Eastern Shore of the Bay.

Owing to the wealth of fresh seafood, fowl, game, and produce on the peninsula, some of the finest examples of Chesapeake cookery are found in the recipes of the Tilghman community. Platters of oyster fritters, green tomato fritters, and crab ball appetizers will be found gracing the tables of the region. The tidewater areas are home to all types of waterfowl that end up in such local recipes as mallards roasted with a spiced wine (see page 150). And birds are not the only thing they stuff around here, as their stuffed rockfish attests (see page 94).

1 cup all-purpose flour
1¹/₂ teaspoons baking powder
¹/₂ teaspoon salt
¹/₄ teaspoon freshly ground
    black pepper
2 eggs, beaten

1 cup milk
1 quart shucked oysters with
    liquor
Vegetable oil, for frying
Tartar Sauce (page 34)

Mix together the flour, baking powder, salt, and pepper in a large bowl. In a small bowl, mix together the eggs and milk. Beat the egg mixture into the dry ingredients until a smooth batter is formed. Stir in the oysters.

Pour oil into a skillet to a depth of 1 inch and heat until very hot, about 375°F. For each fritter, scoop out 3 to 4 oysters with batter. Fry until golden brown on both sides, about 5 minutes. Remove with a slotted utensil to paper towels to drain. Serve with Tartar Sauce.

Mrs. Harrison's Oyster Fritters

The late Alice Harrison was an institution on Tilghman Island. The matriarch of the ever-popular Harrison's Chesapeake House Restaurant on the island, "Miss Alice," as she was referred to by her friends and customers, came from humble beginnings. She worked at waterfront canneries and crab-picking houses and went on, with her husband, Levin, to build a charter fishing business, resort hotel, and the renowned restaurant. She worked in the restaurant kitchen making batches of her legendary crab imperial right up to the time of her passing at the age of ninety-two. Some years ago, Mrs. Harrison provided me with this recipe for her light oyster fritters, which she served with chicken salad.

Serves 6 to 8

Chincoteague Single-Fried Oysters

Chincoteague, Virginia, is home to the famous oysters that bear its name. These oysters have a wonderfully briny flavor due to the high salinity of the local waters. Often locals on the island will eat fried oysters with little more than a squeeze of lemon, but Alma Madanick, a shining star of the Chincoteague culinary world, has designed some incredibly tasty dipping sauces for them. Her husband, John, says that "Alma's not happy until she jazzes something up." Well, she's jazzed up these briny morsels just fine.

Single refers to each oyster being fried individually, as opposed to a fritter, which contains several oysters in a batter.

Serves 4

1 pint shucked oysters
1 cup cracker meal made from saltines, crushed fine
1 cup all-purpose flour
Vegetable oil, for frying

Salt and freshly ground black pepper, to taste
Horseradish Sauce, for dipping (recipe follows)
Tarragon Tartar Sauce, for dipping (recipe follows)

Drain the oysters, reserving the liquor, if desired (see Note). Combine the cracker crumbs and flour. Dust the oysters in the crumb mixture, one at a time. Set aside the oysters for several minutes to dry.

Pour oil into a frying pan to a depth of $^1/_2$ inch. Heat the oil and sauté the oysters for about 5 minutes, or until golden brown. Do not overcrowd the skillet. Add more oil as needed. Remove the oysters with a slotted utensil to paper towels and drain well. Season with salt and pepper.

Note: Oyster liquor may be added to dishes for heightened flavor.

Horseradish Sauce   Makes 1³/₄ cups

1 cup sour cream
$^1/_2$ cup ketchup
3 tablespoons prepared horseradish, drained

1 tablespoon chopped parsley
Freshly ground black pepper, to taste
Cayenne, to taste

Combine all the ingredients in a small bowl and mix well. Cover and refrigerate for at least 1 hour before serving.

Tarragon Tartar Sauce   Makes 1¹/₂ cups

1 cup mayonnaise
$^1/_4$ cup minced sweet pickles
1 tablespoon sweet pickle juice
1 small shallot, minced
1 tablespoon chopped chives

2 tablespoons minced parsley
1 tablespoon minced tarragon
1 tablespoon drained capers, minced

Combine all the ingredients in a small bowl and mix well. Cover and refrigerate for at least 1 hour before serving.

Butter Sauce (recipe follows)
20 oysters, washed
Juice of 1 lemon
1 pound spinach, stemmed
Salt and freshly ground black
    pepper, to taste
1 fennel bulb, cut into strips
2 medium carrots, cut into
    strips
1 leek, cut into strips

4 ounces snow peas
1 cup heavy (whipping) cream
$^1/_2$ cup dry champagne
2 ounces prosciutto or
    Smithfield ham, cut into
    fine strips
$^1/_2$ clove garlic, chopped
1 pound seaweed, for garnish
    (optional)
20 sprigs of chervil, for garnish

Prepare the Butter Sauce and set aside until needed.

Shuck the oysters, reserving the oyster liquor. Set aside the deep part of the shells of the oysters.

Add a little salted water and the lemon juice to a pot and wash the oysters. Remove the oysters and set aside. Add the rinse water to the reserved oyster liquor and set aside.

Pick over the spinach leaves and discard any wilted ones. Wash the spinach and steam for about 1 minute. Refresh in ice water. Remove and squeeze out any excess liquid. Season lightly with salt and pepper. Set aside.

Steam the fennel, carrots, leek, and snow peas for 2 to 3 minutes, making sure each vegetable is still crunchy. Lightly season with salt and pepper. Set aside.

Combine the heavy cream, champagne, and reserved oyster juice in a saucepan. Cook over medium heat and reduce until a quarter of the cooking liquid remains. Lower the heat and add the oysters. Gently poach for 2 to 3 minutes. Remove from the heat and stir in the Butter Sauce. Add the spinach, then sprinkle in the prosciutto and garlic.

If using seaweed, blanch enough to cover the base of 4 plates. Lay the oyster shells on the seaweed. Fill half of each oyster shell with spinach and prosciutto removed from the sauce, top with oysters removed from the sauce, and spoon sauce over. Place a small spoonful of steamed vegetables on top of each oyster serving. Garnish with the chervil.

Oysters Poached in Champagne

During Chesapeake oyster season, guests who are enjoying a relaxing getaway at Sir Bernard Ashley's picture-perfect Inn at Perry Cabin on Maryland's Eastern Shore are treated to this rendering of oysters in champagne. The recipe may seem a bit complicated upon reading, but don't worry: Take your time and take it step-by-step. I can assure you that this dish is well worth the effort.

Serves 4 to 5

Butter Sauce Makes 1 cup

2 shallots, finely chopped
1 cup white wine
$^1/_4$ cup heavy cream
$^1/_2$ pound (2 sticks) butter, cut
    into bits

Salt and freshly ground black
    pepper, to taste

Place the shallots and white wine in a heavy saucepan. Reduce over medium-high heat until about 1 tablespoon of liquid remains. Add the heavy cream and bring to a boil for 1 minute. Remove from the heat and slowly whisk in bits of butter to make an emulsified sauce. Season with salt and pepper.

Revitalizing an Aphrodisiac

After a hundred-plus years of being the country's largest oyster producer, the Chesapeake Bay, along with many other fisheries worldwide, has experienced a vastly diminished supply of once plentiful local seafood. Overfishing, pollution, and natural forces have all contributed to the demise of the Chesapeake oyster industry. Recently a consortium of watermen, environmentalists, scientists, and government officials joined forces to form the Oyster Recovery Project. Their mission is to bring back the Chesapeake Bay oyster.

They have already begun their experimental plan to restore the oyster population in six Chesapeake rivers. Watermen with the help of young volunteers are planting oyster seedlings, called spats, and rebuilding damaged oyster reefs where the spats attach themselves and grow to maturity. It is an ambitious project, and while it's much too early to declare it a success, the current oyster catch in 1997 has been the best in fifteen years.

Seafood

Aquick drive from just about any town in the Chesapeake region will get you to the water. The nearly forty-six hundred miles of tidewater shoreline on the Chesapeake, including its far-reaching tributaries, translate into seafood galore; previous generations told tales of crabs with shell spans two feet across and inlets so densely laden with rockfish a grown man could walk from one shore to another on top of the fish. The Chesapeake's watermen's skill and prowess are also legendary, but watermen are not the only Chesapeake folk to work the water. Almost anyone who calls the Chesapeake home has a rod and reel—complete with tackle box—close at hand. Boats are everywhere, with folks fishing from sunup to sundown, and even the lack of a boat doesn't put a damper on fishing—rows of fishing rods line bridges and public access areas with locals ready to spend the better part of the day trying out their best lures for a plentiful catch. People around here love their seafood. Catching, cleaning, and cooking it is all part of the Chesapeake Bay seafood ritual.

All these fishing-folk know the Chesapeake is blessed with a myriad of seafood. Bluefish, catfish, flounder, herring, trout, spot, perch, and shad, to name just a few. Of course, the largest and most famous catches of the Bay are crabs and oysters, but also abundant are hard-shell clams, such as cherrystone, littleneck, and surf, which are an integral part of Chesapeake cuisine. Hard-shell clams are found in many dishes, including chowders and stews filled with plump clam meat and briny clam juices; bowls of steamed clams with melted lemon butter on the side for dipping; and crisp strips of fried clams served with a horseradish-infused cocktail sauce. And let us not forget the most popular manner of clam consumption: raw, on the half shell.

Another variety of clam from the Bay is the soft-shell clam, or manninose. These peculiar-looking clams, also known as steamers, have thin shells and elongated bodies. Traditionally, they were not eaten but were used as "trash-fish" or "bait-fish." Yet, these same clams are the ones loved by New Englanders for steamers—which proves that one man's trash is another's treasure. Nowadays, soft-shell clams as an edible item are slowly gaining respect from Chesapeake locals.

Rockfish is another high-profile Chesapeake seafood eagerly sought after by cooks up and down the East Coast. Its firm, meaty flesh and mild taste make it a favorite for grilling, but the more common method of preparation is baking. I have fond memories from my youth of watching my grandmother carefully prepare a large whole rockfish. She would place the fish in a baking pan, season it lightly with salt and pepper, and generously splash milk on it to keep the fish moist during baking. For the finale, she would lay strips of thinly sliced hickory-smoked bacon on top of the rockfish so the smoky taste of the bacon would permeate the fish as it baked.

Some may not think of shrimp as part of the Chesapeake seafood repertoire but, judging by the tonnage of shrimp consumed by locals, that's simply not the case. While the number of shrimp caught off the coast where the Chesapeake meets the Atlantic is not nearly the quantity produced by the Gulf fisheries, shrimp is, and always has been, a staple of Chesapeake fare. A favorite local dish is peeled jumbo shrimp stuffed with herbed crabmeat, and just about every neighborhood bar and tavern in the Chesapeake has a "raw-bar" that serves freshly shucked clams and oysters accompanied by mounds of hot steamed shrimp and pitchers of cold beer.

Seafood from the Bay

The Chesapeake Bay is home to numerous varieties of fin- and shellfish. Here is a list of the most popular and readily available types.

Bay Clams come in many sizes and shapes, but the locals keep it simple. They refer to them as either soft-shell clams (manninose or manos) or hard-shell clams. The latter includes anything that's not a soft-shell.

Soft-shell clams, also called steamers, have a thin shell and an elongated body. They are readily identifiable by their protruding snouts. Traditionally Chesapeake residents have not ranked them as good enough to eat, relegating them to the bait box. New Englanders vehemently disagree. For generations they have been importing vast quantities of the Bay's soft-shell clams for their clambakes and fried clams.

Chesapeake hard-shell clams include cherrystone, littleneck, and surf clams. All are enjoyed raw on the half shell, steamed, and fried and in chowders and stews.

Shrimp are enthusiastically eaten at tables around the Chesapeake. They are not fished from the Bay but in the ocean waters just beyond where the Bay meets the Atlantic Ocean. Most of the shrimp used in Bay recipes are medium to jumbo size, from the Atlantic or the Gulf of Mexico.

Terrapins are small turtles that inhabit the Bay tributaries. Diamondback terrapins were widely available at one time, but in recent years as tastes have changed, demand has drastically declined. Terrapin is one of the legendary delicacies of the Chesapeake. It possesses a strong flavor that one either adores or abhors. A generation ago these turtles were always sold live, but now the meat is sold precooked, either frozen or canned.

Black Sea Bass is fished at the mouth of the Bay in ocean waters and is available year-round. It is used as a substitute for rockfish in many local recipes. The flaky white meat of the fillet is excellent broiled or baked and lends itself well to fish stews and chowders.

Bluefish, a Bay staple, is a strong-tasting, oily fish with a dark and moist meat. Available year-round, it is most commonly grilled or baked. It does not freeze well and should be purchased only when very fresh. The high fat content makes bluefish a good candidate for smoking. Bluefish is unique, and there is no substitute.

Catfish, if wild, comes from the tributaries and slow-moving creeks emptying into the Bay. Prime availability of wild catfish is during the summer months, although farm-raised catfish, a huge Bay area business, can now be found throughout the year. According to my fishmonger friends, farm-raised catfish is a popular seller with younger customers who prefer its mild flavor and uniformly white meat to that of the muddier-tasting wild catfish. Frying is regarded by many cooks as the best way to prepare catfish, but baked or braised catfish is also good. Catfish can be substituted in recipes calling for perch and lake trout.

Chesapeake Croakers, or hardheads, are fished mostly from Virginia waters. The tender flesh is similar to that of a sea trout and is best fried or broiled. The name croaker comes from an air bladder that makes a sort of croaking sound. Croakers also have a stonelike knot on the top of their heads, thus the name hardheads. They can be substituted for rockfish.

Eel is the second-largest commercial finfish in Maryland. It is not tremendously popular with local diners, however. Most of the catch is exported to Europe, where oily-fleshed fish is highly prized. Locally, eels are used for crab bait. They are especially good smoked, but are also tasty when fried and braised.

Flounder, of various types, is also fished from the Bay and is generally sold year-round. Mild-tasting, fine-textured flounder can be broiled or fried whole or filleted. It is an excellent stand-in for sole. Any flatfish will substitute nicely in recipes calling for flounder.

Herring run up the Bay and into the tributaries every spring. It is a rather oily fish, and the most popular methods of preparation are smoked, salted, and pickled. Herring roe is eaten fried or baked. As the older generations of Chesapeake locals die off, so does the demand for herring. Its culinary roots lie in western and eastern Europe; nineteenth- and early-twentieth-century immigrants used the preserving techniques of their homelands to process these small fish.

Lake Trout, or whiting, has just one bone up the back, which makes it easy to prepare. Locals refer to this mild-flavored fish as lake trout but the fish is neither from a lake nor is it an actual trout. It is a saltwater fish that used to come to the docks on boats arriving late in the day. As the boats were being unloaded, workers would yell out "late trout." Perhaps because of the Chesapeake regional accent, it was thought they were calling "lake trout," and the name stuck. It is favored for fish and chips and neighborhood fish frys. Flounder, perch, or catfish fillets serve well in place of lake trout.

Norfolk Spot is a small croaker with tender, delicate, mild-tasting flesh. Available in the summer months, the Norfolk spot tastes best when fried or broiled. Spot is a good substitute in rockfish recipes, and bass will substitute nicely for spot.

Perch comes in two varieties, yellow and white. Both are fished in Bay estuaries year-round. Perch is an extremely popular local fish, with a white sweet-tasting meat. It is generally panfried, baked, or broiled. Perch roe is a highly regarded delicacy. The sacks of roe are much smaller than those of shad, but can be prepared in the same manner. Flounder or orange roughy work well in place of perch fillets.

Rockfish takes its name from a local legend. Actually a striped bass, folks recall that these fish were once so plentiful in the waters of Rock Hall, Maryland, that they were virtually "jumping into the boats." Rock has traditionally been the most popular finfish from Chesapeake waters. Over-fishing dramatically decreased the rockfish population in the Chesapeake, but after a successful conservation project was implemented in the 1980s the numbers have steadily risen. There are also many aquaculture farms springing up around the Bay, producing a good-tasting farm-raised product. Rockfish has slightly oily, white, flaky flesh with a marvelous taste. Rockfish are commonly baked whole and are sometimes stuffed. Black sea bass or croakers can be substituted.

Sea Trout, or weakfish, a member of the drum family, is another tender, delicate, fine-tasting Bay fish containing few bones. A saltwater fish most commonly fished near Crisfield, Maryland, it is small in size and usually sold whole. Locals prefer it baked or broiled whole; however, filleted sea trout panfries splendidly. Blackfish or redfish substitute well.

Shad is perhaps the most sought-after delicacy of the Bay. It has a short-lived availability because it runs only in the spring, primarily in March. Shad tend to be quite bony, and an old Chesapeake wives' tale recalls a method of baking whole shad for eight hours in lemon juice, during which time the bones miraculously disappear. The same thing happens when the fish is slow cooked for $2^1/_2$ to 3 hours. However, I find it best prepared with fillets that are broiled, grilled, or sautéed—just don't over-cook. Have your fishmonger do the job of filleting and deboning the fish, as it is a difficult process, given the delicate bone structure of shad. The legendary shad roe is the object of fanatical demand each spring and is a true Bay specialty. There is no substitute for shad.

Tilapia, a farm-raised fish, is not historically a Chesapeake product, but with the advent of large aqua farms in the region it is quickly becoming popular with the locals. Also known as Saint Peter's fish, it is sold in fillets and has a sweet and meaty texture that lends itself well to broiling, sautéing, frying, and baking. Snapper and sea bass substitute well for this fish.

4 eggs, beaten

1 cup milk

1½ teaspoons salt

½ teaspoon freshly ground
black pepper

1 cup all-purpose flour

1 cup yellow cornmeal

Vegetable oil, for frying

4 cups shucked soft-shell clams
(manos)

Tartar Sauce (page 34) or
Skipjack Salsa (page 118)
and lemon wedges, for
accompaniment

Mix the eggs, milk, salt, and pepper together in a bowl. In another bowl, mix the flour and cornmeal together.

Pour the oil into a deep skillet to a depth of 1½ inches and heat until very hot, about 375°F. Dip the clams into the egg mixture, toss them in the cornmeal mixture, and shake off the excess. Fry, a few at a time, for 1 to 1½ minutes, or until golden brown. Do not overcook because it toughens the clams. Remove with a slotted utensil to paper towels to drain. Serve with Tartar Sauce or Skipjack Salsa and plenty of lemon wedges.

Fried Soft-Shell Clams

Soft-shell clams from the Chesapeake are known as manninose, or manos for short. With a protruding neck and thin elongated shell, these mollusks can be fried as well as steamed. Here the shucked clam meat is coated with a cornmeal mixture and lightly fried; to ensure perfectly tender fried clams, take care not to overcook. Tartar Sauce is normally served with the clams, but for a refreshing change of pace try having a bowl of Skipjack Salsa on hand for dipping.

Serves 4 to 6

Steamed Soft-Shell Clams

These soft-shell clams are steamed in an aromatic broth of wine and vegetables, then served piping hot in their shells with plenty of drawn butter and cooking broth for dipping. Be sure to take the time to prepare the clams properly.

To savor every bit of the clam, hold it by the snout, dip it into the hot broth, then dip it into the butter. After eating the body of the clam, peel the skin from the snout, dip it in the broth and butter, and eat that, too.

Serves 5 to 6

8 tablespoons (1 stick) butter
1 small onion, finely chopped
$1/4$ cup chopped celery
$1/4$ cup chopped carrot
2 tablespoons chopped garlic
$1^1/2$ cups dry white wine or water
$1/2$ teaspoon salt
$1/4$ teaspoon freshly ground black pepper
1 bay leaf
6 to 7 dozen soft-shell clams (manos), cleaned (see Note)
Hot melted butter and lemon wedges, for accompaniment

Melt the butter in a large heavy-bottomed pot. Add the onion, celery, carrot, and garlic and cook for several minutes. Add the wine, salt, pepper, and bay leaf. Bring to a rolling boil and add the clams. Cover tightly and steam just until clams open, about 10 to 12 minutes. Do not overcook. Using a slotted utensil, remove the clams from the broth. Remove and discard the bay leaf.

Serve clams with the steaming broth on the side, some hot melted butter, if desired, and lemon wedges.

Note: To clean the clams scrub them well several times under cold water. Place them in a large pot of cold water, add a handful of cornmeal and a tablespoon of salt, and let them sit for 4 to 5 hours. This process purges the clams to ensure a grit-free bowl of steamed clams.

1 bottle (12 ounces) flat beer
    (see page 27)
1 cup white wine vinegar
1 onion, sliced
2 stalks celery, chopped
3 tablespoons Chesapeake
    seasoning
2 teaspoons pickling spice

1 teaspoon whole black
    peppercorns
2 pounds medium to large
    shrimp, in the shell
Tangy Cocktail Sauce (recipe
    follows) and lemon wedges,
    for accompaniment

Combine the beer, vinegar, onion, celery, Chesapeake seasoning, pickling spice, and peppercorns in a large pot. Bring to a boil, add the shrimp, stir, and cover. Cook over high heat, stirring occasionally, until the shrimp turn a bright pink, 4 to 5 minutes. Drain shrimp. Serve hot or cold with plenty of cocktail sauce and lemon wedges.

Tangy Cocktail Sauce   Makes about 2¹/₂ cups

2 cups ketchup
¹/₂ cup prepared horseradish
2 tablespoons Worcestershire
    sauce

1 teaspoon Tabasco Sauce
Juice of 1 lemon

Combine all the ingredients in a bowl and mix well.

Steamed Shrimp

From the barrooms to the backyards of Baltimore, you'll find these spicy critters aplenty. Except for blue crab, there's not a seafood treat the locals prize more highly. I suggest you eat them fast, for they have a tendency to disappear before your eyes. Rule of thumb for a shrimp feast: You snooze, you lose.

Serves 6 to 8

Shrimp Stuffed with Crabmeat à la Dolores

*Y*ou can tell by the aroma pulling you up the steps of Dolores Keh's row house in Baltimore's Little Italy that there's some good cooking going on inside. Her hearty, infectious laughter lights up the kitchen as she sets platter after platter in front of her guests. Not only is Dolores a wizard in the kitchen, but she married one as well: Her husband, Rolando, is a chef for the United States Congress in Washington, D.C. Dolores suggests serving these stuffed shrimp with Tangy Cocktail Sauce, macaroni and cheese, steamed broccoli, and corn bread. After all that good eating it'll be hard to tell who's stuffed, the shrimp or you.

Serves 4 to 5

1 pound jumbo shrimp
1 egg
2 heaping tablespoons mayonnaise
1 teaspoon prepared mustard
2 tablespoons Chesapeake seasoning
1 teaspoon Worcestershire sauce
1/4 cup chopped parsley
1 pound backfin crabmeat, picked over
2 slices of white bread, diced and soaked in milk just to cover

COATING
1 cup all-purpose flour seasoned with salt and freshly ground black pepper
3 eggs, beaten
1 cup fine dry bread crumbs

Vegetable oil, for frying
Lemon wedges and Tangy Cocktail Sauce (page 87), for accompaniment

Peel the shrimp, leaving on the last ring of shell and the tail. Devein and then butterfly along the inside curve of the body. Set aside.

Combine the egg, mayonnaise, mustard, Chesapeake seasoning, Worcestershire, and parsley in a small bowl. Mix well. Place the crabmeat and soaked bread in a large mixing bowl and pour the egg mixture over the top. Toss gently, taking care not to break up the lumps of crabmeat. Arrange the shrimp on a baking sheet or platter, flattening the bodies. Firmly mound some of the crab mixture on each shrimp.

To coat the shrimp, dust them with the seasoned flour, dip them in the beaten egg, and lightly coat them with the bread crumbs.

Pour the oil into a large skillet to a depth of 1 inch and heat over medium-high heat until very hot, about 375°F. Add the shrimp and fry, turning occasionally, until golden brown, about 3 to 5 minutes. Remove to paper towels to drain briefly. Serve at once with the lemon wedges and Tangy Cocktail Sauce.

1 cup backfin or jumbo lump
   crabmeat, picked over
$^1/_2$ cup finely diced Smithfield
   ham
$^1/_2$ cup chopped steamed peeled
   shrimp
3 tablespoons butter
3 tablespoons flour

1 cup milk
2 tablespoons dry sherry
4 egg yolks
Salt, black pepper, and ground
   nutmeg, to taste
$^1/_4$ teaspoon Tabasco Sauce
$^2/_3$ cup grated swiss cheese
6 egg whites

Norfolk Seafood Soufflé

The culinary world is very familiar with the distinctive flavor of the Norfolk cooking style: Smithfield ham paired with fresh seafood. This rather elegant dish embraces that savory combination, blending generous lumps of crabmeat with aged Smithfield ham and steamed shrimp, to create a seafood soufflé that showcases the refinement of the Old South.

Serves 4

Preheat the oven to 375°F.

Toss together the crabmeat, ham, and shrimp in a bowl. Set aside.

Melt the butter in a heavy-bottomed saucepan and whisk in the flour. Cook for 2 minutes, stirring constantly. Do not brown the flour. Remove from the heat and gradually whisk in the milk and sherry. Return to the heat and bring almost to a boil, stirring constantly. Reduce the heat and continue to simmer, stirring frequently, for 2 minutes longer. Remove from the heat and beat in the egg yolks, one at a time. Season well with salt, pepper, and nutmeg. Stir in the Tabasco and all but 3 tablespoons of the cheese. Gently fold in the crabmeat mixture. Beat the egg whites until stiff peaks form and gently fold into soufflé mixture.

Butter a 2-quart soufflé dish and sprinkle the reserved cheese on the bottom. Pour in the soufflé mixture. Bake for about 30 minutes, or until nicely browned and firm. Serve at once.

Big Boats, Big City

Hampton Roads encompasses a large metropolitan area in Virginia. Here, where the waters of the Chesapeake Bay merge with the Atlantic Ocean, sit the cities of Virginia Beach, Portsmouth, Newport News, Hampton, and Norfolk. Before World War II, Norfolk was a small Southern city whose primary commerce was its shipping port and a fishing industry. Now, as site of the world's largest naval base and home of the Atlantic headquarters of NATO, the city has become quite prosperous and cosmopolitan. Its history and Southern charm can, however, still be experienced through the style and flavor of its cooking.

Smith Island Clam Pie

This clam pie is the creation of Mrs. Frances Kitching, the world-renowned Smith Island cook who operates a small inn and restaurant on the remote island. The pie is fashioned from hard shell clams harvested from the Chesapeake, as opposed to the soft-shell variety. I find the pie, accompanied by a garden salad of assorted lettuces, makes for a completely satisfying meal.

Serves 4 to 6

Pastry Dough for a Double-
    Crust Pie (page 244)
8 to 10 hard (chowder) clams,
    shucked with juices reserved
³/₄ cup milk
2 eggs, well beaten
¹/₂ cup soda cracker crumbs
1 teaspoon salt
¹/₄ teaspoon freshly ground
    black pepper
2 tablespoons butter, cut into
    small pieces

Preheat the oven to 450°F.

Prepare the pastry, roll out half the dough, and line a 9-inch pie plate. Roll out the top crust and put aside.

Combine the clams, reserved clam juice, milk, eggs, cracker crumbs, salt, and pepper in a mixing bowl. Pour into the pie shell and dot with the butter. Cover with the top crust, trimming the overhanging pastry to ¹/₂ inch. Flute the edges of the crust and make several 1-inch slits near the center of the pie so that the steam can escape during baking.

Place the pie in the oven and bake for 15 minutes. Reduce the heat to 350°F. Continue baking for 30 minutes longer. Remove from the oven and allow to stand for 10 minutes before serving.

Fish Cakes

These fish cakes can be further enhanced by substituting smoked rockfish or smoked trout for half of the cooked rockfish. Either way they provide a delightfully satisfying meal. If you do use smoked fish, go light on the salt when seasoning the mixture.

Serves 6 to 8

2 cups cooked rockfish or other
    firm fish fillet
2 cups mashed potatoes
2 tablespoons bacon drippings
2 tablespoons butter
1 onion, finely minced
1 egg, beaten
¹/₂ teaspoon Worcestershire
    sauce
¹/₄ teaspoon Tabasco Sauce
Pinch of ground nutmeg
Salt and freshly ground black
    pepper, to taste
3 tablespoons chopped parsley
4 tablespoons butter or bacon
    drippings, for frying cakes

Mix together the rockfish and potatoes in a bowl.

Heat the bacon drippings and 2 tablespoons butter in a skillet. Add the onion and sauté until soft. Add to the rockfish mixture. Add the egg, Worcestershire, Tabasco, nutmeg, salt, pepper, and parsley and mix well. Form the mixture into 12 to 16 cakes. Melt the 4 tablespoons butter in a skillet. Brown the fish cakes on both sides, 3 minutes per side. Drain on paper towels. Serve right away.

1 egg
1 heaping tablespoon
    mayonnaise
1 tablespoon dry mustard
$^1/_2$ teaspoon salt
$^1/_2$ teaspoon freshly ground
    black pepper
$^1/_4$ teaspoon cayenne
1 teaspoon dried tarragon
3 tablespoons chopped parsley
1 pound backfin or claw
    crabmeat, picked over

$1^1/_2$ pounds fish fillets, such as
    blue gill, crappie, flounder,
    or any small whitefish fillets,
    cut into 3 × 1-inch pieces
2 cups Bisquick
$1^3/_4$ cups ice water
Vegetable oil, for frying
Lemon wedges, for
    accompaniment

Combine the egg, mayonnaise, mustard, salt, pepper, cayenne, tarragon, and parsley in a small bowl. Mix well. Place the crabmeat in a large mixing bowl and pour the egg mixture over the top. Mix gently, taking care not to break up the lumps of crabmeat. Line a baking sheet with wax paper. Arrange the fish fillets on the baking sheet. Mound some of the crab mixture evenly on top of each fillet. It should be about $^1/_4$ inch high. Place the baking sheet in the freezer until the fish and crab mixture is stiff, about 45 minutes.

Make a thin tempura-like batter out of the Bisquick and ice water. Pour oil into a heavy skillet until it reaches a depth of about 1 inch and heat until very hot, about 375°F. Dip each fillet into the batter, coating completely, and slip it into the pan, crab-side down. Do not crowd the pan. Fry, turning each fillet once, until golden brown, 2 to 3 minutes on each side. Remove the fillets to paper towels to drain. If all the fillets do not fit in the skillet at once, hold the cooked fillets in a warm oven while the others are being fried. Serve hot with lemon wedges.

Mr. Paul's Fish Sticks

Not many fellows round the Chesapeake Bay know more about what the fish are thinking or where they're hiding than Michael Paul Dahl. He likes nothing better than to spend a day on the water. This recipe came to him while he was fishing blue gills. As Michael fished, other locals caught crabs, and at the end of the day there was a pile of crabs and blue gills on the dock, which started Michael thinking. This pairing of crab and blue gill has heretofore eluded the cooks of the Chesapeake, but now the two will be seeing each other more frequently, thanks to Michael's creation.

Blue gills are a small fish found in Bay tributaries, ponds, and lakes. Blue gills are usually not sold commercially, so if you don't want to spend a day on the water, buy a whitefish fillet, as it will work well in this recipe.

Serves 6 to 8

Bluefish Baked with Tomatoes and Capers

Bluefish is an extremely popular Chesapeake fish that has a dark, rather oily meat. Here its strong taste is complemented by the fragrant combination of tomatoes, capers, wine, and herbs. Covering the dish with wax paper during baking lets the aromas steam through the fillets, infusing the fish with flavor and keeping it moist. Serve this saucy dish with white rice.

Serves 4

1/4 cup olive oil
1 onion, diced
2 stalks celery, diced
2 tablespoons chopped garlic
1/4 cup chopped green onions
1 1/2 pounds tomatoes, peeled and chopped, with juice (about 3 cups)
1 cup dry white wine
3 tablespoons capers, drained and coarsely chopped
1/2 teaspoon dried thyme leaves
1 bay leaf
Juice of 1 lemon
Salt and freshly ground black pepper, to taste
4 bluefish fillets (6 to 7 ounces each)

Preheat the oven to 375°F.

Heat the oil in a heavy pot and sauté the onion, celery, garlic, and green onions until limp. Add the tomatoes, wine, capers, thyme, bay leaf, and lemon juice. Simmer for 45 minutes. Season with salt and pepper.

Spread half of the tomato sauce in the bottom of a 13 × 9 × 2-inch glass baking dish. Arrange the fillets on top. Spoon the remaining sauce over the fish. Butter 1 side of a sheet of wax paper large enough to cover the dish. Cover the dish with the wax paper, buttered side down. Bake for 20 to 30 minutes, or until the fish flakes at touch of a fork.

Remove the fish fillets to a heated platter. Remove and discard the bay leaf and spoon the tomato sauce over the fish. Serve at once.

1/2 cup vegetable oil or butter
plus oil for frying
1 yellow onion, diced
6 green onions, finely chopped
1 green bell pepper, diced
1 red bell pepper, diced
2 stalks celery, diced
2 tablespoons chopped garlic
2 to 3 chilies, minced (see Note)
4 large ripe tomatoes, chopped
1/2 cup tomato juice
1/2 cup white wine
Juice of 1 lemon
1 teaspoon Worcestershire sauce
1 bay leaf
Salt, freshly ground black
pepper, and Tabasco Sauce,
to taste
2 pounds perch fillets
All-purpose flour seasoned with
salt and freshly ground
black pepper
Milk, as needed
Yellow cornmeal, for coating

Heat the 1/2 cup oil in a pot. Cook the yellow and green onions, bell peppers, and celery over low heat for 10 minutes. Add the garlic, chilies, tomatoes, tomato juice, wine, lemon juice, Worcestershire, and bay leaf. Bring to a boil. Season with salt, pepper, and Tabasco. Reduce the heat and simmer for about 1 hour.

For the fish, pour oil into a large skillet to a depth of about 1/2 inch. Dust the fillets with the seasoned flour. Dip the fillets first in milk and then in cornmeal, shaking off the excess. Fry until golden brown and crisp, 2 to 3 minutes per side. Transfer the fillets to a heated platter. Remove and discard the bay leaf and serve the fish topped with the tomato sauce.

Note: When choosing what kind and how many chilies to use, know their strength. If you want to minimize the fire, remove the seeds of the chili. If fresh chilies are not available, 1/4 to 1/2 teaspoon crushed red pepper may be substituted.

Perch Till It Hurts

Tina Louise Jackson, from outside Darlington, Maryland, gave me this recipe. She got it from her mother who said that if it was hot enough, you'd feel like the Holy Ghost had got hold of you. Now that's a gastronomic moment bordering on a religious experience. The chili-fired tomato sauce is also perfect with sautéed shrimp and most other firm-fleshed fish that have been fried or grilled.

Serves 6 to 7

Baked Stuffed Rockfish

Several winters ago I was carting a few freshly caught rockfish up to the mountains of western Maryland to share with a friend who had moved there from the Eastern Shore and missed his ration of baked rock. The night I arrived, a blizzard hit and we found ourselves snowed in. We weathered it well, though, with no cabin fever: We had three days of rockfish meals—baked, sautéed, and chowder. Not a bad way to spend a blizzard.

In summer I stuff rockfish with backfin crabmeat and cover it with hickory-smoked bacon. If rockfish is not available, substitute snapper, grouper, or black sea bass.

Serves 4

1 pound backfin crabmeat, picked over
6 tablespoons (³/₄ stick) butter, melted and cooled
Juice of 1 lemon
Salt and freshly ground black pepper, to taste
2 tablespoons chopped parsley
1 whole rockfish (3 to 3¹/₂ pounds), boned
Milk, as needed
4 strips of hickory-smoked bacon

Preheat the oven to 350°F.

Place the crabmeat in a bowl, pour the melted butter and lemon juice over the top, and toss. Season with salt and pepper. Mix in the parsley. Stuff the crab mixture inside the fish and secure with skewers or toothpicks. Cover the bottom of a baking dish large enough to hold the fish comfortably with milk about ¹/₄ inch deep. Place the fish in the dish. Sprinkle lightly with salt and pepper. Top with the bacon.

Bake for 40 to 45 minutes, or until the fish flakes at the touch of a fork. Baste occasionally during baking with the milk from the dish. When done, transfer the fish to a serving platter. Remove the bacon and discard. Pour any remaining cooking liquid over the fish and serve.

Back Where It Belongs

Twenty years ago it seemed that the Chesapeake rockfish was soon to be a fish of the past. The catches had dwindled to virtually nothing and the prospects of recovering the rockfish population looked grim. Undaunted by local pessimism, the state of Maryland, the watermen's association, and a number of local environmental organizations decided to take action. The state called for a complete moratorium on catching rockfish, by both commercial and sports fishermen. The Chesapeake Bay Foundation led the way, undertaking conservation measures and studies that would gradually help replenish the rockfish population. Today, the rockfish numbers are once again running high in the Bay, and the ban has been lifted, but with strict limits placed on seasonal commercial and sports catches.

During the years of the ban, the business of rockfish aquaculture boomed in the Chesapeake region. The farm-raised fish are now quite popular, their very white flesh possessing a milder flavor than those caught in the wild. During rockfish season, both farmed and wild fish are sold side by side, thereby reducing the demand for the wild ones.

Stuffed Rockfish with Smoked Corn Salsa

Does the thought of a salsa with house-smoked corn get your heart palpitating? Does your mouth start watering if that salsa is piled on a baked freshly caught rockfish stuffed with a moist oyster and corn bread stuffing? Then get your feet moving to Windows Restaurant on St. Michaels Harbor, where executive chef Chris Moyer presides. Chris knows his seafood: He graduated from the Culinary Institute of America and later worked at a highly regarded seafood restaurant in Key West, Florida. Lucky for us locals, he returned not long ago to his boyhood home on the Chesapeake Bay to work his magic in St. Michaels, where he concocted this recipe.

Serves 6

Smoked Corn Salsa (recipe
  follows)
6 rockfish fillets (8 ounces each)
Oyster and Corn Bread Stuffing
  (recipe follows)

Salt and freshly ground black
  pepper, to taste
Melted butter, for brushing fish

Prepare the salsa and let stand for at least 1 hour.

Preheat the oven to 350°F.

Cut a pocket lengthwise in each of the fillets to hold the stuffing. With a small spoon fill the pockets with stuffing, about $^1/_2$ cup per fillet. Place the fillets in a well-buttered 13 × 9 × 2-inch glass baking pan. Brush the fish with a little melted butter and season with salt and pepper.

Bake for about 20 minutes, or until nicely browned on top. Place the fillets on dinner plates and top with a generous dollop of salsa. Serve at once.

Smoked Corn Salsa   Makes 2 cups

1 cup fresh corn kernels
Wood chips
$^1/_4$ cup diced green bell pepper
$^1/_4$ cup diced red onion
$^1/_4$ cup chopped tomatoes,
  peeled and seeded

2 tablespoons chopped cilantro
2 tablespoons tomato juice
2 tablespoons fresh lemon juice
5 dashes of Tabasco Sauce
Salt and freshly ground black
  pepper, to taste

Place the corn in a shallow perforated pan that sits in a deeper solid pan. Place a couple of handfuls of wood chips (hickory works well) in the deeper pan. Put the perforated pan into the deep pan and cover with a lid or foil. Place on the stove over medium heat. Checking frequently, let the corn smoke until it has turned a nice light brown color. Remove from the heat and transfer the corn to a mixing bowl. Add the remaining ingredients and mix thoroughly. Let stand for at least 1 hour before using, to allow the flavors to blend.

Oyster Corn Bread Stuffing Makes 3 cups

4 tablespoons (¹/₂ stick) butter
¹/₂ cup diced onion
¹/₂ cup diced celery
¹/₂ cup diced carrot
2 tablespoons chopped bacon
¹/₂ cup dry sherry

1 cup chopped oysters
¹/₄ cup chopped parsley
2 cups crumbled Two O'Clock
    Club Corn Bread (page 226)
Salt and freshly ground black
    pepper, to taste

Melt the butter in a skillet and sauté the onion, celery, carrot, and bacon until the onions are transparent, about 5 minutes. Add the sherry, oysters, and parsley. Remove the skillet from the heat and mix in enough corn bread to reach a firm, yet somewhat moist texture. Season with salt and pepper.

Rockfish Braised in Gravy with Crabmeat

*F*ish in gravy?
*Absolutely, especially
when my favorite cook,
Mealy Sartori, is at the
stove. Mealy learned the
cooking trade from her
mother, an Italian
immigrant who made her
way to Baltimore. As is
common with Mediter-
ranean cooking, the seafood
is cooked in a rich, garlic-
scented tomato sauce. With
this recipe Mealy does the
Chesapeake proud as her
robust gravy bathes the
moist rockfish. The gravy
recipe makes more sauce
than needed in this recipe;
however, Mealy suggests
making a full batch of
sauce, as it can be used
with pasta and almost any
other recipe calling for an
herbed tomato sauce. Serve
this with spaghetti or
fettuccine dressed with olive
oil and garlic.*

Serves 6 to 8

2 rockfish or bass (3 to 4
    pounds each), cleaned
Salt and freshly ground black
    pepper, to taste
4 cups Gravy (recipe follows)

1 bay leaf
1 pound backfin crabmeat,
    picked over

Preheat the oven to 350°F.

Cut off the head and tail of each fish. Place the fish side by side in a large ovenproof glass dish. Season with salt and pepper. Cover the fish two thirds of the way up with the gravy, add the bay leaf, and cover the pan tightly with foil. Place in the oven.

After the fish has cooked for 30 minutes, remove the dish from the oven and add the crabmeat. Cover with the remaining gravy. Cover and continue to bake for 15 minutes.

Place the fish on a large serving platter and top with crabmeat. Remove the bay leaf and pour the gravy over the fish. Serve at once.

Gravy Makes about 8 cups

$^1/_4$ cup olive oil
4 cloves garlic, minced
1 onion, finely chopped
$^1/_2$ teaspoon crushed red pepper
1 can (6 ounces) tomato paste
3 cups water
1 can (8 ounces) tomato sauce

1 can (28 ounces) crushed
    tomatoes
1 teaspoon dried oregano
1 teaspoon dried basil
1 teaspoon salt, or to taste
2 teaspoons sugar

Heat the oil in a pot and sauté the garlic, onion, and crushed red pepper until golden. Stir in the tomato paste. Rinse the can with the water and add to the pot. Simmer for 30 minutes.

Add all the remaining ingredients. Simmer for $1^1/_2$ to 2 hours. If you have more time, simmer a little longer. Remove from the heat and use the sauce needed for the rockfish recipe.

Allow the remaining sauce to cool completely before storing. If the additional sauce is going to be used within several days, it may be covered and refrigerated. Otherwise, place it in a container with a tight-fitting lid and store in the freezer.

Mealy Sartori of Baltimore's Little Italy

Carmella "Mealy" Sartori is one of my culinary heroes from whom I've learned much about the ways of the kitchen, the garden, and life. I often find Mealy sitting in her kitchen in the home that she and her late husband, Pete, built by hand some forty years ago, ready to talk: "I grew up living right next to the harbor in Little Italy, in the early 1900s. There were ships from everywhere, loading and unloading stuff. The smells! There were banana boats from South America, boats of vegetables and fruits from the Eastern Shore, and watermelons—they were floating everywhere. As kids we loved to sit on the docks and watch the melons bobbing up and down in the water. The boys would try to spear them."

Mealy's mother emigrated from Italy to Baltimore, and Mealy says her mother was a great cook from whom Mealy learned the tricks of the trade: "We never wasted nothing. Hell, you couldn't afford to! By the time I was married and had the kids I was making my own breads, goat cheeses, ricotta, and pasta. I kept goats, chickens, ducks, and rabbits. Yeah, right here in the backyard. I had a garden bigger than this one. It had everything! Fed us during the summer and gave us enough to put up for the winter. I love to cook! You know, you gotta love it. Nobody wants to bother with it no more. I don't know what's wrong with them. They don't want to take the time to make something good, or take the time to sit with the family and eat. How are you going to get to know each other? I think they're all going crazy."

After watching Mealy enthusiastically prepare her food—truly a reflection of her Italian heritage and Chesapeake homeland—and then tasting the results, I know she loves to cook. You know, you gotta love it.

An Italian Dinner with Mealy Sartori

Escarole Soup (page 128)
Rockfish Braised in Gravy with Crabmeat
Stewed Fresh Figs in a Warm Marsala
Zabaglione (page 262)

Rockfish with Baby Bok Choy and Herbed Mashed Potatoes

Mark Salter, executive chef of the Inn at Perry Cabin in St. Michaels, Maryland, developed this recipe shortly after he caught his first rockfish from the pier behind the inn. The entree was a hit and soon found its way onto the Inn's dinner menu. Fortunately for Mark, he does not have to personally catch all the rockfish needed for the guests at Perry Cabin.

Serves 4

1 1/2 pounds Yukon Gold potatoes, peeled
4 tablespoons (1/2 stick) butter
1 cup heavy (whipping) cream, heated
1 tablespoon chopped mixed herbs (parsley, chives, cilantro, and basil)
Salt, freshly ground black pepper, and grated nutmeg, to taste
2 heads baby bok choy, cut lengthwise in half

2 teaspoons olive oil
1/2 cup dry bread crumbs
1 teaspoon chopped mixed herbs (equal amounts thyme, chervil, and chives)
4 rockfish fillets (6 ounces each)
Olive oil, for sautéing
Scallion Crust Topping (recipe follows)
Bouillabaisse Sauce (recipe follows)
Sprigs of chervil, for garnish
Diced plum tomato, for garnish

Preheat the oven to 375°F.

Place the potatoes in a pot of salted boiling water and simmer until just cooked, about 20 to 25 minutes. Drain. Pass the potatoes through a ricer into a bowl. While the potatoes are still hot, beat in the butter and cream, beating until smooth. Mix in the 1 tablespoon of mixed herbs and season with salt, pepper, and nutmeg. Set aside.

Blanch the bok choy in lightly salted boiling water for about 3 minutes. Refresh in ice water. Drain and pat dry with a cloth. Set aside.

Heat the 2 teaspoons of olive oil in a sauté pan until hot. Add the bread crumbs and herbs. Sauté briefly to coat the bread crumbs well.

Pipe the mashed potatoes onto the bok choy halves and top with the bread crumbs.

Season the rockfish fillets with salt and pepper. Pour the olive oil into a well-heated ovenproof skillet to a depth of 1/8 inch and heat until hot. Place the fillets in the skillet and sear on both sides. Remove from the heat and cover the surface of the fillets with the Scallion Crust Topping. Bake for 10 minutes, or until the fish is just cooked.

While the fish is cooking, place the bok choy halves in a baking pan large enough to hold them comfortably. Pour a small amount of water into the pan to prevent the bok choy from drying out when baked. Bake for 10 minutes, or until the top of the potatoes is golden brown.

Arrange a fish fillet and a bok choy half on each of 4 serving plates. Spoon a small amount of Bouillabaisse Sauce over the fillet. Garnish with chervil sprigs and diced fresh plum tomato. Serve immediately.

Scallion Crust Topping Makes ¾ cup

½ teaspoon Dijon mustard
¼ cup mayonnaise
1 tablespoon olive oil

2 tablespoons finely chopped
   green onions
½ teaspoon minced garlic
½ cup dry bread crumbs

Mix together the mustard and mayonnaise in a small bowl. Heat the olive oil in a sauté pan. With a paper towel, pat dry the green onions. Sauté the green onions and garlic for 2 to 3 minutes, or until soft. Remove from the heat and add to the mayonnaise mixture. Mix in the bread crumbs. Set aside until needed.

Bouillabaisse Sauce Makes about 10 cups

2 tablespoons olive oil
1 onion, chopped
1 carrot, chopped
½ leek, well washed and chopped
1 stalk celery, chopped
1 small fennel bulb, chopped
2 cloves garlic, minced
1 cup white wine
1 pound ripe tomatoes, peeled,
   seeded, and chopped

Pinch of saffron
2 cans (28 ounces each) crushed
   tomatoes
2 cups tomato juice
½ teaspoon sugar
8 cups Fish Stock (page 109)
½ teaspoon dried thyme leaves
1 bay leaf
Salt and freshly ground black
   pepper, to taste

Heat the olive oil in a saucepan over low heat and cook the onion, carrot, leek, celery, fennel, and garlic for about 7 minutes, or until slightly softened. Raise the heat to high and deglaze with the white wine. Reduce by about one third, then add the fresh tomatoes, saffron, crushed tomatoes, tomato juice, and sugar. Add the Fish Stock, thyme, and bay leaf. Simmer for 1 hour. Strain into another saucepan and return to the heat. Cook until the sauce is reduced by one half. Remove from the heat. Season to taste with salt and pepper and set aside.

This recipe makes more sauce than needed, and the remaining sauce should be allowed to cool completely before storing. If the sauce will be used within several days, refrigerate it in a tightly covered container; otherwise, place it in a container with a tight-fitting lid and store in the freezer.

Chef Mark Salter of the Inn at Perry Cabin, St. Michaels, Maryland

The Inn at Perry Cabin, named the fifth best resort in the United States by *Condé Nast* magazine, is Sir Bernard Ashley's (of Laura Ashley fame) world-class resort in St. Michaels, Maryland. The Inn is an attractive yet unassuming large country home, surrounded by manicured lawns and brightly colored flowers and plants, in a tranquil setting on the Miles River. There is nothing hotel-like about it—the elegantly furnished entryway could be someone's parlor. The sunlit sitting room, completely decorated in Laura Ashley fabrics and designs, affords a picturesque view of the water. Comfortably ensconced in a plush, oversized armchair enjoying tea and scones, I quickly became one of the many ardent admirers of the Inn, and of its employees. The staff has a casual British way of making you feel as if you are a personal guest, rather than a customer.

Perry Cabin's amiable executive chef Mark Salter has trained and worked extensively in the United Kingdom and on the Continent. His credentials are impressive, including positions at top-rated hotels in Switzerland, the Black Forest in Germany, and the south of France. Mark's impeccable culinary reputation prompted Sir Bernard Ashley to approach him to take the helm of Llangoed Hall in Wales, Sir Bernard's flagship hotel.

Now as executive chef at Perry Cabin, Mark has combined his expertise in preparing European cuisine, game, and waterfowl with all the Chesapeake Bay has to offer to develop his own Chesapeake-style repertoire. Mark works closely with the local farmers and watermen; every day they bring in vegetables, fruits, salad greens, and seafood, understanding Mark's demand for perfection. Taking the seafood and produce of the Bay, he transforms them into works of culinary art. His kitchen runs smoothly, with chefs who have a great love of their craft and none of the arrogance or pretense sometimes found in kitchens of other world-class restaurants. Mark reminds me of a benevolent symphony conductor as he leads the different sections of his kitchen into the creation of true dining masterpieces.

The Inn at Perry Cabin with Chef Mark Salter

Crab Spring Roll (page 60)

Oysters Poached in Champagne (page 77)

Rockfish with Baby Bok Choy and Herbed Mashed Potatoes

4 slices of bacon
12 tablespoons (1¹/₂ sticks)
    butter
1¹/₂ cups thinly sliced
    mushrooms (about 6
    ounces)

Salt and freshly ground black
    pepper, to taste
4 pairs of shad roe
Juice of 1 lemon
1 tablespoon chopped parsley

Fry the bacon in a skillet until fairly crisp. Remove to paper towels to drain, leaving the drippings in the skillet.

Melt 3 tablespoons of the butter in the skillet with the drippings. Sauté the mushrooms for 2 to 3 minutes, or until cooked. Season with salt and pepper. Remove from the skillet and keep warm.

Melt 6 tablespoons of the remaining butter in the same skillet. Sprinkle the roe with salt and pepper. When the butter is hot, add the roe. Cook the roe, covered, over medium-low heat, turning now and then for about 10 to 12 minutes, or until the inside of the roe is no longer pink. Remove the roe from the skillet and place on a heated platter. Top with the mushrooms and bacon strips. Keep warm.

Pour off any excess grease and melt the remaining 3 tablespoons of butter in the skillet over high heat. When melted and just beginning to brown, add the lemon juice and parsley. Remove from the heat immediately and pour over the roe. Serve at once.

Shad Roe with Bacon and Mushrooms

Those shad are quick, so you better get them while you can. They run in the Bay and its tributaries only during the spring, primarily March, making them a short-lived delicacy. In this recipe, smokehouse bacon is featured to give the dish a distinctive Chesapeake flair. It is a very simple preparation of shad roe, so keep that in mind. The two most important things to remember when cooking shad roe are: Don't overcook them; stand back from the stove when cooking, so you don't get burned when the sacks of roe start to pop during sautéing. This dish goes nicely with Lena's Spicy Rice (page 204) or buttered boiled potatoes and a fresh vegetable.

Serves 4

Sole Fillets Stuffed with Crabmeat and Saffron Cream Sauce

crabmeat imperial–like mixture is stuffed into fresh sole fillets, which are then baked in wine and topped with an aromatic saffron sauce. This type of dish is usually found in finer Chesapeake restaurants, but it is actually quite simple to prepare at home. For a more dapper presentation, top each sauced fillet with a thin strip of sautéed red bell pepper.

Serves 6

4 tablespoons (¹/₂ stick) butter
¹/₄ cup diced red bell pepper or pimiento
¹/₄ cup diced green bell pepper
¹/₃ cup mayonnaise
¹/₂ teaspoon dry mustard
¹/₂ teaspoon salt plus salt to taste
¹/₄ teaspoon white pepper plus white pepper to taste
2 lemons
2 tablespoons chopped dill or parsley
1 pound backfin crabmeat, picked over
6 sole or flounder fillets (about 4 to 5 ounces each)
1¹/₂ cups dry white wine, heated to the boiling point
Saffron Cream Sauce (recipe follows)
Chopped fresh parsley, for garnish

Preheat the oven to 375°F.

Melt 2 tablespoons of the butter in a small skillet over low heat and sauté the bell peppers until soft. Combine the mayonnaise, mustard, ¹/₂ teaspoon salt, ¹/₄ teaspoon white pepper, the juice of 1 lemon, and the dill in a small bowl. Add the sautéed peppers and mix well. Place the crabmeat in a bowl and pour the mixture over the top. Gently toss together.

Spread the fillets with the crabmeat mixture and roll up. Arrange, seam side down, in a glass baking dish large enough to hold the rolls comfortably. Melt the remaining butter and brush the tops of rolled fillets. Sprinkle lightly with salt and pepper. Top each fillet with a squeeze of juice from the remaining lemon. Pour the hot wine into the bottom of the baking dish. Cover the dish with aluminum foil and bake for 20 to 25 minutes, or until the fish is cooked through. Remove the fillets with a slotted utensil to a heated platter and keep warm while making the sauce. Strain the cooking juices to use for making the sauce. Ladle the sauce over the fillets and garnish with parsley. Serve immediately.

Saffron Cream Sauce Makes about 1 cup

2 tablespoons butter
1 teaspoon minced shallot
1½ tablespoons flour
Strained pan juices or ¼ cup
    Fish Stock (page 109)
2 to 3 threads of saffron, soaked
    in 3 tablespoons warm water
    for at least 10 minutes

1 cup heavy (whipping) cream
Salt and freshly ground black
    pepper, to taste
1 tablespoon fresh lemon juice

Melt the butter in a saucepan over low heat and sauté the shallots for 2 minutes. Whisk in the flour. Cook, stirring, for 1 to 2 minutes. Do not brown the flour. Remove from the heat and stir in the pan juices, saffron, and cream. Return to the heat and bring to a boil. Season with salt, pepper, and lemon juice. Simmer for 5 minutes.

Panfried Lake Trout

*I*n eateries and fish
markets around the Bay,
signs advertise fresh lake
trout. Actually whiting,
these fish come from the
Bay and its tributaries—
and have never seen a
lake. Seems they got their
name from fishmongers'
cries of yesteryear (see page
83).

This fish has a nice
firm flesh, making it a
perfect candidate for frying;
in fact, it often graces the
tables of church hall fish
frys around the
Chesapeake. If you can't
find so-called lake trout in
your area, try flounder,
perch, or catfish as a
substitute.

Serves 6

2 pounds lake trout fillets
Milk, as needed
1$^1/_2$ cups yellow cornmeal
1$^1/_2$ cups all-purpose flour
Salt, freshly ground black
    pepper, and Chesapeake
    seasoning, to taste

Vegetable oil, for frying
Lemon wedges and Tabasco
    Sauce, vinegar, or Tartar
    Sauce (page 34), for
    accompaniment

Soak the trout fillets in milk to cover in a shallow dish for 1 hour.

In a second dish, mix the cornmeal and flour together. Season with salt, pepper, and Chesapeake seasoning. Remove the fish from the milk, 1 fillet at a time, letting the excess milk drip back into the dish. Coat well with the cornmeal mixture.

Pour oil into a frying pan to a depth of $^1/_2$ inch and place over medium heat. When the oil is hot, add as many fillets as the pan will allow. Fry about 3 to 4 minutes on each side, or until golden brown. Remove the fish from the pan and drain well on paper towels. Serve with lemon wedges, Tabasco Sauce, vinegar, and Tartar Sauce on the side.

Soups and Stews

Without a doubt, soups and stews are my favorite dishes, both to eat and to prepare. This preference is due in no small part to the fact that I grew up on the Chesapeake Bay where these savory concoctions are a staple of local kitchens. I believe that the overall expertise of a kitchen and a cook can be judged solely on the merits of their soups and that much about a regional cuisine can be discerned simply by the results of its soup kettles.

For me, the warm, homey aromas rising from time-worn Chesapeake family soup pots are beyond comparison. And, as one would imagine, seafood soups and stews are the mainstay of the Chesapeake's soup repertoire, with plenty of crab soup recipes. There are two basic types of crab soup. One type is made with a fortified vegetable base that is scented with crab claws and lumps of sweet crabmeat. The other is a richer cream-based soup, or bisque, which is traditionally reserved for more formal dining occasions.

Crab is not the only seafood to make its way into the kettle. On the Eastern Shore the oyster has always ruled supreme, and the watermen's legendary oyster stews bear witness to that fact. Such stews are prepared simply and with great care to respect the integrity of the oyster. The plump juicy oysters are not cooked, but rather are bathed in an aromatically infused milk or cream in which they are barely heated—just until their edges begin to curl slightly. Shucked hard-shell clams are also used in stews and soups, the meat and briny juices of the clams turned into chowders that are thickened by the starch from diced potatoes and scented with hardwood-smoked bacon or ham.

Chesapeake soup makers are also blessed with a wealth of fresh produce from the fertile bayside farmland, yielding dishes such as champagne-based cantaloupe soup in summer and delicate asparagus soup in spring.

In all these soup and stew creations, the primary ingredient of each—be it seafood, vegetable, or fruit—is allowed to shine through; Chesapeake cooks take great pains not to overpower the intrinsic flavor and texture of the main ingredient.

6 tablespoons (³/₄ stick) butter
1 large onion, diced
1 green bell pepper, diced
4 cups sliced okra (about 1 pound)
1 tablespoon chopped garlic
Fish Stock (recipe follows)
4 large ripe tomatoes, diced, or 1 can (14¹/₂ ounces) whole tomatoes, diced, with their juice

1 tablespoon Worcestershire sauce
1 teaspoon dried thyme leaves
1 bay leaf
1 cup white rice
1 pound claw crabmeat, picked over
Salt and freshly ground black pepper, to taste

Eastern Shore Crab Soup

Almost every region around the Bay has its own version of crab soup, and the Eastern Shore, known for its quintessential Chesapeake cooking style, is no exception. Okra and rice set this soup a world apart from the heavier, ham-based crab soups prepared elsewhere on the Bay.

Serves 6 to 8

Melt the butter in a large pot. Add the onion, bell pepper, okra, and garlic. Cook over low heat, stirring occasionally, for 15 minutes. Add the stock, tomatoes, Worcestershire, thyme, and bay leaf and bring to a boil. Reduce the heat and simmer for 20 minutes.

Add the rice and continue to cook for 30 minutes. Add the crabmeat and simmer for 5 minutes longer. Remove the bay leaf and season with salt and pepper. Serve hot.

Fish Stock Makes about 2 quarts

3¹/₂ to 4 pounds fish heads, bones, or trimmings
10 cups cold water
2 onions, sliced
3 stalks celery, chopped
2 carrots, chopped

4 cloves garlic, unpeeled
2 bay leaves
1 tablespoon black peppercorns
2 teaspoons dried thyme leaves
4 sprigs of parsley

Combine all the ingredients in a large pot and bring to a boil. Simmer over medium heat for 30 minutes, skimming off surface foam frequently. Strain through a fine sieve or cheesecloth. Cool completely and refrigerate if not using immediately.

Crab Soup at Cross Street Market

Located in south Baltimore, a stone's throw from Camden Yards, the home of the Orioles, Cross Street Market carries the visitor back in time. At the turn of the century, Cross Street was an open-air market, with stalls displaying fish, meats, poultry, vegetables, and dairy products. Nowadays it has a roof to keep shoppers and vendors sheltered from the elements, but many of the stalls are still run by the same families that operated them nearly one hundred years ago.

Jean Chagouris of Nick's Inner Harbor Seafood stall shared her locally famous recipe for crab soup. She said the recipe is not written in stone, so feel free to vary the amounts of crab or vegetables to your taste.

Serves 12 to 15

4 quarts water

5 cups peeled tomatoes or 2 cans (28 ounces each) tomatoes

1 can (8 ounces) tomato sauce

2 bay leaves

1/2 cup pearl barley

1/2 cup chopped parsley

1 tablespoon Chesapeake seasoning

3 stalks celery, diced

1 large onion, chopped

2 ham hocks

1 beef bone

Salt and freshly ground black pepper, to taste

8 live blue crabs, cleaned and quartered, backs reserved (see Note)

1/2 head cabbage, chopped

2 medium potatoes, peeled and diced

4 cups fresh or frozen mixed vegetables, such as diced carrots, cut-up green beans, corn kernels, shelled peas, and lima beans, in any combination

2 pounds claw crabmeat, picked over

Combine the water, tomatoes, tomato sauce, bay leaves, barley, parsley, Chesapeake seasoning, celery, onion, ham hocks, beef bone, salt, and pepper in a large soup pot. Bring to a boil, reduce the heat, and simmer for 1 hour.

Add the crabs and backs. Continue cooking for another 30 minutes. Add the cabbage, potatoes, and mixed vegetables. When the vegetables are tender, remove the ham hocks and pick the meat off the bone. Return picked meat to the soup. Discard the bay leaves and backs. Add the claw meat and simmer 10 minutes longer. Serve at once (soup may be prepared in advance to this stage and gently reheated before serving).

Note: Blue crabs used in soup recipes are usually whole blue crabs that are female or too small for steaming. To prepare crabs for use in a soup, drop the crabs into

Take Me Out to the Ball Game

Camden Yards, home of the Baltimore Orioles ball club, is the crown jewel of Baltimore's Inner Harbor renaissance. Considered one of the best ballparks in America (some say *the* best), Camden Yards is located in the heart of Baltimore's bustling harbor and financial district and affords spectacular views of Baltimore's skyline, including the famous Bromo Seltzer Tower. (This tower is an enduring Renaissance-style monument to the popular stomach-settler, commissioned by a local businessman to be an exact replica of a tower in Florence, Italy.) The baseball stadium was built in the late 1980s, yet it has an old-time ballpark feel, similar to Wrigley Field in Chicago. And the huge success of Camden Yards has inspired a new genre of ballparks in Denver, Cleveland, and Texas.

In addition to the excitement of an American league baseball game, there is some great Chesapeake eating to be had at the park as well. As might be expected the luxury skyboxes have the market covered on the ultimate in Chesapeake Bay fare. Perfectly seasoned jumbo crab cakes comprised entirely of lump crabmeat are served to VIPs and reporters—you won't find a speck of crab shell in these cakes. Down in the stands the fans are treated to quite respectable crab cakes—perhaps not made with lump crabmeat—but instead, fashioned with backfin crabmeat blended with special and claw. There is spicy steamed shrimp to be eaten, as well as several styles of local sausages grilled with slightly caramelized onions and peppers. A Camden Yards culinary must is to sample the famous tangy barbecue of the legendary Oriole slugger Boog Powell at his smoked-filled stall on the eating concourse. At Boog's Barbecue you'll likely find the amiable Boog in attendance. He comes to most of the games, greeting fans and making sure the barbecue is up to his high standards.

a pot of boiling water and allow to cook for 5 minutes. Rinse in cold water until cool enough to handle. Remove top shell of crabs, reserving shells for soup, as they add flavor to the soup as it cooks. Clean the body of the crab by removing the gills and innards (see page 45). Break the crabs into quarters, and they are ready for use in a soup.

Cream of Crab Soup

When people from the Chesapeake refer to crab soup, they're often talking about the vegetable-based style. When they refer to cream of crab, they mean this soup. The Maryland Seafood Festival, held each year on the shores of the Bay at Sandy Point State Park, sponsors a crab soup contest with only two categories: crab and cream of crab. This version of cream of crab is much lighter and more refined than others I have sampled in my travels around the Bay. Creamed crab soups are usually reserved for more formal dining occasions; that's why the choice of crabmeat in this soup is the more costly backfin, rather than claw meat, which is used in everyday crab soup.

Serves 4 to 5

4 tablespoons ($^1/_2$ stick) butter
1 small onion, finely diced
$^1/_4$ cup minced shallots
2 tablespoons flour
2 cups Fish Stock (page 109)
2 cups heavy (whipping) cream
1 teaspoon Worcestershire sauce
1 teaspoon salt
$^1/_8$ teaspoon white pepper
1 bay leaf
Dash of Tabasco Sauce
1 pound backfin crabmeat, picked over
$^1/_4$ cup sherry
Lightly whipped cream and paprika, for garnish

Melt the butter in a pot over low heat and sauté the onion and shallots until tender. Whisk in the flour and cook over medium heat, stirring constantly, for about 2 minutes. Do not brown the flour. Remove from the heat and whisk in the stock and cream. Return to medium heat and stir frequently until the mixture thickens, about 8 to 10 minutes. Add the Worcestershire, salt, pepper, bay leaf, Tabasco, crabmeat, and sherry. Lower the heat and simmer for 20 minutes. Remove the bay leaf, ladle into soup bowls, and garnish with whipped cream and paprika.

12 live female blue crabs (sooks)
8 tablespoons (1 stick) butter
1 small onion, finely diced
3 tablespoons flour
2 cups Fish Stock (page 109)
2 cups heavy (whipping) cream
1 teaspoon Worcestershire sauce
1/4 teaspoon Tabasco Sauce

1 teaspoon salt
Ground white pepper, to taste
1/4 cup dry sherry
Juice of 1 lemon
1 tablespoon minced shallot
1/2 cup heavy (whipping) cream,
    lightly whipped, for garnish
Cayenne, for garnish

Virginia She-Crab Soup

In the tradition of the Old South, this soup is a roe-laden cream of crab scented with sherry, fish broth, and lemon juice. Pass around some additional dry sherry so that your guests may add a touch to their bowls of steaming soup.

Serves 6

Pour water into a steamer pot or other large heavy pot with a tight-fitting lid to a depth of 2 to 3 inches. Put a round raised rack that is tall enough to clear the liquid into the pot. Bring to a rolling boil. Place the crabs on the rack, cover, and steam over medium-high heat until the crabs are bright red, about 20 minutes. Remove the crabs from the rack. When cool enough to handle, pick out the meat and orange roe. Set aside.

Melt 4 tablespoons of the butter in a heavy-bottomed pot over medium heat, add the onion, and sauté until tender, about 5 minutes. Whisk in the flour and cook over medium heat, stirring constantly, 2 to 3 minutes. Take care not to brown the mixture. Remove from the heat and slowly whisk in the stock and cream. Add the Worcestershire and Tabasco. Return the pot to medium heat and stir frequently until the mixture thickens, about 20 minutes. Add the salt, pepper, sherry, and lemon juice. Simmer for 25 minutes. Remove from the heat.

Heat the remaining 4 tablespoons butter in a sauté pan over medium-high heat. Add the shallot and sauté for about 1 minute. Add the reserved crabmeat and roe. Heat for 1 to 2 minutes, tossing the crabmeat in the butter to coat evenly. Add the crabmeat mixture to the soup and re-heat until hot.

Ladle into soup bowls and top with whipped cream and a light sprinkling of cayenne.

Pauleen's Seafood Gumbo

Mumbo jumbo who's got the gumbo? Well, Miss Pauleen Lee, down in Pocomoke City, Maryland, does. She confides, "Darling, it's all in the roux. Don't want it looking like oatmeal and don't want it burnt to the devil. Got to be the color of a rusty old nail." In case you're fresh out of rusty nails, the shade you're aiming for is a dark reddish brown. The roux not only thickens the gumbo and gives it its color, it also imparts a distinctive nutty flavor to the dish.

Cook up a big pot of white rice while the gumbo is simmering. Serve the gumbo ladled over the rice and pass plenty of hot Old-fashioned Skillet Corn Bread (page 227).

Serves 15 to 20

³/₄ cup vegetable oil
¹/₄ cup bacon drippings or rendered chicken fat
1 cup all-purpose flour
1 large onion, cut into ¹/₄-inch dice
1 cup diced celery (¹/₄-inch dice)
1 green bell pepper, seeded, deveined, and cut into ¹/₄-inch dice
1 cup finely chopped green onions
3 tablespoons minced garlic
2 cups chopped peeled ripe fresh tomatoes, or 2 cans (16 ounces each) diced tomatoes
8 live blue crabs, cleaned and cut in half (see page 45)
5 cups water or Fish Stock (page 109)

1 teaspoon salt
¹/₂ teaspoon freshly ground black pepper
¹/₂ teaspoon dried thyme leaves
¹/₂ teaspoon dried basil
¹/₂ teaspoon dried oregano
1 bay leaf
¹/₄ teaspoon cayenne
¹/₂ teaspoon Tabasco Sauce
1¹/₂ pounds kielbasa or andouille sausage
¹/₂ pound okra, cut into pieces
1 pound shrimp, peeled and deveined
1 pound claw crabmeat, picked over
1 pint shucked oysters and their liquor

Heat the oil and bacon drippings in a heavy-bottomed soup pot (not cast-iron) until smoking hot. Whisk in the flour and stir constantly over medium-high heat until the mixture turns a dark reddish brown, about 3 to 5 minutes. Keep whisking the roux or it will burn and stick to the bottom. Be careful not to splash it on your skin.

When the roux is properly browned, turn off the heat and stir in the onion, celery, bell pepper, green onions, and garlic. Return to medium heat and cook, stirring constantly, until the vegetables are soft and browned, 6 to 8 minutes.

Add the tomatoes, crabs, water, salt, black pepper, thyme, basil, oregano, bay leaf, cayenne, and Tabasco. Add whole pieces of sausage. Bring to a boil, reduce the heat, and simmer, uncovered, for 1 hour. Remove whole sausage and cut into thin (¹/₄-inch) pieces and return to pot.

Stir in the okra and simmer for 30 minutes more. Add the shrimp, crabmeat, and oysters with their liquor and bring almost to the boil. Remove from the heat and serve at once.

6 tablespoons (³/₄ stick) butter
¹/₂ cup diced onion
¹/₄ cup diced celery
¹/₄ cup diced carrot
1 quart shucked oysters, with
    liquor
4 cups Fish Stock (page 109)
¹/₂ cup white rice

Salt, to taste
2 cups heavy (whipping) cream
Freshly ground black pepper, to
    taste
Few dashes of Tabasco Sauce
Whipped cream and cayenne,
    for garnish

Melt the butter in a skillet over low heat and sauté the onion, celery, and carrot for 5 minutes. Drain the oysters, reserving their liquor. Chop 3 or 4 oysters and set the remaining oysters aside. Add the chopped oysters to the skillet and cook for 3 minutes. Bring the stock to a boil in a pot. Add the rice, 1 teaspoon salt, and the sautéed vegetables and oysters. Reduce the heat and simmer for 40 minutes.

In a blender, puree the soup in batches and press the soup through a fine sieve. Return to the pot and place over the heat. Add the cream and reserved oyster liquor. Season with salt, pepper, and Tabasco. Simmer for 15 minutes. Add the reserved oysters and heat briefly until the edges of the oysters begin to curl.

Serve the bisque in bowls. Garnish each serving with a dollop of whipped cream and a sprinkling of cayenne.

Oyster Bisque

Originally the term "bisque" referred to a method of preparing soup by thickening it with bread crumbs; over the years, it has become synonymous with a type of creamy soup made with shellfish. Many oyster bisques have found their way to the tables of Washington, D.C., state dinners where chefs use them to showcase the famous Chesapeake oysters. This recipe makes a rich and creamy bisque, delicately flavored with sautéed vegetables and the oyster's own liquor. Note that once the whole oysters are added, the bisque is only heated briefly so as to not overcook the oysters.

Serves 10 to 12

Power on the Potomac

The Potomac River is the second largest river pouring into the Chesapeake Bay and with it flow generations of American history. Up river, past George Washington's Mount Vernon residence, lies the nation's capital, Washington, D.C. Washington *is* a Chesapeake city. There's so much power up there that people often forget it is an historic old town that has been linked to the Chesapeake since its birth.

From the beginning the capital's kitchens and chefs have been serving the bounties of the Bay to dignitaries and visitors from all around the globe. To many of these guests the food they were enjoying defined American cuisine: deviled crab, terrapin soup, roast wild goose, and briny Chesapeake oysters. Chesapeake cuisine has always been one of the cornerstones of classic American cooking. Lawmakers who make the District of Columbia their residence nowadays should keep in mind where their city lies: The Potomac River and the Chesapeake Bay give Washington its substance—be nice to them.

Sailing down the Potomac along the picturesque Virginia Northern Neck you'll pass by Oak Grove, the birthplace of George Washington, and shortly thereafter, Stratford Hall Plantation, one of the great houses of American history and the birthplace of Robert E. Lee. Thousands of farmland acres border the Potomac here, with golden fields of corn, wheat, barley, and oats.

½ pound slab bacon
1 cup finely minced onion
1 cup finely minced celery
2 quarts half-and-half
1 quart shucked oysters, with liquor
3 tablespoons flour

Salt and white pepper, to taste
Cayenne, to taste
1 teaspoon Chesapeake seasoning
2 tablespoons Worcestershire sauce
1 tablespoon butter

Chill the bacon in the freezer for 20 minutes, then slice into thin strips. In a heavy-bottomed pan, fry the bacon until crisp. Remove with a slotted utensil to paper towels to drain. Leave the bacon drippings in the pan. Add the onion and celery and cook in the bacon fat, stirring now and then, until their shapes almost disappear, about 4 to 5 minutes.

In a separate pan, heat the half-and-half, stirring, until quite hot.

Heat the oysters with liquor in a separate pan, just until the edges begin to curl. Immediately drain the liquor into the hot half-and-half. Cover the oysters and set aside.

Blend the flour into the vegetables and cook, stirring, over low heat for 2 minutes.

Stir the hot half-and-half mixture into the vegetable mixture. Cook over medium heat, stirring constantly, until slightly thickened, about 5 minutes. Season lightly with salt, white pepper, cayenne, Chesapeake seasoning, and Worcestershire. The stew should be very savory but not salty.

To serve, pour the stew into a soup tureen, add the oysters, and stir. Drop the butter into the center and sprinkle with cayenne. Ladle into bowls and crumble the reserved bacon over the top.

Chesapeake Oyster Stew

Master chef and dinner designer William Taylor hosted the prestigious St. Mary's County Oyster Festival for many years, so, as you can imagine, this man knows his stews. Oyster stews originated on the workboats of Chesapeake watermen where they were made with freshly shucked oysters cooked with little more than potatoes and water. The stews have evolved over the years and now have a much richer and aromatic flavor with the addition of vegetables, seasonings, and sometimes bacon. Bill explained to me that in the old days oyster crackers were passed at the table so that they could be crumbled into the hot stew to thicken it. This stew, however, should never be served with oyster crackers because it is already properly thickened.

Serves 8 to 10

Captain Ed's Newfangled Oyster Stew

Watermen are renowned for their skills in preparing seafood stews, and Captain Ed Farley of the skipjack H.M. Krentz is no exception. Traditional Chesapeake oyster stews consist of little more than freshly shucked oysters and milk. Captain Ed created this new version of that Chesapeake classic, and it proves to be yet another example of a waterman's excellent culinary skills. This simple dish showcases the Chesapeake oyster at its finest. Ever the gastronomic improviser, Captain Ed says he has been known on occasion to add sour cream, parmesan cheese, or even some leftover mashed potatoes. This stew is hearty enough for an entree when served with a salad and warm crusty bread.

Serves 3 to 4

3 tablespoons butter plus butter
    for garnish
1/3 cup finely chopped onion
1/3 cup finely chopped green
    bell pepper
3 cups milk, heated

Salt and freshly ground black
    pepper, to taste
1 pint shucked oysters, with
    liquor
1/2 cup Skipjack Salsa (recipe
    follows)
Chopped parsley, for garnish

Melt the butter in a heavy-bottomed pot. Sauté the onion and bell pepper until limp. Add the hot milk, salt, and pepper, and simmer over low heat for 10 minutes. Add the oysters and the liquor to the pot and continue to simmer until the edges of the oysters begin to curl. Remove from the heat and stir in the salsa. Garnish with chopped parsley and serve at once.

Skipjack Salsa Makes about 2 cups

1 pound ripe red tomatoes,
    peeled, seeded, and chopped
2 to 3 cloves garlic, minced
3 tablespoons minced green
    onion
1 tablespoon minced jalapeño
    or serrano chili, or to taste

1 teaspoon red wine vinegar
Salt and freshly ground black
    pepper, to taste
3 tablespoons chopped basil or
    cilantro (optional)

Combine all the ingredients in a bowl and mix well. Cover and refrigerate for at least 1 hour before using. The salsa is best served the day it is made.

Workboats Under Sail

Sitting on the banks of the Chesapeake at Tilghman Island on a cool, crisp fall morning, you may still witness the awesome sight of several majestic Chesapeake skipjacks gracefully gliding along the horizon under full sail. These beautiful ships became popular near the end of the nineteenth century and rapidly became the primary style of boat used in the once enormous and wealthy Chesapeake oyster industry. Today these sailing workboats of the Bay are gradually disappearing with the decline in harvests of oysters from the Chesapeake. They constitute the last fleet in the nation still operating solely under sail power. Their current existence is partly due to a legality: Decades ago in an effort to conserve the Chesapeake oyster, the Maryland legislature passed a law requiring all oyster dredging be done by using only wind power.

Skipjacks are built for speed and maneuverability, and Deal Island, Maryland, is the host of the Chesapeake Skipjack Races. Each Labor Day weekend, many of the remaining skipjacks and their longtime captains come to these races to demonstrate sailing and docking skills and their maritime prowess.

Islands in the Bay: Tangier Island
Fifty Clam Chowder Serves 6

Tangier Island, Virginia, and Smith Island, Maryland, are isolated spots found right smack in the middle of the Bay, requiring a substantial boat or ferry ride to reach them from the mainland. Both islands are totally dependent on the Chesapeake Bay for their survival. Until recently, these communities were virtually cut off from the outside world. In response to their sometimes harsh climate and environment, these islands at the mouth of the Chesapeake breed a hardy people with a partially learned, partially inherent respect for the Bay. This respect is evident in the honest preparation of their foods, resulting in simple yet delicious dishes.

Lifelong Tangier Island resident Alva Crockett gives the lowdown on how to make an authentic waterman's clam chowder.

2 onions	24 hard clams, well washed, shucked,
1/4 pound salt pork, cut into 1/4-inch	and liquor reserved
squares	Salt and freshly ground black pepper,
4 large potatoes, peeled	to taste
	Crackers, for accompaniment

"Cut the onions into little diced pieces, real fine like. The finer the better.

"Fry out the salt pork in your frying pan. Add the onions and cook them for a few minutes.

"Use good-size potatoes and cut them in little squares, no more than an inch.

"In a pot, mix your cooked onions and diced potatoes together. Cover with the clam liquor you saved and enough water to cover it all. Milk is good for babies and on cereal. That's about it, not in this chowder. Simmer until potatoes are tender.

"Cut each clam into 6 to 8 pieces. Add to the chowder and cook for about 3 minutes. Don't cook too long. You can overcook clams so they're as tough as wood on a bar.

"Season with salt and pepper. Serve with crackers."

Colonial Preservation, and Sailing, Too?

When you enter the old town of Annapolis, you are immediately struck by a sense of history. It is one of the oldest cities in the United States, looking the same as it did when George Washington walked its streets. Situated on the Chesapeake, at the mouth of the Severn River, the town of Annapolis is full of streets lined with grand old homes, possibly the best-preserved collection in the country, dating back to the days before the American Revolution.

Although today it is the state capital of Maryland, Annapolis once served briefly as the capital of the United States, prior to the state giving up the land that became the District of Columbia. The presence of the United States Naval Academy, which was founded to "create a select group of gentleman and scholar officers," adds to the sense of tradition and chivalry that has always been a strong part of the city's culture.

Instead of tearing down and burying the past as so many other cities have done, Annapolis residents are devoted to the preservation and restoration of their city's proud history. Annapolis cooking reflects this heritage with an air of elegance and refinement. In the eighteenth century, Britain's influence undoubtedly shaped the styles of society and cuisine, but the fashions and flavors of France made their way into the manors and dining halls of Annapolis's most prominent families.

Annapolis is not totally absorbed in history, however. Do not forget the boats, for Annapolis is the most boat-oriented town on the East Coast. The locals are a sophisticated, pleasure-seeking lot whose leisure time is tied to the water. There are plenty of "weekend captains" on the waters surrounding Annapolis, sharpening their boating skills at the helm as well as reaping the riches of the Chesapeake Bay.

Chesapeake Bay Seafood Stew

During the eighteenth century, French cuisine was the order of the day in Annapolis, Maryland, which then was considered the cosmopolitan city. Gourmets from all over the new republic made their way to this colonial city to sample the tastes of French fare, including George Washington and Thomas Jefferson. In fact, Jefferson, a devotee of fine cuisine, insisted that all his chefs at his Monticello estate be trained in French cookery in Annapolis.

This version of a Chesapeake Bay bouillabaisse, teeming with fresh clams and crabmeat in a saffron-scented tomato broth, is a dish typical of Annapolis. The Rouille, a classic French accompaniment to fish stew, is mayonnaise-like in texture and made from chilies, garlic, and olive oil. Pass around plenty of hot, crusty bread for dipping in the broth.

Serves 8 to 10

$^1/_4$ cup olive oil
1 large onion, diced
6 cloves garlic, unpeeled
2 leeks, well washed, halved, and cut into pieces
$^1/_3$ cup chopped fennel bulb, or 1 tablespoon fennel seed
5 pounds ripe tomatoes, chopped
2 small potatoes, peeled and diced
2 cups dry white wine
3 cups Fish Stock (page 109)
1 teaspoon dried thyme leaves
1 teaspoon dried oregano
1 bay leaf
Grated zest of 1 orange
3 or 4 threads of saffron
Salt and freshly ground black pepper, to taste
8 to 10 pieces of French bread, sliced on the diagonal
Melted butter and chopped garlic, for toast
2 pounds bass, rockfish, bluefish, or other firm-fleshed fillets
1 pound backfin crabmeat, picked over
$1^1/_2$ pounds small hard-shell clams, well scrubbed
Rouille (recipe follows)
Chopped parsley

Heat the oil in a heavy pot and sauté the onion, garlic, leeks, and fennel until slightly softened, about 8 to 10 minutes. Add the tomatoes, potatoes, wine, stock, thyme, oregano, and bay leaf. Bring to a boil, reduce the heat, and simmer for 30 minutes.

Puree the mixture in a blender or food processor. Pour through a fine sieve and return to the pot. Add the orange zest, saffron, salt, and pepper. Cook over medium-low heat, stirring frequently, until somewhat reduced, about 20 to 30 minutes.

Meanwhile, preheat the oven to 375°F.

Brush the bread slices with melted butter and top with garlic. Toast in the oven until browned.

Cut the fish in chunks about 2 inches square. Add to the sauce and cook for 8 to 10 minutes, or until the fish is almost done.

Add the crabmeat and clams. Stir, then cover. Cook until the clams have opened. Reserve 1 cup of the liquid for making Rouille.

Prepare the Rouille. Place 1 piece of garlic bread in each bowl, then spoon in the fish and broth. Arrange the clams on top. Garnish with parsley. Serve the Rouille on the side.

Rouille Makes about 1½ cups

1 small potato, peeled
1 cup broth from Chesapeake
    Bay Seafood Stew
6 cloves garlic

4 fresh or dried red chilies
1 teaspoon Tabasco Sauce
½ cup olive oil
Salt, to taste

Quarter the potato and cook in the reserved broth. Drain, reserving the liquid. Finely chop the garlic and peppers in a blender or a food processor. Add the potato, Tabasco, and oil. Process until the mixture forms a paste. Slowly add enough of the reserved liquid to give the mixture the consistency of mayonnaise. Season with salt.

Café Metropol's Smoked Rockfish Chowder

The charmingly eclectic Café Metropol, a café and art gallery, is owned and operated by Odessa Dunson and Barbara Lahnstein. They designed a smoker to wood smoke poultry and seafood in order to satisfy Barbara's craving for the smoked fish she enjoyed in Europe and could not find here. But their smoked products caught on with the locals and are now prominently featured at the Metropol and sold at local farmers' markets.

Odessa and Barbara created this soup to showcase the local ingredients of the Chesapeake. They purchase all their ingredients right at the farmers' market, except for the fish, which they get from their favorite fishmonger.

Serves 6 to 8

1 large smoked rockfish (2¹/₂ to 3 pounds), including head
3 tablespoons butter
3 medium potatoes, peeled and diced
3 tablespoons flour
4 cups Rockfish Chowder Stock (recipe follows)
1 carrot, diced
1 leek, well washed, halved and diced
1 medium fennel bulb, diced, sprigs reserved, for garnish
1 cup fresh corn kernels (about 2 ears)
1 large Golden Delicious apple, peeled, cored, and diced
2 cups heavy (whipping) cream, heated
2 tablespoons fresh lemon juice
¹/₄ cup applejack or apple brandy
Salt and freshly ground black pepper, to taste
Cayenne and ¹/₄ cup toasted slivered almonds, for garnish

Remove the head from the smoked rockfish and wrap the head in cheesecloth, tying securely. Set aside. Remove the skin from the rockfish and carefully remove the flesh of the fish from the bones. Gently flake the fish into pieces and set aside. Discard the skin and the bones.

Melt the butter in a heavy pot and add the potatoes. Cook over medium heat for 3 minutes. Sprinkle the flour over the potatoes and stir well. Continue to cook for 2 minutes, stirring constantly. Remove from the heat and slowly stir in the Rockfish Chowder Stock. Return to the heat and add the cheesecloth-wrapped rockfish head. Add the carrot, leek, fennel, and corn. Cook over medium heat for 12 to 15 minutes, or until the potatoes are tender. Add the apple, hot cream, lemon juice, and flaked rockfish. Stir well and remove from heat. Remove the cheesecloth-wrapped fish head and discard.

Place a saucepan with the applejack over high heat and bring to a full boil. Remove from heat and add to the chowder. Season with salt and pepper. Ladle the soup into bowls and garnish each bowl with a light dusting of cayenne, toasted almonds, and a small sprig of fennel.

Rockfish Chowder Stock Makes 4 to 5 cups stock

1 tablespoon butter
2 large carrots, chopped
1 small fennel bulb
2 leeks, washed well and
    chopped

3 shallots, chopped
2 pounds fish bones
10 cherrystone clams
1 cup dry white wine
3 bay leaves

Melt the butter in a large pot over low heat and add the carrots, fennel, leeks, and shallots. Cook for 2 minutes, stirring often. Add the fish bones, clams, 5 cups of water, wine, and bay leaves. Bring just barely to a boil. Cover the pot and reduce the heat. Simmer for 45 minutes.

Remove from the heat and let cool to room temperature before straining. Strain the stock and set aside until ready to use. This stock can be made 1 day in advance and stored in the refrigerator until the chowder is prepared.

Maryland Diamondback Terrapin Soup Serves 6 to 8

The diamondback terrapin, a water turtle, is one of the stars of Chesapeake Bay cuisine. This recipe is from the late Mrs. J. Millard Tawes, a former first lady of Maryland; she served the soup at formal dinners at the executive mansion. She also would regularly send batches to Sir Winston Churchill, who was a great admirer of her recipe.

The terrapin, once the toast of presidents, governors, and crowned heads of Europe, is no longer as popular as it once was, and as demand for the turtle waned, availability diminished. Today, only the older generations can recall the times when this delicacy was regularly pulled from the Bay waters. Since the turtle is less readily available, I have included the recipe primarily for its historical importance in Chesapeake cookery.

3 live diamondback terrapins, 5 to 7
   inches across
Boiling water
8 tablespoons (1 stick) butter
4 tablespoons all-purpose flour
4 cups milk

6 hard-cooked eggs
1 cup heavy (whipping) cream
1/2 cup dry sherry
Salt and freshly ground black pepper,
   to taste

To prepare the terrapins, place them in a large pot filled with enough boiling water to cover the turtles completely. Cover and cook until tender, about 1 hour. To test, stick a fork into the sides. It will pierce the skin easily when the turtles are done. Remove them from the water and let cool. When cool enough to handle, remove the top and bottom shells, scraping them for any adhering meat. Pull off the legs and remove the meat from the top of the leg. Remove the liver, taking care not to break the bile pocket. Cut out and discard the bile pocket. Chop the liver and add to picked meat. Skin the legs and cut off the nails. If the meat is still somewhat tough, cook it in a little water.

Melt the butter in a saucepan and whisk in the flour. Cook for 1 to 2 minutes, stirring constantly. Do not brown the flour. Gradually stir in the milk. Chop the egg whites and add to the saucepan. Mash the egg yolks and add them with the terrapin meat. Simmer, stirring constantly, until thickened, about 8 to 10 minutes. Add the cream, sherry, salt, and pepper. Heat through and ladle into soup bowls.

2 pounds asparagus
5 tablespoons butter
1 small onion, sliced
2 tablespoons chopped shallots
1 tablespoon chopped garlic
1/4 cup all-purpose flour
4 cups Chicken Stock (recipe
    follows)

1/2 teaspoon dried thyme leaves
1 cup heavy (whipping) cream
    or milk
2 tablespoons fresh lemon juice
Salt and freshly ground black
    pepper, to taste
Lightly whipped cream, for
    garnish

Cream of Asparagus Soup

The Chesapeake's Eastern Shore has perfect sandy soil for growing what many believe to be the best asparagus to be found. The vegetable is harvested for only a short time each spring, and locals use as much as they can during those precious weeks.

Serves 6 to 8

Cut the tips off the asparagus. Bring a saucepan of water to a boil and blanch the asparagus tips for 3 to 4 minutes. Drain and cool in ice water. Drain and reserve.

Cut off and discard the tough bottoms of the asparagus. Chop the remaining portions into pieces.

Melt the butter in a soup pot and sauté the onion, shallots, and garlic for 5 minutes, or until softened. Whisk in the flour and cook, stirring, for 2 to 3 minutes. Gradually whisk in the stock and then add the thyme. Add the asparagus pieces (not tips) and bring to a boil, stirring often.

Simmer for 20 to 30 minutes, or until tender. Remove from the heat and puree in a blender or food processor. Pass through a sieve and return to the pot. Add the cream and heat almost to the boiling point. Now add the asparagus tips, reserving 6 to 8 for garnish. Season with lemon juice, salt, and pepper. Ladle into bowls and garnish with whipped cream and reserved tips.

Chicken Stock Makes about 8 cups

2 to 2 1/2 pounds chicken backs
    or necks
10 cups water
2 onions, sliced
3 stalks celery, chopped

2 carrots, chopped
4 cloves garlic, unpeeled
2 bay leaves
2 teaspoons dried thyme leaves
4 sprigs of parsley

Combine all the ingredients in large pot and bring to a boil. Simmer, uncovered, for 4 to 5 hours, skimming off surface foam frequently. Strain through a fine sieve or cheesecloth. Chill and degrease. Stock that will not be used within 4 to 5 days may be frozen.

Hominy Cheese Soup

*H*ere's a full-flavored, not full-figured, creamy hominy potage. It is a light, aromatic broth enriched with hominy and fresh kernels of golden corn. When serving, cheese lovers can add a bit more grated cheese to their bowl. I also like mine with a dollop of Skipjack Salsa (page 118).

Serves 6 to 8

Vegetable oil spray
½ small yellow onion, finely diced
1 medium red bell pepper, diced
1 clove garlic, minced
1 cup finely chopped green onions
1 can (20 ounces) hominy, broken apart with a fork
2 cups fresh corn kernels (4 ears), or 2 cups frozen
1½ cups low-fat milk
1 cup shredded low-fat cheddar cheese, plus extra for garnish
Salt and freshly ground black pepper, to taste

Spray the bottom of a medium saucepan well with vegetable oil. Heat the pan and sauté the onion, bell pepper, garlic, and green onions for about 3 minutes. Add the hominy, corn, and milk. Cook over high heat, stirring constantly, until soup comes almost to a boil. Remove from the heat and stir in the grated cheese. Season with salt and pepper and serve.

Escarole Soup

*M*amma Mealy Sartori of Little Italy in Baltimore prepares this soup when expecting special guests. She says it's an Italian wedding soup and is actually very easy to prepare. In lieu of a prosciutto bone I have used the bone from a salty Smithfield ham, achieving equally excellent results. If the bone is too long for your pot, have the butcher cut it into several smaller pieces.

Serves 6 to 8

4 quarts water
½ prosciutto bone, cut into several pieces
1 large onion, finely chopped
3 heads escarole, cored, washed, and coarsely chopped
3 eggs, lightly beaten
1 cup grated parmesan
Freshly ground black pepper, to taste

Bring the water and prosciutto bone to a boil in a soup pot. Reduce the heat and simmer, uncovered, for 2½ to 3 hours. Remove the bone and pick off any pieces of meat. Add the meat to the pot. Bring the liquid back to a boil and add the onion and escarole. Lower the heat and simmer for 15 minutes.

Mix together the eggs and parmesan in a bowl. While the soup is simmering, pour in the egg mixture in a slow stream, stirring constantly. Remove from the heat and ladle into soup bowls. Top with freshly ground pepper.

Chicken and Game Birds

If the adage "you are what you eat" is true, then I am a big old bird. I could eat chicken seven days a week and be completely satisfied, so it is my good fortune to live in close proximity to the Chesapeake's Eastern Shore of the Delmarva (*De*laware, *Mar*yland, and *Vir*gini*a*) peninsula. The large flat expanse of the Eastern Shore is perfect not only for crop farming but poultry farming as well. For generations the Delmarva has been known for its superb quality of poultry, and its reputation has been pushed to the forefront even further by poultry magnate Frank Perdue: His entrepreneurial spirit has made the Chesapeake's Eastern Shore synonymous with poultry.

Around these parts, locals utilize a myriad of methods for serving chicken: grilled chicken basted with tangy barbecue sauces; potpies filled with moist chicken and tender vegetables tucked under a flaky pastry lid; and creamy chicken salad paired with crisp fried oysters. Yes, there's roasted, stewed, grilled, and poached chicken, but the most famous, and my absolute favorite kind, is fried chicken.

The cooking techniques of Maryland- and Southern-style fried chicken are quickly becoming a lost art because the Chesapeake residents of today are not frying up chicken as often as locals did years back. Despite this, fried chicken recipes still arouse the type of regional fervor usually reserved for crab cake recipes. Every family has what it considers *the* best recipe, and will unwaveringly protect their seasoning and cooking techniques from wandering eyes.

Traditionally, fried chicken is prepared in big, well-seasoned cast-iron skillets. Many locals claim the secret is in the fat, and old-timers insist on frying chicken in lard to get the proper flavor. I find using lard alone gives the chicken a heavy flavor, so I use vegetable oil with just a touch of lard to add taste and color. Then comes another great controversy: gravy or dry. Residents of the Bay's northern towns prefer a plain fried chicken, and serve gravy only to top mounds of buttery mashed potatoes. But in the southern part of the Bay, residents like their chicken smothered in a cream gravy—with extra gravy for the potatoes.

The wetlands and marshes of the Chesapeake are a hunter's paradise, where flocks of migrating birds often block out the sun. During various times of the year, there are Canada geese, mallard ducks, black ducks, and wild pheasant to be had. Chesapeake folks usually prepare these birds simply, with roasting being the preferred method. I find that roasting works exceptionally well for pheasant, especially if it is a young bird that weighs about $2^1/_2$ to 3 pounds. For larger, older birds—which have a tendency to be a bit tough when roasted—it is better to use a recipe in which the bird is gently stewed with a red wine and game stock enhanced by aromatic vegetables and spices.

Chicken and Game Birds

1 frying chicken (3 to 4
   pounds), cut into serving
   pieces

MARINADE
1 quart buttermilk
1 teaspoon salt
1 teaspoon Chesapeake
   seasoning
$^1/_2$ teaspoon cracked black
   pepper
$^1/_2$ teaspoon Tabasco Sauce
3 cloves garlic, peeled and cut in
   half
Juice of 1 lemon

COATING
2 cups all-purpose flour
1 tablespoon salt
2 teaspoons Chesapeake
   seasoning
1 teaspoon freshly ground black
   pepper
1 teaspoon rubbed sage
$^1/_2$ teaspoon powdered thyme
$^1/_2$ teaspoon cayenne

Vegetable oil (and lard, optional,
   3 parts oil to 1 part lard),
   for frying
Cream Gravy (recipe follows),
   for accompaniment

Maryland Panfried Chicken

You'll have no trouble getting people to the table with this one. In fact, it'll take a lot of shooing to keep them out of the kitchen while you're frying. This world-famous dish puts the Colonel to shame. When you put the chicken pieces in the bag, it's your basic "shake and bake" technique—but you don't bake. You brown the chicken in very hot oil, then cover the pan and reduce the heat to steam the chicken; this keeps the meat moist while producing a crisp coating. I serve my panfried chicken with buttery mashed potatoes, and country greens (see page 196).

Serves 4

Place the chicken pieces in a shallow dish. To prepare the marinade, pour the buttermilk in a bowl and add the Chesapeake seasoning, cracked black pepper, Tabasco, garlic, and lemon juice. Mix well and pour the mixture over the chicken to cover. Cover the dish and refrigerate overnight.

For the coating, put the flour in a bowl and add the salt, Chesapeake seasoning, ground black pepper, sage, thyme, and cayenne. Mix together well and transfer to a strong paper bag or large, heavy-duty plastic bag. When ready to fry, remove the chicken from the buttermilk and wipe off the excess. Place the chicken in the bag of seasoned flour and shake to coat well.

Pour vegetable oil into a large cast-iron skillet to a depth of about $1^1/_4$ inches. Heat until very hot but not smoking. Add the chicken and brown on both sides, turning frequently. Do not crowd the pan. Reduce the heat to medium and cover the skillet. Cook the chicken, turning occasionally, for about 25 minutes. Remove the chicken with a slotted utensil to paper towels to drain. Reserve the cooking fat. Serve with Cream Gravy on the side.

"That's One Big Ole Frying Pan"

I reminisce about the days when Chesapeake cooks would haul out their big frying pans to cook up a generous helping of chicken for Sunday supper, but just the sight of the gargantuan frying pan used by the Delmarva Poultry Festival would have my grandmother Nanny Shields pass right out from the thought of coating and frying all those birds. There's a whole lot of chicken frying going on at this Chesapeake community get-together.

This frying pan is not something you'd keep in the kitchen cupboard or have hanging behind the stove. It sits on a concrete base, measures 10 feet in diameter, and is 8 inches deep. It could keep a pot holder company working overtime, with a handle that measures in at 8 feet long. I cringe thinking how many trips to the grocery store it would take to tote 180 gallons of cooking oil, which is how much this frying pan requires.

The Delmarva Poultry Festival is a rambunctious two-day event held annually in June on the Delmarva Peninsula, the thin strip of land that separates the Chesapeake Bay from the Atlantic Ocean. Chicken rules the roost on the peninsula, as the peninsula is one of the country's largest poultry producers, and you can be sure that during the gala celebration there is a lot of frying. Depending on appetites, between eight and ten thousand pieces of chicken are panfried, translating into 370 pounds of flour, 60 pounds of salt, 30 pounds of pepper, and, for color, 30 pounds of paprika.

Cream Gravy Makes about 2 cups

Reserved cooking fat
$^1/_3$ cup all-purpose flour
2 cups milk

Salt and freshly ground black
pepper, to taste

Pour off all but 3 tablespoons of the cooking fat. Stir in the flour and cook, stirring, for 1 to 2 minutes. Slowly whisk in the milk. Stir constantly until thickened, about 4 to 5 minutes. Season with salt and pepper.

BARBECUE SAUCE

$^1/_2$ cup ketchup

$^1/_4$ cup apple cider vinegar

1 tablespoon brown sugar

$^1/_4$ cup water

1 tablespoon Worcestershire
  sauce

2 tablespoons fresh lemon juice

2 tablespoons grated onion

1 teaspoon chopped garlic

2 teaspoons dry mustard

$^1/_4$ teaspoon cayenne

Tabasco Sauce, to taste

2 frying chickens (3 to 4 pounds
  each), cut into quarters

Vegetable oil or melted butter

Combine all the barbecue sauce ingredients in a small pot. Simmer for 15 minutes. Remove from the heat and let stand for at least 1 hour before using.

Meanwhile, preheat the oven to 400°F.

Put the chicken in a roasting pan and brush the skin with oil. Place in the oven and roast for about 1 hour. Baste the chicken occasionally with the pan juices during the first 40 minutes. Baste it with the barbecue sauce the last 20 minutes. Serve with plenty of napkins for sticky fingers.

Miss Lorraine's Barbecued Chicken

Miss Lorraine is notorious for her Rappahannock River cookouts. She used to love getting her grill hot and loading it up with chicken while sipping beer. Once, when she piled too much chicken on the grill, the flames shot up and her wig caught fire, which she recalls as "quite the sight." Due to her now-jangled nerves, she's adapted the recipe for the oven.

For you outdoor barbecuers, don't pile too much chicken on at one time, and only baste the chicken with the sauce during the last ten to fifteen minutes. Once you start basting, keep the chicken moving, as it tends to burn. And make up a batch of Father Joe's Favorite Potato Salad (page 176) to go along with the birds.

Serves 5 or 6

Roast Chicken with Sage Butter and Corn Bread Stuffing

The Eastern Shore of the Chesapeake has been historically a travel destination for those in search of tranquility, relaxation, and natural beauty, and by food lovers seeking the best the Bay has to offer. In the early 1900s, when the hot, humid Baltimore air would take its toll on the population, hordes of breeze seekers would set sail on one of the many ferryboats that crossed the Bay and find relief on the cool shores of Betterton. After a relaxing afternoon lying on the beach at the mouth of the Sassafras River, visitors would return to their Victorian hotels to change into evening wear and enjoy a savory chicken dish just like this one.

Serves 6

1 roasting chicken (5 to 6 pounds)
Salt and freshly ground black pepper, to taste
3 tablespoons butter, softened
1 tablespoon finely chopped fresh sage or dried rubbed sage
Corn Bread Stuffing (recipe follows)
Pan Gravy (page 161), optional

Preheat the oven to 400°F.

Wash the cavity of the chicken with cold water and dry with paper towels. Sprinkle the cavity with salt and pepper. Insert your index finger between the skin and breast to separate. Mix together the butter, sage, salt, and pepper in a small bowl. Push the butter under the skin covering the breast.

Stuff the chicken with the Corn Bread Stuffing. (If there is any extra dressing, bake separately in a buttered pan during the last 30 minutes the chicken is roasting.) Truss the chicken. Place the chicken on a rack in a roasting pan. Place in the oven and immediately reduce the heat to 350°F. Bake for 25 minutes per pound, basting occasionally. When finished cooking, loosely cover the chicken with aluminum foil and let stand 10 minutes before carving. If desired, make gravy.

Corn Bread Stuffing Makes about 4 cups

6 tablespoons (3/4 stick) butter or bacon drippings
1 small onion, finely diced
3 stalks celery, finely diced
1/2 cup cooked corn kernels
3 cups corn bread pieces
1 egg, beaten
Salt and freshly ground black pepper, to taste
Milk

Melt the butter in a skillet and sauté the onion and celery for 5 minutes. Transfer to a bowl and mix with the remaining ingredients, using only as much milk as needed to lightly moisten.

1 roasting chicken (5 to 6 pounds)

Salt and freshly ground black pepper, to taste

4 cups Chicken Stock, (page 127), or canned, heated

1 bay leaf

1 onion, peeled and sliced

2 cloves garlic

Drop Dumplings (recipe follows)

Pan Gravy (page 161)

Preheat the oven to 400°F.

Dry the chicken with paper towels. Season with salt and pepper. Place it in a deep roasting pan and bake, uncovered, for 20 minutes. Pour in the hot stock. Add the bay leaf, onion, and garlic. Cover, reduce the heat to 325°F., and continue to cook for 1¹/₂ hours, or until the chicken is tender.

Remove the chicken to a heated platter. Skim the fat from the pan juices. Prepare the dumpling dough. Bring the juices to a simmer and cook the dumplings in the roasting pan as directed. After all the dumplings have been cooked, strain the juices and thicken for gravy. Season to taste. Slice the chicken and place on a large platter surrounded by the dumplings. Serve hot gravy on the side.

Drop Dumplings Makes about 16

2 cups all-purpose flour, sifted

1 tablespoon baking powder

1 teaspoon salt

1 tablespoon butter

1 egg, beaten

³/₄ cup milk

Sift together the flour, baking powder, and salt in a large mixing bowl. Work in the butter with your fingertips. In a separate bowl, mix together the egg and milk. Gradually add to the dry ingredients, mixing to make a soft dough.

Drop the dough by the tablespoonful into simmering pan juices. Cover and cook until firm, about 12 to 15 minutes.

Mom-Mom's Braised Chicken and Drop Dumplings

My mother is a woman of many names. "Mom-Mom" came about with the arrival of her grandchildren. Monday night is roast chicken night at the homestead, and Mom-Mom is quite agitated with me for calling her famous roast chicken "braised," but that's the truth of the matter. It's one of my favorites and I know you'll like it, too. Fill the bird with your tastiest stuffing, if you like.

Serves 6

Chicken Stewed with Tomatoes and Okra

When those sweet summertime Eastern Shore tomatoes and field fresh okra get together with a plump roasting chicken, one-pot cooking never tasted so fine. After a slow cook with the team of fresh vegetables, the meat of the chicken is picked from the bone and returned to the pot. The resulting aromatic ragout is served over rice with a basket of warm Old-fashioned Skillet Corn Bread (page 227).

Serves 5 to 6

6 tablespoons bacon drippings or butter
1 roasting chicken (5 to 6 pounds)
1 large onion, chopped
3 stalks celery, diced
2 tablespoons chopped garlic
1 pound okra, cut into 1/2-inch pieces
2 cups chopped tomatoes with their juice
2 1/2 to 3 cups Chicken Stock (page 127) or water
Salt, to taste
2 teaspoons sugar
1 bay leaf
1/2 teaspoon dried marjoram
1/4 teaspoon ground nutmeg
1 1/2 cups corn kernels
Freshly ground black pepper, to taste
Cooked white rice, for accompaniment

Heat the bacon drippings in a heavy-bottomed pot and brown the chicken on all sides. Remove from the pot and set aside.

Add the onion, celery, and garlic to the pot and sauté for 4 to 5 minutes. Add the okra, cover, and simmer for 20 minutes. Stir in the tomatoes and return the chicken to the pot. Pour in enough stock to reach three quarters of the way up the side of the chicken. Add 1 teaspoon of salt, the sugar, bay leaf, marjoram, and nutmeg. Cover and simmer for about 1 1/2 hours, or until the chicken is tender.

Remove the chicken from the pot and discard the bay leaf. Add the corn to the pot and simmer, uncovered, for 10 minutes. Pick the meat from the chicken and put it back in the pot. Heat through and season with salt and pepper. Serve over rice.

Graceful Living

A drive through St. Mary's County brings to mind bygone days. One imagines families sitting on broad plantation porches in retreat from the summer sun, sipping iced tea and mint juleps, or sultry July picnics beneath a sprawling shade tree with everyone eating from platters of fried chicken and assorted salads. The smells, tastes, and graceful manner of living that elude most of today's world are still alive and well on the shores of St. Mary's County.

Down south on the western shore of the Chesapeake Bay is St. Mary's City, a bit of living history right on the shores of the St. Mary's River, which flows into the nearby Potomac. In 1634 two ships, the *Ark* and the *Dove,* arrived from England to the shores of what was to become the first settlement of the Maryland colony. St. Mary's City was originally a Catholic settlement, but the Protestants got wind of the crabs, oysters, and other delights being pulled from the Bay, and it wasn't long before the culinary gold rush was on. As more colonists arrived, and new and larger towns and ports sprang up along the shore, St. Mary's City began losing its rank as the center of the colony. Today work has begun on excavating and restoring the site of the city.

Tobacco is king in the surrounding St. Mary's County. It has been and still is one of the primary cash crops on the southern part of the Bay. The old tobacco plantations were also the source of smoked hams, sausages, and a rich bounty of fruits and vegetables.

Bordered by the Chesapeake Bay and the Patuxent and Potomac rivers, this area has numerous inlets and creeks along its shores. The locals fish, crab, and harvest the surrounding waters and fields, providing some of the finest seafood, ham, game, waterfowl, and agricultural products of the Bay region. These culinary resources join to create a gastronomic experience that is marked by the tastes and flavors of the Old South. Full-bodied country hams become the focal point of a St. Mary's breakfast, which might include fried tomatoes and a cream gravy. A Southern barbecue sauce atop briny Chesapeake oysters translates into the locally famous barbecued oysters. And the many sauces and gravies of the St. Mary's repertoire of recipes all beg for sopping up with legendary Maryland beaten biscuits.

Smoked Chicken Potpie with Sweet Potato Pastry

*P*otpies are a staple of Chesapeake kitchens: Oysters, fish, game, and waterfowl are bathed in rich sauces and covered with a layer of flaky pastry. This chicken potpie is a creation from the smokehouse experts of St. Mary's County and is perhaps the most popular of the potpie family. In this recipe, a small amount of smoked chicken is added to the creamy poached chicken filling to impart a hint of smokiness to the pie. The topping is an innovative pastry enriched by the earthy flavor of sweet potatoes.

Serves 6 to 8

Salt
1 large chicken (4 to 4^1/$_2$ pounds)
1 large onion, sliced
2 whole cloves
Sweet Potato Pastry (recipe follows)
15 pearl onions
1 cup medium diced carrots
1 cup medium diced celery

1 cup corn kernels
1 cup fresh peas
1 cup coarsely cut smoked chicken meat
8 tablespoons (1 stick) butter
^{1}/$_2$ cup all-purpose flour
1 cup heavy (whipping) cream
Freshly ground black pepper and ground nutmeg, to taste

Bring a large pot filled with salted water to a boil and add the chicken, sliced onion, and cloves. Reduce the heat and simmer until the chicken is tender, 1 to 1^1/$_2$ hours. While the chicken is cooking, cook and chill the sweet potatoes for the pastry. Remove the chicken from the pot and pick off the meat. Set aside. Strain and reserve the liquid from the cooking pot. Skim off the fat.

Combine the pearl onions, carrots, celery, corn, and peas in a saucepan. Pour in only enough of the strained cooking liquid to cover. Simmer until tender. Drain, reserving the cooking liquid.

Preheat the oven to 350°F.

Arrange the reserved chicken meat, smoked chicken, and vegetables in a 4-quart baking dish.

To make the sauce, melt the butter in a saucepan and whisk in the flour. Cook, stirring 2 to 3 minutes. Gradually whisk in 3 cups of the cooking liquid and the cream. Bring to a boil, reduce heat, and continue to simmer for 3 minutes. Season well with salt, pepper, and nutmeg. Pour over the chicken and vegetables. Finish making the pastry and fit it on the top of the baking dish. Crimp the edges of the pastry.

Bake the pie for about 45 minutes, or until the top is nicely browned and filling is piping hot. Remove from oven and let stand for 5 minutes before serving.

Sweet Potato Pastry Makes one 12-inch crust

1 to 2 sweet potatoes (enough
    to yield 1^1/$_2$ cups mashed)
1^1/$_2$ cups all-purpose flour
1 teaspoon salt

2 teaspoons baking powder
^{1}/$_2$ cup vegetable shortening
2 eggs, beaten

Preheat the oven to 400°F.

Bake the sweet potatoes until soft, 40 to 60 minutes, depending on the size. Prick with a fork when half-cooked to prevent the potatoes from bursting. When cool enough to handle, scoop out the flesh and mash. Chill.

Sift together the flour, salt, and baking powder in a large bowl. Add the chilled yams, shortening, and eggs, and with a pastry blender, two knives, or fingertips, work into the flour. Turn the dough out onto a lightly floured surface and roll it to a size that will cover the baking dish.

Chicken Breasts with Crabmeat and Mozzarella

These mouthwatering bundles of crabmeat and melted cheese surrounded by moist and tender chicken take some time to prepare, but they are more than worth the effort. When fresh basil is available, I like to substitute a few chopped leaves in place of the thyme. This dish is good with pasta tossed with olive oil and garlic. For a vegetable I suggest serving Fried Watercress (page 197).

Serves 6

1 tablespoon butter
5 to 6 tablespoons olive oil
$^1/_2$ cup tomato sauce or Gravy (page 98)
$^1/_2$ pound backfin crabmeat, picked over
8 ounces mozzarella cheese, coarsely shredded
Salt and freshly ground black pepper, to taste
3 boneless and skinless chicken breasts, halved and pounded thin

All-purpose flour seasoned with salt and pepper
8 ounces mushrooms, cut into quarters or sixths
3 tomatoes, peeled, seeded, and chopped
1 tablespoon chopped garlic
$^3/_4$ cup dry Marsala
$^1/_2$ cup coarsely chopped basil

Heat the butter and 1 tablespoon of the olive oil in a small pan. Stir in the tomato sauce and cook for 1 to 2 minutes. Remove from heat. Gently mix together the crabmeat and cheese in a bowl. Pour the sauce over and toss to mix. Season with salt and pepper.

Spread each chicken scaloppine with some of the crab mixture, leaving a bit of room at the edges. Roll up and tie with kitchen string.

Heat 4 tablespoons of olive oil in a skillet. Lightly roll the packets in the seasoned flour and brown the rolls well on all sides. Remove from the pan. Adding more olive oil to the pan as needed, sauté the mushrooms briefly. Add the tomatoes, garlic, Marsala, and basil. Bring to a boil and return chicken rolls to pan. Cover and continue cooking for 5 minutes, turning the packets occasionally.

With a slotted utensil, remove chicken packets to a platter. Remove the string with kitchen scissors. Increase the heat and reduce the juices until a slightly creamy sauce forms. Adjust the seasonings and serve the sauce over the chicken.

³/₄ cup all-purpose flour
1¹/₂ teaspoons baking powder
¹/₂ teaspoon salt
2 eggs, beaten
¹/₂ cup milk
1 tablespoon grated onion
2 tablespoons chopped chives or
    parsley
Pinch of ground nutmeg

³/₄ cup coarsely chopped
    cooked chicken meat
    (¹/₂-inch pieces)
¹/₂ cup corn kernels
Vegetable oil, for deep-frying
Green Tomato and Apple
    Chutney (page 268), for
    accompaniment

Sift together the flour, baking powder, and salt in a large bowl. Stir in the eggs. Beat in the milk, onion, chives, and nutmeg. Add the chicken and corn.

Pour oil into a heavy skillet to a depth of 1 inch, and heat until very hot, about 375°F. Drop the batter in by the tablespoonful, a few fritters at a time, and fry until golden brown, 2 to 3 minutes. Remove with a slotted utensil to paper towels to drain. Serve with chutney for dipping.

Chicken and Corn Fritters

Every summer during my childhood, we would head to the Eastern Shore resort town of Betterton, Maryland. Just anticipating the boat trip and a stay at the old Victorian-style hotel with its big screened porches would leave me sleepless for days before our actual departure. I still remember the sumptuous meals served in the elegant dining room of the hotel. Biting into these light and fluffy fritters takes me back to those enchanting summer excursions. Although not traditional, an apple chutney served on the side goes well with these tasty morsels.

Serves 5 to 6

Rock Cornish Game Hens with Savory Stuffing

This game hen recipe is the centerpiece of a colonial menu that Marjorie Steen of Annapolis has re-created to demonstrate open-hearth cookery with historical accounts of the cuisine. While conducting cooking classes, she demonstrates both the colonial method of preparation as well as an updated version for the kitchens of today. Here is her twentieth-century version for a conventional oven, along with a few tips on how you might cook this recipe in a fireplace.

Serves 2

2 Rock Cornish game hens
Salt and freshly ground black
    pepper, to taste
3 cups dry or soft bread
    crumbs, soaked in brandy or
    milk

1 egg, beaten
1 teaspoon rubbed sage
$1/2$ teaspoon dried oregano
$1/4$ teaspoon ground mace
$1/4$ teaspoon ground nutmeg
2 tablespoons butter, softened

Preheat the oven to 400°F.

Wash out the cavities of the hens and rub inside and out with a small amount of salt and pepper. In a medium bowl, combine the soaked bread crumbs and the soaking liquid with all the remaining ingredients except the butter. If the mixture is too wet, add more bread crumbs. Season with salt and pepper. This mixture should be sufficient for 2 Cornish hens and the Poor Man's Pudding (page 146). Stuff both openings of the hens and truss closed. Rub the outside of the hens with softened butter.

Bake until the hens are tender and browned, 40 to 45 minutes. When they are done, remove them from the oven and cut away the trussing. Strain the pan juices and spoon over hens. Serve at once with stuffing still inside bird.

Note: If a fireplace is available for cooking, wrap the hens with strong cord (grocer's twine) and suspend them 8 to 12 inches above the fire. Roast until no juices run when a thigh is pierced with a fork. The heat of the fire will cause the birds to rotate on their cords. If they become dry before they are finished cooking, brush with more butter.

1 turkey (10 to 12 pounds)
Salt and freshly ground black
    pepper, to taste

Oyster Dressing (recipe follows)
2 tablespoons butter, softened

Preheat the oven to 325°F.

Wash the cavity of the turkey with cold water and dry with paper towels. Sprinkle the cavity with salt and pepper and stuff loosely with the dressing. If there is any extra dressing, bake it separately in a buttered pan during the last hour the turkey is roasting. Truss the turkey. Rub the skin with butter. Place the turkey on a rack, breast side down, in a roasting pan.

Roast 25 minutes per pound. Turn the turkey over after 2 hours. When done, remove the turkey from the oven and let stand, loosely covered with aluminum foil, for 15 to 20 minutes before carving.

Oyster Dressing Makes 10 cups

$^1/_2$ pound (2 sticks) butter
1 cup chopped onion
1 cup chopped celery
7 cups day-old bread cubes
$2^1/_2$ teaspoons salt
$^1/_2$ teaspoon freshly ground
    black pepper

$^1/_4$ teaspoon ground mace
1 pint shucked oysters, drained,
    liquor reserved, and
    chopped
1 cup milk, as needed

Melt the butter in a skillet and sauté the onion and celery until soft. Combine the onion, celery, bread cubes, salt, pepper, mace, and chopped oysters in a bowl. Mix well. Pour in the oyster liquor, then slowly add enough milk to moisten stuffing. Do not make it too wet.

Roast Turkey with Oyster Dressing

Quite often turkey and oysters find themselves paired together around these parts. Signs for community suppers herald "Turkey and Oyster Dinner," and advertisements from local dining establishments announce "Turkey Stuffed with Oyster Dressing" with each approaching Thanksgiving. Chesapeake locals take great pride in this regional stuffing, and with good reason: It is a unique eating experience. The flavor of the Chesapeake oysters imparts a subtle seafood tang to the dressing, complementing the succulent meat of the roast turkey.

Serves 10 to 12

Poor Man's Pudding   Serves 4

Savory puddings were quite common in Chesapeake fare during the 1700s, keeping in tradition with the tastes of the early English settlers. This versatile pudding can be served as a sweetened dessert or mixed with leftover meats to make a hearty entree. Marjorie Steen provided this technique, which would have been used for colonial fireplace cooking.

2 cups leftover stuffing from Rock
    Cornish Game Hens with Savory
    Stuffing
1 egg, beaten
1/4 cup sugar
1 teaspoon ground cinnamon,
    nutmeg, or mace (see Note)

1 apple, peeled, cored, and chopped
1/2 cup raisins
2 tablespoons vegetable oil
2 tablespoons butter, cut into small
    pieces

Preheat the oven to 350°F.

Combine the stuffing, egg, sugar, cinnamon, apple, and raisins in a bowl.

If baking in an oven: Pour the oil into a small cast-iron skillet and place the skillet in the oven until it is very hot. Remove from the oven and pour in the pudding mixture. Smooth the top so it is flat and dot with butter. Return to the oven and bake about 20 minutes, or until set.

If baking in a fireplace: Pour the oil into a dutch oven with a lid and heat it in the fireplace. Add the pudding, smooth the top, cover with the lid, and return to the fireplace. Heap coals on the lid, then remove from fire. Allow the pudding to cook at the edge of the fireplace, replacing the coals on the lid if they stop glowing. Check the pudding after about 20 minutes. If not yet set, repeat the process.

Note: If instead of a "warm" spice you use a "heavy" spice, such as thyme, sage, tarragon, or rosemary, add black pepper and chopped onion as well. Omit the sugar and serve this as a savory side dish. If bits of cooked meat, especially roast beef, are added with the onion and spice, this pudding can serve as a main dish.

Crab Cake Platter

Clams and Oysters on the half shell

Chesapeake **Bay Seafood Stew** (page 122)

Miss Lorraine's Barbecued Chicken (page 133)

Maryland Panfried Chicken (page 131), **Jimmy Le Blue's Barbecued Ribs** (page 164), and Sweet Summer Corn on the Cob (page 189)

Stuffed Tomatoes (page 190) and Green Beans with Country Ham

and Sautéed Peanuts (page 195)

Eastern Shore Crab Salad with Cantaloupe (page 180)

Lady Baltimore Cake (page 238)

4 tablespoons (1/2 stick) butter
2 pheasants (about 2 1/2 pounds each), cut into serving pieces
2 large onions, sliced 1/4 inch thick
3 carrots, sliced 1/4 inch thick
3 stalks celery, diced
2 cups dry red wine

1 teaspoon rubbed sage
1/2 teaspoon dried marjoram
1/4 teaspoon ground mace
2 teaspoons salt
1/2 teaspoon freshly ground black pepper
2 tablespoons flour
1 cup walnut pieces
1 cup sour cream

Pheasant with Red Wine and Walnuts

Light the fire in the fireplace and disconnect the phone if you serve this romantic dish on a winter's night. The pheasant slowly stews with red wine, aromatic vegetables, and spices, and the thickened stewing juices are finished with sour cream and walnuts.
Serves 4

Melt the butter in a flameproof casserole or dutch oven and over medium heat brown the pheasant pieces on both sides. Then remove the pheasant and add the onions to the pot, sautéing for 3 minutes. Add the carrots, celery, and pheasant pieces. Pour in the wine and add enough water to cover birds. Add the sage, marjoram, mace, salt, and pepper and bring to a boil. Cover and simmer for about 1 1/2 hours, or until the pheasant pieces are tender.

Remove the pieces to a platter and keep warm. Mix together the flour, walnuts, and sour cream in a small bowl. Stir into the juices and simmer for 5 minutes over low heat to thicken juices. Adjust the seasonings. Remove from the heat and let cool somewhat. Serve the pheasant pieces with the sauce spooned over them.

A Living Museum

The York, James, and Rappahannock rivers are three principal waterways in Tidewater Virginia. During colonial times, the first English settlement was founded at Jamestown on the James River, and not much later the town of Williamsburg, Virginia, was built, nestled between the James and Fork rivers. Historic buildings, inns, and taverns abound in this captivating region, quite possibly outnumbering the new. Nowadays Williamsburg is a living museum, with residents acting out the lives of colonial settlers for visitors. Many of the reconstructed homes and taverns feature colonial kitchens, where food is prepared using the same methods as in the 1700s. A visit to Williamsburg is a fascinating look at the development of both Chesapeake Bay and Southern styles of cookery.

Roast Wild Goose with Apple-Chestnut Stuffing

When approaching a wild goose with the intent of cooking it, a good idea is to check its credentials, such as age. Senior birds are best stewed or braised, while younger ones are better for roasting. If a goose weighs over 5 pounds and was bagged in the fall, it is most likely an older bird. A farm-raised goose has a sweeter, less gamy flavor than the wild goose, but it requires a slightly longer cooking time (about twenty minutes per pound) since it is not so lean as a wild bird. This traditional apple-chestnut stuffing is perfect for accentuating the dark, succulent meat.

Serves 4

1 goose (4 to 5 pounds)
Salt and freshly ground black
    pepper, to taste
1 onion, halved

Apple-Chestnut Stuffing (recipe
    follows)
3 tablespoons flour

Preheat the oven to 400°F.

Wash the cavity of the bird with cold water and dry with paper towels. Sprinkle the cavity with salt and pepper. Rub the goose with the onion. Fill the cavity with stuffing and truss. Place on a rack in a shallow roasting pan.

Put the pan in the oven. Reduce the heat to 375°F. and cook for 2 hours, basting frequently. For the first hour, place an aluminum foil tent over the goose. Remove it after an hour. Remove the goose to a heated platter and keep warm. Pour the pan juices into a pitcher and degrease, reserving about 3 tablespoons of the fat. Heat the reserved fat in a saucepan and whisk in the flour. Cook, stirring, for 2 to 3 minutes. Stir in 2 cups of pan juices (add water or chicken stock to supplement) and whisk over medium heat until thickened, about 3 to 5 minutes. Carve the goose and serve with stuffing and pan gravy.

Apple-Chestnut Stuffing Makes 7 cups

6 tablespoons (^{3}/$_4$ stick) butter
1 onion, diced
2 stalks celery, diced
2 cups peeled and sliced apples
2 cups bread cubes
1 cup chestnut pieces (see Note)

2 tablespoons dried sage
^{1}/$_2$ teaspoon dried thyme leaves
1 egg, beaten
^{1}/$_2$ cup milk or water, as needed
Salt and freshly ground black
    pepper, to taste

Melt the butter in a small skillet and sauté the onion and celery until soft. Mix together the apples, bread cubes, chestnuts, sage, and thyme in a bowl. Add the sautéed vegetables and egg. Toss well. Sprinkle in as much milk as needed to moisten. Season with salt and pepper.

Note: Jars of whole peeled chestnuts may be found at many specialty food shops. If not, to shell chestnuts, cut an X on the flat side of each nut and place on a pan in a preheated 425°F. oven for about 15 minutes. Remove and, when cool enough to handle, peel away the outer shell and fuzzy membrane.

where we lived—Chesapeake menus have always relied heavily on local meats, as the Chesapeake region is primarily an agricultural center. Dotting the countryside are farming communities raising large herds of beef cattle and lamb.

Pork is important in Chesapeake cuisine, too, and hardly any self-respecting resident in the rural parts would be found without at least one or two hogs in residence. In fact, the Chesapeake Bay region is one of the largest producers of country ham—pork that has been cured and smoked—in the country. This fascination with pork, and cured and smoked pork products, dates back to the seventeenth century, when most of rural life centered around plantations or large estates, each one equipped with its own smokehouse. They each had their own curing and smoking techniques, which were closely guarded secrets, and every town and village was known for the type of country ham it produced. Ham made practical sense in those times: There was no refrigeration as we know it today, and the early settlers could preserve that cut of pork by curing it.

Chesapeake country hams may be served on their own as entrees, or the bones, skin, and meat may be used for flavor in vegetables, soups, stews, and other one-pot dishes. The Smithfield region on the James River in Virginia has maintained its own unique style of curing and smoking pork for nearly three hundred years and produces highly salted aged hams that are enjoyed worldwide. Chefs often favorably compare Smithfield ham to the prosciutto of Italy and the Bayonne ham of France.

1 aged country ham	Dry mustard, to taste
1 part cider vinegar	Whole cloves
4 parts brown sugar	

Scrub the ham well with a stiff brush. Place in a large container and add water to cover. Soak for 24 to 48 hours.

Place the ham in a large pot, throw out the soaking water, and re-cover with fresh water. Bring to a boil, reduce the heat, and simmer for 2 to 2½ hours, or until the bone becomes loose. Let the ham cool in the cooking liquid.

Preheat the oven to 350°F.

Make a paste of the vinegar, brown sugar, and mustard. Carefully remove the skin from the ham while still warm, but do not remove the fat. Cover the ham with the paste. Stick whole cloves into the fat.

Bake, basting often, for 20 to 30 minutes, or until the glaze has browned. Let the ham sit for at least 30 minutes before slicing. Cut into thin slices and serve warm or cold.

Baked Maryland Ham

How long to presoak your ham depends largely on its age. Country hams are aged anywhere from three months to three years, but the tastier hams have been aged for at least nine months and require a minimum twenty-four hours of soaking. If a ham is older, it is a good idea to soak it for two full days. While Chesapeake country hams are dry-cured, some hams are sweet-pickled cured, and it is important to read the accompanying instructions before cooking to know which type you have purchased. This recipe is for the more traditional dry-cured kind, which always requires a good scrubbing and a soak in cold water.

Whole hams with the bone in serve 2 persons per pound; a boneless ham serves 3 to 4 persons per pound

Ham It Up

Confused about hams? Below is a list of terms and their meanings to help you navigate through the world of hams. When purchasing a ham, talk to your butcher and always read the labels and instructions carefully so you know what you're buying. Keep in mind that since producers of ham each have their own length of time and technique that they use when curing, smoking, and aging the ham, the resulting flavors will vary widely. A general rule of thumb: The longer the aging process, the stronger the taste and drier the flesh.

Aging: the length of time a ham is stored.

Brine: a solution of water and salt for preserving; sometimes sugar is also added.

Brining: curing by immersing in a sweet brine with added seasonings.

Corned ham: a ham cured by brining; usually smoked but not aged.

Country ham: a dry-cured and smoked ham.

Cured ham: one that has been preserved by a curing technique.

Dry-curing: curing by salting the surface thoroughly; sometimes a mixture of salt, sugar, and spices is used.

Fresh ham: unprocessed meat; it has not been cured.

Ham: the cut of meat from a hog's hind leg.

Injection-curing: curing by injecting with brine.

Pork: any cut of meat from a hog.

Smithfield ham: a country ham that is aged for a minimum of six months in Smithfield, Virginia.

Smoking: various techniques are used; adds flavor to the ham.

1/2 bushel (about 8 pounds) kale, thick stems removed

2 medium cabbages, cored and cut into wedges

12 bunches of wild field cress, if possible, or watercress, tough stems removed

12 bunches of green onions

1 bunch of celery

1/2 cup salt

2 tins (1 1/4 ounces each) mustard seed

1/4 cup crushed red pepper

1 corned ham (20 pounds), fat removed, boned, and tied

1 clean, extra-large white cotton T-shirt

Bunches of watercress and sliced ripe tomatoes, for garnish

Clean and coarsely grind or chop all the vegetables. Put them in a large deep tub and work in the salt, mustard seed, and red pepper with your hands. Place the ham on a large baking sheet or tray with an edge. With a boning knife, cut deep half-moon slits in the ham. Starting at the butt end, make a row with 4 slits, about 2 inches apart, across the ham. Move about 2 inches down and make a second row across with 3 slits, making sure the slits are not parallel to the first row. The following row below will have 4 slits, and the next row 3 and, if room, a final row with 4 slits. It will create a checkerboard effect. With your fingers, poke some of the vegetables into the holes, filling them. Turn the ham over and repeat the process of cutting the slits and filling them.

Spread out the T-shirt on a clean tray. With scissors cut it up the front and lay it open. Spread half of the remaining vegetables on the T-shirt and place the stuffed ham on the vegetables. Pack the rest of the vegetables over the top of the ham. Bring up the T-shirt over the ham, stretching it. Tie the ham round and round with strong twine, adding a loop for lifting.

Put a small rack in the bottom of a deep canning kettle and half fill the kettle with cold water. Put in the ham and add additional water to cover. Put a lid on the kettle and bring to a boil. Lower the heat and simmer slowly 4 hours. After 4 hours, remove from the heat and take the lid off the kettle. Leave the ham in the pot liquor overnight.

In the morning, drain well, put the ham in a plastic bag, and refrigerate for 1 day. To serve, cut away the T-shirt and lift the ham onto a large platter. Scoop up any vegetables remaining on the shirt and pat them all over the top of the ham and around the edges. Decorate the platter with watercress and tomatoes. Carve the ham into thin slices, exposing the green veining. Serve ham cold or slightly warm with the extra greens.

St. Mary's County Stuffed Ham

Stuffed ham is a grand culinary tradition of southern Maryland. If a corned ham is not available from the butcher, substitute a fresh ham. A fresh ham is the same cut of meat as a corned ham, only the latter has been cured in a brining solution.

Stuffed ham is served cold and sliced very thin; however, ham slices may be placed on small biscuits or rolls, slathered with mayonnaise, and then heated very slightly in a moderate oven. Because this recipe makes such a large quantity, it is best suited for a well-attended party or large family gathering.

Serves 20 to 25, with some left over

William Taylor
of St. Mary's County

A trip to southern Maryland would not be complete without a visit and meal with William Taylor. Bill resides in St. Mary's County at Klahanie, his beautiful cottage home sitting in a grove of trees on the edge of Nat Creek. Mr. Taylor is the full-time goodwill ambassador of St. Mary's County. His gracious manner, quick wit, and winning smile are the epitome of Southern hospitality—and Mr. Taylor has the hospitality market covered. He is a much-sought-after Chesapeake food designer, cooking instructor, and foremost expert on both the old and new cooking styles and recipes of St. Mary's.

At historic Sotterley, the oldest working plantation on the Chesapeake and a place where southern Maryland country hams are still smoked in the traditional manner, one can easily imagine Mr. Taylor as the master of the plantation in a bygone era. Here he can often be found hosting clients, students, and visiting dignitaries at afternoon teas, eighteenth-century–style candlelight dinners, and the Grand Oyster Gala Dinner, the annual feast for the National Oyster Festival.

St. Mary's County Stuffed Ham is legendary in the Old South and serves as the focal point in Mr. Taylor's country buffet menu. He offers remarkably detailed, yet manageable instructions on the preparation and cooking of the ham. Perhaps due to today's heightened pace of life, such culinary treasures are becoming harder to find.

A Country Buffet with William Taylor

Chesapeake Oyster Stew (page 117)
St. Mary's County Stuffed Ham
Green Beans with Country Ham and Sautéed
Peanuts (page 195)
Bourbon-Apple Crisp (page 253)

Pastry Dough for a Single-Crust Pie (page 247)
6 tablespoons ($^3/_4$ stick) butter
1 cup sliced leeks
6 ounces Roquefort cheese, softened
6 ounces cream cheese, softened
$^1/_4$ cup heavy (whipping) cream
3 eggs, lightly beaten
Salt and freshly ground black pepper, to taste
$1^1/_4$ cups diced country ham

Preheat the oven to 425°F.

Prepare the pastry dough, roll it out, and line a 9-inch pie pan. Flute the edge of the shell. Prick the bottom of the shell with a fork. Press aluminum foil into the bottom and sides of the shell and cover the foil with pie weights or raw rice or dried beans to weight the pastry and prevent the crust from swelling during baking. Bake for 8 minutes. Remove the foil and continue to bake for another 5 minutes. Let cool before filling.

Preheat the oven to 350°F.

Melt 3 tablespoons of the butter in a skillet. Add the leeks and cook over medium heat until soft. While the leeks are cooking, cream the remaining 3 tablespoons butter, Roquefort, and cream cheese together in a medium bowl. Beat in the cream and eggs and mix until smooth. Season to taste.

Arrange the ham and leeks in the bottom of the pastry shell and pour in the cheese mixture.

Bake for 35 to 40 minutes, or until nicely browned. Remove the pie from the oven and allow to stand for at least 5 minutes. Cut into 6 or 8 slices and serve warm.

Smoked Country Ham and Roquefort Pie

This rich, creamy cheese pie, an unusual blend of hickory-cured ham and pungent Roquefort, can be served as an appetizer or as an entree with a garden salad and hot rolls.

Serves 6 to 8

Ham Pâté

In colonial times the word "pâté" referred to foods encased in dough. Often the crust was hard enough to be a storage container for fruits and meats for months at a time. These crusts were either thrown away or used as plates or serving dishes for the meal that they had just cooked. Later, eighteenth-century recipes described pâtés as "fine crusts [that are] crispy and tender enough for eating." Such are the crusts we are now familiar with today.

This recipe does not contain one of the concrete-hard crusts of colonial times, but rather, a fine flaky crust, which envelops seasoned layers of sliced baked ham and ground turkey for a generous amount of pâté, perfect for a large gathering. A Dijon or coarse-grain mustard goes well with this pâté.

Serves 20

2 teaspoons ground ginger
1 medium ham (6 to 8 pounds), boned
12 to 16 whole cloves
Fine Crust Pastry (recipe follows)
2 pounds ground turkey
2 cups soft bread crumbs, soaked in half-and-half to cover
3 egg whites
Salt and freshly ground black pepper, to taste
Pinch of ground nutmeg
1 egg, beaten
Mixture of 1 part brandy to 4 parts dry white wine, as needed

Preheat the oven to 325°F.

Rub the ground ginger into the outer skin of the ham and stud the ham with the whole cloves. Bake for 2^1/$_2$ hours, cool, and thinly slice.

Prepare the pastry, wrap, and chill.

Preheat the oven to 350°F.

Divide the pastry into 2 balls, one slightly larger than the other. On a lightly floured surface, roll out the smaller ball ^{1}/$_4$ inch thick and large enough to line the bottom of a 13 × 9 × 2-inch baking pan. Line the pan as for a pie, covering the bottom and sides.

Mix together the turkey, soaked crumbs, egg whites, 1 teaspoon salt, ^{1}/$_2$ teaspoon pepper, and nutmeg in a bowl.

Place a 1- to 1^1/$_2$-inch-thick layer of the turkey mixture on the pastry. Top with a ^{1}/$_4$- to ^{1}/$_3$-inch-thick layer of thin ham slices. Sprinkle with a small amount of salt and pepper. Repeat layers of turkey mixture and ham slices until all is used, ending with a layer of turkey on top and a generous amount of turkey along the sides. Roll out the remaining pastry ^{1}/$_4$ inch thick and cover pan with it. Crimp the edges, moistened with water, to ensure a good seal. Reroll any pastry scraps, make small cutouts, and use to decorate top of pastry. Brush with beaten egg. Make a hole in the middle of the crown, or perhaps 2 or 3, if the dish is long and narrow.

Bake for 1 hour. Remove from the oven and place a funnel in the pastry hole. Slowly pour in as much of the brandy-wine mixture as the dish will allow. Return to the oven for 1 hour more.

When done, remove from the oven and allow to stand for 20 to 30 minutes before serving. Pâté may be served warm, or it may be refrigerated and served later at room temperature. Slice the pâté to reveal the ham layers.

Fine Crust Pastry Makes enough pastry to line and top a 13 × 9 × 2-inch baking pan

4 cups all-purpose flour
1 teaspoon salt
1¹/₂ cups vegetable shortening

¹/₃ cup cold water
2 tablespoons distilled white vinegar

Mix the flour and salt together in a large bowl. Cut in the shortening with your fingertips or a pastry blender until mixture has the consistency of coarse meal. Mix together the water and vinegar and work in the mixture. Form into a ball, wrap, and refrigerate for at least 1 hour.

1 smoked pork butt (2 to 3 pounds)
2 bay leaves
1 onion, sliced
²/₃ cup red wine vinegar

1 medium cabbage, cored and cut into wedges
Prepared horseradish and mustard, for accompaniment

Place the pork butt in a pot and add water to cover. Bring to a boil and add the bay leaves, onion, and vinegar. Return to a boil, cover, reduce the heat, and simmer about 20 minutes per pound. Add the cabbage to the pot during the last 30 minutes of cooking. Remove the meat from pot and allow to sit for 10 to 15 minutes before slicing. Discard the bay leaves.

Arrange the sliced meat on a platter with the cabbage and buttered boiled potatoes. Serve horseradish and mustard on the side.

Smoked Neck and Cabbage

Confusing as it may sound, smoked neck is sometimes sold as smoked pork butt or smoked shoulder, but all three are the same product: a cut of meat from the shoulder portion. The cooking process is similar to the preparation of corned beef and cabbage. Serve with buttered boiled potatoes.

Serves 4 to 5

Smithfield Ham and Potato Casserole

Smithfield, Virginia, is without a doubt the Ham Capital of the U.S. of A. Jackie Swann of Olde Smithfield Farms, purveyors of fine Smithfield hams, says this recipe is one of her family favorites. Serve this casserole as a side dish, or as a main course with a generous garden salad. Use leftovers at breakfast as a substitute for home fries—just reheat and serve with eggs.

Serves 6 to 8

8 large potatoes, peeled and
  sliced about ⅛ inch thick
1 pound sharp cheddar cheese,
  grated

1 cup mayonnaise
2 cups diced Smithfield ham
1 small onion, minced

Preheat the oven to 325°F.

Cook the potatoes in lightly salted water until just barely tender, about 10 minutes. Drain and place in a large mixing bowl. Add the remaining ingredients and mix together. Place in a well-greased 9 × 13-inch pan. Bake for 30 to 35 minutes. Jackie adds to "watch closely so the cheese doesn't burn." If necessary, cover the casserole for the last few minutes if it appears it is getting too brown. Remove from the oven and let stand for 5 minutes before serving.

1 large (8 to 16 pounds) fresh
    ham
3 cloves garlic, cut into slivers

1 medium rubbed sage
Salt and pepper, to taste

Roast Fresh Ham with Fried Apples

Preheat the oven to 350°F.

Score the skin of the ham with a sharp knife. Push slivers of garlic under the skin, then rub skin with sage, salt, and pepper. Place the ham on a rack in a shallow baking pan. Reduce the heat to 325°F.

Bake for 20 minutes per pound. Remove the ham to a platter and keep it warm. Make a gravy from pan juices (see below) and cook the Fried Apples. Carve the ham and serve with gravy and apples on the side.

One is hard-pressed to find a more typical Bay country pork dish than this one. A fresh ham is sheer gastronomic bliss and has been to Chesapeake folk for generations. A fresh ham is the same cut of meat as a country ham, that is, taken from the rear quarter of the hog, but it has not been brined or dry cured. It is like a pork roast. Serve it with the Fried Apples (page 201) and mashed potatoes.

Serves 12

Pan Gravy

After roasting or braising meats, fowl, or poultry, drain off all the liquid from the pan and skim the fat off the top. For 1 cup of gravy, put 2 tablespoons of the fat back into the pan and heat on the top of the stove. Whisk in 2 tablespoons flour and cook over a medium heat for 2 minutes until slightly browned—this is a roux. Remove from the heat and whisk in 1 cup of the reserved cooking liquid (or stock or water if that's all you have). Bring to a boil, stirring constantly, reduce the heat, and simmer for 5 minutes. Season to taste with salt and pepper, herbs, or spices.

Pork Chops with Apples and Rye Whiskey

This traditional Maryland recipe is just the thing for a crisp fall night. The whiskey-scented apples sweetened with brown sugar are an exceptional topping to the chops. This dish goes well with Sauerkraut and Apples (page 201), mashed potatoes, and pan gravy, which will pick up a trace of the cooked apples.

Serves 6

$^1/_4$ cup vegetable oil
6 thick loin pork chops
All-purpose flour seasoned with salt and freshly ground black pepper
4 tablespoons ($^1/_2$ stick) butter
4 tart apples, peeled, cored, and sliced $^1/_4$ inch thick

$^1/_2$ cup (firmly packed) brown sugar
2 tablespoons fresh lemon juice
Freshly grated nutmeg, to taste
$^1/_4$ cup rye whiskey
Salt and freshly ground black pepper, to taste

Heat the oil in a heavy skillet. Lightly dust the pork chops with the seasoned flour. Brown on both sides and continue to cook for about 20 to 25 minutes, turning now and then for even cooking. Remove the chops from the skillet and pour off most of the fat, saving some for pan gravy, if desired.

Melt the butter in the skillet. Add the apples and sauté briefly. Sprinkle the apples with sugar, lemon juice, and a touch of nutmeg. When the apples are just about tender, about 3 minutes, increase the heat and pour in the whiskey. Cook for 1 to 2 minutes. Return the chops to the skillet, cover, and cook over low heat for 5 minutes. Season with salt and pepper to taste. Serve the chops on a heated platter, topped with apples. If desired prepare a pan gravy (see page 161).

4 loin pork chops, about 1 inch
   thick
4 tablespoons ($^1/_2$ stick) butter
$^1/_2$ cup finely chopped onion
$^1/_4$ cup finely chopped celery
1 cup dry corn bread crumbs or
   pieces
1 cup diced ripe pears

$^1/_2$ teaspoon dried sage
$^1/_4$ teaspoon ground nutmeg
Milk, as needed
Salt and freshly ground black
   pepper, to taste
6 tablespoons vegetable oil
Chicken Stock (page 127), if
   needed

Pork Chops with Corn Bread and Pear Stuffing

Here is a marvelous stuffing for big, fat, juicy chops, a perfect dish for a late fall or winter dinner. Should the pears not be quite soft, sauté them in a little butter until tender. Serve with country greens (see page 196) and Fried Apples (page 201).

Serves 4

Have your butcher cut pockets in the pork chops. Melt the butter in a skillet. Add the onion and celery and sauté until soft, about 3 to 4 minutes. Mix the crumbs and pears together in a bowl and add the sautéed onion and celery. Add the sage and nutmeg. Sprinkle with a little milk to moisten. Season with salt and pepper. Fill the pork chop pockets with stuffing and secure with toothpicks.

Preheat the oven to 350°F.

Heat the oil in a flameproof casserole. Salt and pepper the chops and brown well on both sides. Pour in just enough water to cover the bottom of the casserole. Cover tightly and bake for 45 minutes. Remove the chops and make a pan gravy from the juices (see page 161). If there is not enough liquid, add a little stock to the casserole. Remove toothpicks from chops and serve with the pan gravy on the side.

Jimmy Le Blue's Barbecued Ribs

Jimmy Le Blue and his brother Leroy have had a feud going on for a number of years about how to fix the finest spareribs. Leroy likes to throw them right on the grill. Jimmy twists his face up when he hears that, saying you get a tough, fatty rib that will, "if you ain't careful, fly back and hit you square in the face." Not wanting facial lacerations, I took Jimmy's side. Here is Jimmy's recipe. The ribs turn out as tender as butter and very moist. Sorry, Leroy.

Serves 5 to 6

Salt
5 to 6 pounds pork spareribs
2 onions, sliced
Bay leaf

Jimmy's Barbecue Sauce (recipe
  follows)
Vegetable oil, for marinating
1 tablespoon chopped garlic

Bring a large pot filled with salted water to a boil. Add the ribs, onions, and bay leaf. Cover, reduce the heat, and simmer for 45 minutes. Drain.

Meanwhile, prepare the barbecue sauce and set aside.

Pour a little oil and the chopped garlic into a shallow dish. Add the ribs and marinate until ready to grill, at least 1 hour.

Grill over hot coals for 15 to 20 minutes, turning often. Baste with the barbecue sauce after each turn. Serve with extra sauce on the side.

Jimmy's Barbecue Sauce Makes about 2½ cups

1½ cups ketchup
½ cup cider vinegar
2 tablespoons brown sugar
2 tablespoons dry mustard
2 tablespoons grated onion
1 tablespoon minced garlic
1 tablespoon Worcestershire
  sauce

2 tablespoons prepared
  horseradish
2 tablespoons fresh lemon juice
1 teaspoon salt
3 tablespoons butter

Mix all the ingredients together in a saucepan and bring to a boil. Simmer for 15 minutes. Let stand for at least 1 hour to let the flavors mingle.

3 pounds beef short ribs, cut
    into 3-inch pieces
All-purpose flour seasoned with
    salt, freshly ground black
    pepper, and cayenne
$^1/_4$ cup vegetable oil or rendered
    beef fat
1 onion, finely diced

2 cloves garlic, minced
$^3/_4$ cup beef stock
2 cups peeled and sliced peaches
3 tablespoons dark brown sugar
3 tablespoons cider vinegar
$^1/_2$ teaspoon ground cinnamon
$^1/_4$ teaspoon ground cloves

Tangy Peach Short Ribs of Beef

These ribs, braised in a lightly sweetened stock with spiced peaches, are so tender the meat falls from the bone. As the braising juices cook down during the baking, they thicken into a sweet, tasty sauce that's finger-licking good.

Serves 3 to 4

Preheat the oven to 325°F.

Dust the ribs with the seasoned flour. Heat the oil in a dutch oven and brown the ribs well on all sides. Remove the ribs and set aside. Pour off all but 3 tablespoons of the fat from the pot. Add the onion and garlic to the pot and sauté briefly. Return the ribs to the pot and add all the remaining ingredients. Mix well, bring to a boil, and cover the pot.

Place the pot in the oven and bake for $1^1/_2$ to 2 hours, basting the ribs often. When done, remove the ribs and cut into serving pieces. Let the sauce stand for several minutes and degrease. Pour a small amount of sauce over the ribs and serve remaining sauce on the side.

Grandma Wissman's Sour Beef and Dumplings

The Chesapeake's many communities of German heritage possess an array of recipes for the classic German pot roast, sauerbraten. Although known as sauerbraten to the rest of the world, the locals around the Bay refer to it simply as sour beef. Here is my great-grandmother's recipe for sour beef, which she handed down to my grandmother. After relatives sampled my attempt at her signature dish, I was assured it was every bit as pungent and tender as they remembered. And my relatives, natives of the Chesapeake, know their sour beef: They are regulars at the ever popular sour beef and potato dumpling church hall fundraisers held around the Bay.

Serves 8 to 10

1 rump roast (5 to 6 pounds), or eye of the round
2 cups red wine vinegar
1 cup dry red wine
1½ tablespoons salt
2 cloves garlic, peeled
2 medium onions, sliced
2 stalks celery, chopped
2 carrots, sliced
2 bay leaves
12 black peppercorns
3 whole cloves
3 allspice berries
¼ cup sugar
All-purpose flour, for dredging
½ cup bacon drippings
Potato Dumplings (recipe follows)
3 tablespoons flour
1 cup gingersnaps, finely crushed
⅔ cup sour cream

Put the roast in a deep glass or ceramic bowl. In a saucepan, combine the vinegar, wine, 1 cup water, salt, garlic, onions, celery, carrots, bay leaves, peppercorns, cloves, allspice, and sugar. Bring to a boil and pour over the meat. Cover the bowl and refrigerate in the marinade for 2 to 3 days, turning the meat 2 or 3 times a day with wooden spoons.

Remove the meat from the marinade, reserving the marinade. Wipe meat dry with paper towels. Dredge meat in flour. Melt the bacon drippings in a heavy-bottomed pot. Brown the meat on all sides. Remove the roast, pour off the fat from the pot, and reserve. Return the meat to the pot and pour the reserved marinade over it. Bring to a boil. Cover, reduce the heat to a simmer, and cook for 3 hours, or until tender when pierced with a fork.

Remove the meat to a heated platter and keep it hot. Strain the cooking liquid and reserve. Cook the dumplings and keep warm.

Heat 3 tablespoons of the reserved fat in the pot. Stir in the 3 tablespoons flour and cook for 1 to 2 minutes, stirring constantly. Add the gingersnaps. Whisk in the reserved liquid and heat, stirring, until the sauce thickens. Remove from the heat and stir in the sour cream. Adjust the seasonings. Slice the meat and serve the gravy over the sliced meat and dumplings.

Meat and Game

Potato Dumplings Serves 8 to 10

Salt, to taste

2 pounds potatoes, peeled,
 boiled, and mashed

2 eggs, lightly beaten

Freshly ground black pepper, to
 taste

$^1/_2$ to $^3/_4$ cup dry bread crumbs

Bring a deep pot filled with salted water to a boil. Combine the potatoes, eggs, salt, pepper, and bread crumbs in a mixing bowl, adding only enough bread crumbs so that the mixture can be formed into balls. Using a tablespoon, form mixture into balls, dusting them with bread crumbs as you form them. Gently drop the dumplings into the boiling water. Reduce the heat and simmer uncovered for 6 to 8 minutes, or until floating. Remove with a slotted spoon.

Brunswick Stew

Nowadays most recipes for this stew feature chicken in place of squirrel as the main ingredient. It tastes fine, but truth be told, it just isn't authentic. But if you chicken out, I won't tell: Substitute a 3-pound frying chicken for the squirrel and proceed with the recipe, reducing total cooking time to 1½ hours.

Serves 4

All-purpose flour seasoned with salt and freshly ground black pepper
2 squirrels or 1 frying chicken (about 3 pounds), cut into serving pieces
2 tablespoons butter
2 tablespoons bacon drippings
2½ quarts boiling water (see Note)
1½ cups dried lima beans, soaked in cold water overnight
1 large onion, coarsely chopped
4 large ripe tomatoes, chopped
1½ cups fresh corn kernels (3 ears)
4 potatoes, peeled and cut into quarters
1 teaspoon dried thyme leaves
1 bay leaf
Salt and freshly ground black pepper, to taste

Lightly flour the squirrel pieces. Melt the butter and bacon drippings in a heavy-bottomed pot and brown the squirrel well on all sides. Pour in the water and bring to a boil. Cover, reduce the heat, and simmer for 1½ hours. Drain the lima beans.

Add lima beans and all the remaining ingredients. Cover and continue to simmer over a very low heat for another hour, or until the meat is tender.

Note: For a richer stew, substitute Chicken Stock (page 127) for the water.

Muskrat Love

Squirrel isn't the only rodent Chesapeake residents enjoy on their plates for an unusual meal. Fall to early spring is muskrat season on the marshes of the lower Eastern Shore. These semiaquatic creatures weigh several pounds when mature and have a rich, red meat that is high in protein and low in fat. Muskrat is a traditional Eastern Shore favorite, either braised or stewed. And it has an extremely loyal following that extends around the Bay. Please note, for your sake, that muskrat has musk glands similar to those of a skunk, and these must be removed before cooking. Buy your muskrat from a reputable game or seafood dealer and have him clean and cut the muskrat.

4 venison steaks, 1 to 1¹/₂ inches
    thick
All-purpose flour seasoned with
    salt and freshly ground
    black pepper
3 tablespoons butter

3 tablespoons vegetable oil
2 onions, cut into ¹/₄-inch-thick
    rings
Salt and freshly ground black
    pepper, to taste

Dredge the steaks in the seasoned flour. Heat the butter and oil in a skillet. Fry the steaks about 7 minutes on each side, or a bit longer if you want them well done. Remove the steaks to a heated platter and keep warm.

If necessary, add additional butter to bring the pan drippings to about 6 tablespoons. Heat the drippings, add the onions, salt, and pepper, and cook over medium heat, stirring now and then, until the onions turn a darkish brown or caramel color, about 20 minutes. Serve the onions on top of the steaks. Make a pan gravy (see page 161), if you like.

Venison Steaks with Caramelized Onions

Venison" is not a word heard frequently in these parts. Bay folks use the term "deer" when they refer to this savory, rich-tasting meat, not equating deer with a certain adorable animated creature. Deer hunting season around the Chesapeake brings out the game cook in men who never lift a spatula during the rest of the year. That's not the case with this recipe from my friend Keith Dixon, a dairy farmer and weekend hunter in Kent County. He's a great cook all year round.

Serves 4

Canals and More

Why bother taking a steamer south to Central America to behold the wonder of the Panama Canal? You would need to brave fierce Atlantic storms, avoid the Bermuda Triangle, and be wary of sailing off course to some God-forsaken locale. And need I remind you of mosquitoes and malaria? Enough said. Being afraid as I am of all the afore-mentioned, I highly suggest heading for the upper Chesapeake Bay to pay respects to one of the oldest, still-operating canals in the country. That would be the historic C & D (Chesapeake & Delaware) Canal in Chesapeake City, Maryland, which also happens to be the home of a fascinating canal museum and a recreational boaters' paradise.

A refreshingly simple and honest local cuisine, the food of the region is dominated by the abundance of fresh seafood, game, and produce. The ingredients are showcased in the recipes of the people who work the Bay and the fields. This oyster center has originated such recipes as scalloped oysters and the Eastern Shore oyster roast, both of which have evolved in Chestertown over the centuries. The Amish settled in the area and brought with them a recipe for a molasses-rich pie. And corn is one of the primary farm crops around here, highlighted in sweet corn pudding.

Venison Marinade (recipe
    follows)
3 pounds venison ribs, excess fat
    trimmed off
1 cup apple cider
$^1/_3$ cup cranberry juice
1 teaspoon sugar
$^1/_2$ teaspoon salt
$^1/_2$ teaspoon whole black
    peppercorns

2 cloves garlic, chopped
$^1/_2$ teaspoon ground allspice
1 teaspoon chopped parsley
1 teaspoon tarragon
1 teaspoon Worcestershire sauce
2 shots bourbon whiskey
    (optional)

Prepare the marinade and place in a glass baking dish large enough to hold the ribs. Add the ribs and turn several times, coating well. Turn the ribs meat side down into the marinade, cover, and refrigerate overnight.

When ready to prepare the ribs, place a dutch oven with a tight-fitting lid on the stove. Add all the remaining ingredients and mix well. Place the marinated ribs and marinade in the pot and turn the ribs to coat. Bring almost to a boil. Cover the pot tightly, reduce the heat to very low, and cook for about $2^1/_2$ to 3 hours, or until the meat begins to fall from the bone. Serve ribs hot, with the cooking liquid on the side as a sauce.

Venison Marinade   Makes about 2 cups

1 cup apple cider
$^1/_2$ cup apple cider vinegar
$^1/_3$ cup cranberry juice
2 tablespoons olive oil

1 teaspoon dried tarragon
1 teaspoon chopped parsley
1 bay leaf

Place all the ingredients in a small bowl and mix well.

Pop-Pop Dahl's Slow-Simmered Venison Ribs

Ron "Pop-Pop with No Hair" Dahl calls the Byrd River in the northwest Chesapeake region his home. Known far and wide for his cooking skills, Pop-Pop is now "retired"—but one would be hard-pressed to keep up with this gentleman who fishes, hunts, chops wood to heat his house, grows all his own vegetables, and, during the peak harvest season, puts up preserves and vegetables. There's also always plenty of venison meat on hand at the Dahl household, and Ron developed the recipe for these tender ribs. He suggests serving the ribs with buttered noodles or rice.

Serves 3 to 4

Savory Venison Stew

Too often I have eaten venison dishes that were, in a word, tough. *Game meats need to be prepared correctly—they often require braising or stewing, or even a bit of marinating—before cooking, as they are inherently tougher than domesticated cuts of meat. Stewing is a perfect way to prepare game: Letting the meat simmer and cook in its own juices keeps it from drying out. This simple hearty stew, which comes to me from Miss Lee of Chestertown, is fine game dining, and is even better reheated the next day.*

Serves 6

Lard or vegetable oil, for browning
2 pounds venison rump or round, cut into 1¹/₂-inch cubes
All-purpose flour seasoned with salt and freshly ground black pepper
2 large onions, sliced
4 cups boiling water
4 carrots, sliced
6 potatoes, peeled and cubed
1 teaspoon Chesapeake seasoning
¹/₄ teaspoon freshly ground black pepper
1 bay leaf
Pinch of dried thyme leaves
2 cups fresh or frozen peas
Hot rolls or biscuits, for accompaniment

Heat the lard in a dutch oven. Dust the meat cubes in the seasoned flour and brown well on all sides in the hot fat. Add the onions to the pot and cook for a few minutes with the meat. Pour in the boiling water. Bring to a boil, cover, reduce the heat, and simmer for 1¹/₂ hours.

Add all the remaining ingredients except the peas and simmer, uncovered, for 1 hour and 15 minutes.

Add the peas and continue to simmer for 5 minutes, or until the peas are tender. Adjust the seasonings and serve with hot rolls.

Salads

A large wooden bowl overflowing with freshly picked salad greens on a country farm situated on the banks of the Chesapeake Bay is a lovely image—but it is an image not totally based on fact. The great food writer James Beard in his classic book, *American Cookery*, reminds us that American salads, and that would include Chesapeake salads, have traditionally tended to be "composed salads," with green vegetables, leafy and raw, dressed in sweet-and-sour combinations of vinegar and sugar. One of the earliest forms of this composed salad is coleslaw.

Times have changed as well as eating habits and many small Chesapeake farms now specialize in baby lettuces, tender greens, and edible flowers that satisfy even the most discerning palate. Around the Bay, however, the most popular and most frequently prepared salad dishes are the sturdy, tried-and-true composed salads. The anchors of Chesapeake salads are cabbage- and potato-based salads, such as a creamy country coleslaw, a tart, hot red cabbage slaw, or an old-fashioned, mustard-infused potato salad.

The bounty of the Chesapeake Bay's fields and waters are similarly fashioned into numerous composed salads, including an Eastern Shore crab salad with cantaloupe, the quintessential Chesapeake shrimp salad, a Smithfield ham and crabmeat potato salad, and the Polish-inspired herring salad with apples, beets, and black walnuts.

Hot Red Cabbage Slaw

A dramatic change of pace from mayonnaise-dressed slaw, this dish, served warm, is cooked and dressed all at the same time. I like the slaw best when the cabbage is just slightly cooked. While cooking, I constantly taste the cabbage, making sure it stays on the heat not a minute longer than necessary.

Serves 4 to 6

$^1/_3$ cup red wine vinegar
1 teaspoon prepared mustard
$^1/_2$ teaspoon celery seed
3 tablespoons sugar
1 teaspoon salt
$^1/_4$ cup vegetable oil

$^1/_4$ cup bacon drippings
$^1/_2$ teaspoon freshly ground black pepper
1 small head red cabbage, chopped

Combine all the ingredients except the cabbage in a large pot. Heat, stirring to dissolve the sugar. Add the cabbage and stir to coat. Cover and cook for 8 to 10 minutes, stirring often and checking to make sure cabbage does not overcook. Serve warm.

1 cup mayonnaise

1 tablespoon red wine vinegar

1 teaspoon sugar

1 teaspoon Worcestershire sauce

1 tablespoon prepared
horseradish

1 teaspoon Dijon mustard

Few dashes of Tabasco sauce

Salt and freshly ground black
pepper to taste

1 small head cabbage, thinly
sliced

Combine all the ingredients except the cabbage and carrots in a small bowl and mix well. In a large bowl, toss together cabbage and carrots. Add the dressing and mix thoroughly. Cover and refrigerate at least 1 hour before serving.

Coleslaw

Coleslaw dressings are made either with a spiced mayonnaise base or a German-influenced, sweet and sour oil-and-vinegar mixture. This recipe calls for a tangy mayonnaise base, the type most commonly served around the Bay. Coleslaw goes hand in hand with crab cakes, fried oysters, and any form of fried fish—and around the Chesapeake, to not serve a large bowl of this slaw at a cookout or picnic can mean social ruin.

Serves 4

Father Joe's Favorite Potato Salad

*P*otato salad in all of its numerous manifestations is a staple of Chesapeake Bay fare. As pastor of Saint Ann's Church in Baltimore, Father Joe Muth presided over many a church hall fish fry. His potato salad, a perfect accompaniment to the crisp fillets of panfried fish, graced the buffet tables at the annual event, and the bowl was constantly replenished because it was so popular.

Serves 6

6 medium potatoes, boiled and peeled (see Note)
1 onion, finely chopped
3 stalks celery, finely chopped
$^1/_4$ cup sweet pickle relish
2 tablespoons dry mustard
$^3/_4$ to 1 cup mayonnaise
3 hard-cooked eggs, chopped
$^1/_2$ cup chopped parsley
Salt and freshly ground black pepper, to taste
Paprika, for garnish

Cut the potatoes into bite-size pieces and place in a bowl. Mix together the onion, celery, relish, mustard, and mayonnaise in a small bowl. Fold in the eggs and parsley. Pour over the potatoes and mix well. Season with salt and pepper. Just before serving, garnish with paprika.

Note: Cook the potatoes in their jackets in boiling salted water until easily pierced with a knife, then immerse them in cold water. After the potatoes have cooled slightly the skins can be easily removed. This cooking method makes for a cleaner, less starchy salad.

½ pound goat cheese
12 fresh sage leaves
1 cup olive oil
Sage Dressing (recipe follows)

½ cup dry bread crumbs
4 handfuls mixed salad greens,
    washed

Cut the goat cheese into 4 rounds. Place the cheese and sage leaves in a bowl, then pour olive oil over all. Cover the bowl tightly and refrigerate overnight.

Preheat the oven to 400°F.

Drain the cheese, reserving 6 tablespoons of the olive oil for the dressing (see Note), and lightly coat each slice with bread crumbs, covering both sides. Place the cheese slices on a greased baking sheet and bake for 10 to 12 minutes.

While the cheese is baking, lightly dress the greens and arrange on plates. When finished baking, set a hot cheese slice on each salad plate and serve immediately.

Note: Remaining olive oil may be used at a later time for another dressing or to make salad croutons.

Sage Dressing Makes ½ cup

2 tablespoons white wine
    vinegar
1 clove garlic, minced
1 tablespoon finely chopped
    fresh sage leaves

¼ teaspoon Dijon mustard
6 tablespoons reserved olive oil
Salt and freshly ground black
    pepper, to taste

Mix together the vinegar, garlic, sage, and mustard in a small bowl or blender. Slowly whisk in the olive oil. Season with salt and pepper. Prepare the dressing at least 1 hour before using so that the flavors blend.

Hot Goat Cheese Salad with Sage Dressing

Cinda Sebastian knows her lettuce. Matter of fact, she is the Chesapeake's Lettuce Queen. Along with her husband, Scott Williams, Cinda operates a small farm in Carroll County, Maryland, specializing in herbs, lettuces, and other vegetables. I'm usually out of bed early on Saturday mornings, when I make my way down to the 32nd Street Farmer's Market in Baltimore to see Cinda's stall overflowing with baby lettuces and herbs. Her stand is always my first stop, and by the looks of the lines there, it's a weekly stop for many others who know good food and demand the best.

Serves 4

Millington Chicken Salad

This is a real chicken salad. Many times chicken salad is made with leftovers, almost as an afterthought. The volunteer firefighters at the Millington Fire Hall on the upper Eastern Shore do things differently, using a carefully braised chicken as the starting point. If you attend one of their fundraising suppers you'll find they pair this moist chicken salad with Baked Maryland Ham (page 153) and Slippery Dumplings and Gravy (page 203).

Serves 6 to 8

1 frying chicken (3 to 4 pounds)
8 cups Chicken Stock or water (page 127)
2 onions, sliced
4 stalks celery, chopped
2 carrots, chopped
4 sprigs of parsley
3 cloves garlic
2 bay leaves
Salt and freshly ground black pepper, to taste
Chicken Salad Dressing (recipe follows)

Wash the chicken well in cold water, pat dry, and place in a large pot. Add the stock, onions, celery, carrots, parsley, garlic, and bay leaves. Add 1½ teaspoons salt if the stock is unsalted. Bring to a boil and cover the pot. Reduce the heat and simmer, covered, skimming foam that forms at the top from time to time, for about 1 hour. Carefully remove the chicken from the pot and place on a platter. Set aside to cool. Strain broth from the pot and reserve for another purpose.

While the chicken is cooling, prepare the dressing. After the chicken has completely cooled carefully pick the meat from the bones and place it in a mixing bowl. Cut any large pieces of chicken into bite-size pieces. Add the dressing and gently mix into chicken. Adjust the seasoning and chill the salad for at least 30 minutes before serving.

Chicken Salad Dressing Makes 2 cups

1 cup mayonnaise
1 cup finely diced celery
1 small onion, finely diced
2 tablespoons Dijon mustard
1 clove garlic, minced
Juice of 1 lemon
Salt and freshly ground black pepper, to taste

Combine the mayonnaise, celery, onion, mustard, garlic, and lemon juice in a mixing bowl and mix well. Season with salt and pepper.

6 to 8 medium potatoes, boiled
and peeled (see page 176)
3 stalks celery, diced
1 small yellow onion, finely
chopped
5 green onions, minced
$^1/_2$ cup diced green bell pepper
3 tablespoons dry mustard

$^1/_2$ teaspoon Tabasco Sauce
1 cup mayonnaise
1 pound backfin crabmeat,
picked over
$^1/_3$ pound Smithfield ham, diced
Salt and freshly ground black
pepper, to taste

Cut the potatoes into bite-size pieces for salad and let cool.

Combine the celery, yellow and green onions, bell pepper, mustard, Tabasco, and mayonnaise in a small bowl and mix well. Combine the potatoes, crabmeat, and ham in a large bowl. Add the mayonnaise mixture and toss very gently so as not to break up the crabmeat. Season with salt and pepper. Be careful! Smithfield ham is very salty.

Treasie's Crabmeat and Smithfield Ham Potato Salad

Here is Aunt Treasie Utz-Utz's famous summertime dish—famous up and down her street in Havre de Grace, Maryland, that is. She got her nickname Utz-Utz because of her addiction to the Utz brand of potato chips sold in the Chesapeake region. She likes the taste of potatoes with other things, too, but she prepares this treat only on the Fourth of July, " 'cause it's too expensive to make all the time. Plus, the crabs is running big and heavy by the Fourth." When making this dish Treasie keeps one hand in her ever-present bag of chips, and a watchful eye out for Uncle Elmer, who is disposed to picking the lumps of crabmeat out of the salad when he thinks no one is looking.

Serves 8 to 10

Eastern Shore Crab Salad with Cantaloupe

During a long, hard winter when I'm feeling trapped by the cold and snow, I sometimes picture myself on the shore in the summertime, stopping by a farmer's roadside stand piled high with freshly picked cantaloupes. The soil of the Chesapeake's Eastern Shore produces some of the sweetest, most fragrant summer melons imaginable. This salad pairs sweet melon with firm lumps of crabmeat, a perfect match that, for those of you who have never had the pleasure, goes together like berries and cream.

Serves 6

1 pound backfin crabmeat, picked over
$^1/_4$ cup diced red bell pepper
$^1/_4$ cup diced green bell pepper
2 tablespoons minced green onion
$^1/_4$ cup diced apple
$^3/_4$ cup mayonnaise
$^1/_4$ cup sour cream
1 tablespoon honey
2 tablespoons chopped mint
Dash of Worcestershire sauce
Dash of Tabasco Sauce
Juice of $^1/_2$ lemon
Salt and freshly ground black pepper, to taste
3 small ripe cantaloupe or honeydew melons, halved and seeded
Sprigs of mint, for garnish

Combine the crabmeat, red and green bell peppers, green onion, and apple in a large bowl. In a small bowl, combine the mayonnaise, sour cream, honey, chopped mint, Worcestershire, Tabasco, and lemon juice and mix well. Pour the mayonnaise mixture over the crabmeat mixture and toss gently. Season with salt and pepper.

Place each melon half, cut side up, on an individual salad plate. Divide the salad mixture evenly among the melon halves, mounding the salad in the hollow centers. Garnish with the mint sprigs and serve.

2 pounds medium to large
   shrimp in the shell
¹/₂ to ³/₄ cup mayonnaise
1 teaspoon Chesapeake
   seasoning

1 cup chopped celery
¹/₄ cup minced onion
3 tablespoons minced capers
2 tablespoons chopped parsley
2 tablespoons chopped dill

Steam the shrimp as directed on page 87. Drain, peel, devein, and cut into pieces. Place in a salad bowl. In a small bowl, combine the mayonnaise, Chesapeake seasoning, celery, onion, capers, parsley, dill, and lemon juice and mix well. Pour over the shrimp and mix well. Refrigerate for about 1 hour to let the shrimp absorb the dressing.

Shrimp Salad

Next to crab cakes, shrimp salad is the biggest seller in every bar, restaurant, tavern, and deli in the Chesapeake region. There are numerous versions: some with mayonnaise, others with hard-cooked eggs in an oil-and-vinegar dressing, and others still in a Thousand Island–like sauce. For my money, this is the best, no nonsense, good-eating shrimp salad to be found.

Serves 6 to 8

Northwest Chesapeake, Geographically Speaking

There's something for everyone in this neck of the Bay. You can go to an Orioles' game at Camden Yards, stroll along Baltimore's bustling Inner Harbor, or better yet, take a scenic sail up the Bay to the charming town of Havre de Grace sitting at the mouth of the Susquehanna River. The towns and villages that surround this northern part of the Chesapeake are a far cry from the cosmopolitan hubbub of Baltimore. Drive not even thirty minutes from the city center in any direction, and you'll enter a different world of forests, creeks, quiet docksides, and farms tucked into tranquil rolling hills. No wonder they call the Chesapeake Bay "the land of pleasant living."

Spring Shad and Roe Salad with Spicy Pecans

The Chesapeake shad run, lasting only several weeks, occurs each spring. Locals dine overtime to eat their fill of the shad and their delicate sacks of roe (eggs) during this brief season. Well known for her creative dishes featuring traditional Chesapeake delicacies, Chef Nancy Longo, owner of Pierpoint Restaurant in Baltimore's historic Fells Point neighborhood, created this lovely spring salad, a testament to her skill.

Serves 6

3 pairs shad roe, separated
1¹/₂ pounds shad fillets
1 ear white corn, shucked
¹/₂ cup finely diced Smithfield ham
1 pound spinach
¹/₃ pound frisée or mesclun greens

18 red pear tomatoes, halved
¹/₃ cup sherry wine vinegar
3 tablespoons hard cider
1 tablespoon freshly ground black pepper
¹/₂ cup olive oil
Spicy Pecans (recipe follows)

Preheat the broiler.

Place the shad roe and shad fillets that have been divided into 6 serving portions in a shallow baking pan and cover by one third with cold water. On an open flame, toast the corn, rotating frequently, until lightly charred on the outside. Cut the corn from the cob and mix with the Smithfield ham. Set aside. Trim and discard the stems from the spinach and wash leaves well. Dry in a salad spinner. If necessary, wash the frisée and dry in a salad spinner. Arrange the spinach and frisée on plates and garnish with pear tomato halves.

Combine the vinegar, hard cider, and pepper in a small bowl. To make a dressing for the greens, slowly add the olive oil in a fine, steady stream while whisking constantly.

Place the shad and roe under the broiler and broil until just done, turning once, about 4 minutes on each side. Use a slotted spatula to place the shad and shad roe on top of the salad greens. Spoon the dressing over the top of the fish and roe, allowing it to spill onto the greens. Garnish each plate with the Spicy Pecans and the corn–Smithfield ham mixture.

Spicy Pecans Makes 2 cups

2 cups pecan halves
4 tablespoons melted butter
3 tablespoons sugar
¹/₂ teaspoon salt

¹/₄ teaspoon cayenne pepper
¹/₂ teaspoon ground coriander
¹/₄ teaspoon onion powder

In a bowl mix the pecans and butter together. Place the pecans in a hot skillet and sauté, stirring often, until browned, about 3 minutes. Remove from the heat and season with sugar, salt, cayenne, coriander, and onion powder.

1 pound steamed shrimp, peeled
  and deveined (see page 87)
2 cups small shell macaroni
1 cup sliced celery
1/2 medium green bell pepper,
  finely chopped
1/2 medium red bell pepper,
  finely chopped
1/2 small red onion, finely
  chopped
2 green onions, chopped

2 tablespoons chopped parsley
1/4 cup mayonnaise
1/4 cup Vinaigrette Dressing
  (recipe follows)
1/4 cup sherry
1 tablespoon fresh lemon juice
1 teaspoon Chesapeake
  seasoning
Freshly ground black pepper, to
  taste

Cut the shrimp into pieces about 1/2 inch wide and set aside.

Cook the macaroni in boiling salted water until tender but not
mushy. Drain and rinse with cold water. Put the pasta in a large bowl and
add the celery, green and red bell peppers, red onion, green onion, and
parsley. In a small bowl, mix together the mayonnaise, Vinaigrette Dressing, sherry, lemon juice, and Chesapeake seasoning. Pour the mayonnaise
mixture into the pasta and mix well. Season with pepper. Add the crabmeat and reserved shrimp and fold gently, taking care not to break apart
the lumps of crabmeat. Serve immediately.

Vinaigrette Dressing   Makes 2/3 cup

1 shallot, finely diced
3 tablespoons red wine or
  sherry vinegar

1/4 teaspoon salt
1/2 cup olive oil or vegetable oil

Combine the shallot, vinegar, and salt in a bowl. Slowly pour in the
oil while constantly beating with a wire whisk.

Lady Liberty Seafood Salad

A *family Fourth of July picnic at the Biddlecombs' in Reedville, Virginia, just wouldn't seem right without this colorful salad, a longtime family favorite. Primarily a seafood salad, it contains just a small amount of pasta and fresh, crisp vegetables that are bound together with a light, sherry-flavored vinaigrette.*

Serves 8 to 10

Beverley Biddlecomb (and Family) of Reedville, Virginia

I love to go to a party, so I didn't have to think twice when I received the invite from Beverley to come down and join her and the Biddlecomb family for their annual Fourth of July celebration in Reedville, Virginia. It is a two-day affair with three generations of family getting together for a grand old time. Beverley is a hostess and cook *extraordinaire*—a warm, wonderful woman who makes me feel like a part of her family. She is able to organize and prepare the huge event, host guests, and run her household, all the while working the day-shift as a nurse. I could use some lessons from her on time management.

July 3rd: The evening before the festivities I find myself helping in the kitchen. Beverley shows me the technique for her famous seafood pasta dish—it is so perky and colorful that we dub it "Lady Liberty Seafood Salad." Maria, Beverley's sister-in-law, is busy making her deviled eggs, which are a mainstay of the family outing. I have brought some chicken as my contribution to the affair, and I whip up my friend Miss Lorraine's barbecue sauce, which is reputed to put hair on your chest, need it or not. Desserts galore are concocted and jars of fig preserves and pickled watermelon rind are packed for the festivities.

July 4th: Today we go on an early morning fishing trip and picnic on *The Dudley* (the charter boat of Beverley and her husband, Fred), watch the Reedville Fourth of July parade in the afternoon, and enjoy a nighttime viewing on the water of the town's fireworks. It is a day of early rising and late-night carousing.

Almost everyone wants to fish during the boating voyage. A glorious sunny day on the Bay with just the perfect amount of warm breezes blowing make this day the type of which memories are born. Beverley and I are leaning on the railing of the boat with our fishing lines dropped when, all at once, Beverley calls out that she has something and darn if she doesn't. The hostess of the day wins the annual Biddlecomb Family Fishing Tournament. I catch something too, but it is so small no one can quite make out what it is.

Soon we spread the tablecloths over *The Dudley*'s deck and lay out an incredible assortment of summer dishes. We all dig in and spend the rest of the morning snacking, fishing, and laughing at the antics of the kids on board. Not a bad way to start the Fourth.

July 5th: Day two of the Biddlecomb festivities is centered around a traditional cook-out. The whole gang assembles at a Biddlecomb family member's summer home, nestled on the banks of a little creek. The barbecues are blazing and I get a chance to talk and sling a bit of chicken with the family's barbecue expert, Maria's husband, Ray. He explains the nuances of country-cooking on the open fire—and a few other tales I won't divulge here. We eat and eat. Later, the family has a show-and-tell, each member bringing with them artifacts of family historical significance and tales to accompany them. The stories are remarkable—funny, warm, witty—and told with such a love and respect for their relations that I keep thinking if I am reincarnated I want to come back a Biddlecomb.

A Fourth of July Picnic with the Biddlecomb Family

Miss Lorraine's Barbecued Chicken (page 133)
Lady Liberty Seafood Salad
Pickled Watermelon Rind (page 267)
Sweet Pickled Figs (page 267)

East Baltimore Herring Salad

How much more east Baltimore can you get than this salad? For generations the east side of Baltimore has been home for thousands of Eastern European immigrants, a neighborhood of white marble steps, screen paintings, and a little chopped herring with sweet beets and apples on dark bread. Such things you don't want to miss in this lifetime.

Serves 6 to 8

$1/2$ pound pickled or schmaltz herring fillets, diced
2 cups boiled potatoes, diced
2 cups cooked beets, diced
1 cup apples, peeled, cored, and diced
$1/2$ cup diced yellow onion
$1/2$ cup chopped toasted black walnuts
$1/2$ cup apple cider vinegar

3 tablespoons honey or maple syrup
$2/3$ cup sour cream
Freshly ground black pepper, to taste
$1/2$ cup chopped parsley

Sliced apples and sliced hard-cooked eggs, for garnish (optional)

Combine the herring, potatoes, beets, apples, onion, and black walnuts in a large bowl and mix well. In a small bowl, mix together the vinegar, honey, sour cream, pepper, and parsley. Pour the dressing over the herring mixture and mix well. Refrigerate for several hours before serving. Garnish with sliced apples and hard-cooked eggs, if desired.

Vegetables and Other Side Dishes

Chesapeake folk take their vegetables seriously, expecting high quality at the produce stall and in their own backyards. Domestic vegetable gardens have been extensions of Chesapeake kitchens for generations. Summer months bring bushels of tomatoes to these home gardens, providing plenty for the day's table and surplus for preserving. Each August my family's garden would be heavy with cymling squash, in addition to the tomatoes, and our kitchen turned out plates of steamed squash and several variations of creamy squash and tomato casseroles. Around the turn of the century, the shores of the Patapsco River in the industrial center of Baltimore were lined with canning plants working round the clock to preserve the bumper harvest of Eastern Shore produce, which was brought in on barges.

The abundance of local vegetables provides the basis for a wide array of Chesapeake vegetable dishes, such as simply prepared fresh vegetables laced with lemon butter; long-simmered country greens; freshly picked green beans, sautéed gently with peanuts and julienned slices of smoked country ham; and mace-scented tomato pie. And folks on the Bay eagerly await each year's summer harvest of Silver Queen corn to eat it straight from the cob or to transform it into a delicious succotash or savory pudding. The preparation methods are many and varied, as plentiful and diverse as the local vegetables themselves.

1 cup young lima beans
Salt
1 cup fresh corn kernels (2 ears)
3 tablespoons butter

Juice of ¹/₂ lemon
Freshly ground black pepper, to taste

Put the limas in a saucepan and add water just to cover. Lightly salt the water. Bring to a boil, cover, and simmer until the beans are barely tender, about 15 to 20 minutes. Add the corn and simmer for 10 minutes more. Drain off the water and season with butter, lemon juice, salt, and pepper. Serve right away.

Succotash

This vegetable dish is as Southern as corn bread. The name is said to derive from **msickquatash,** the Narragansett Indians' word for "boiled kernels of corn." Keep in mind that a tasty succotash simply cannot be made from frozen or canned vegetables.

Serves 4

Sweet Summer Corn on the Cob Serves 4

Summer means shucking around these parts, and I'm not talking oysters here. I'm talking sitting on the front porch with a glass of mint-scented iced tea, out of the glare of the hot afternoon sun, with piles of freshly picked sweet corn on the cob. I'm not sure what part I like best—eating the crisp corn right from the cob, or the corn-shucking ritual of filling paper bags with corn silk and husks while chewing the fat with friends during those lazy afternoons.

Blissfully delicious white Silver Queen corn appears in the Bay region's produce stalls in July, producing a fervent response from Chesapeake folks who are eager to sink their teeth into an almost-sugary row of kernels. When preparing this type of corn, no sugar needs to be added to the pot.

¹/₂ cup milk
¹/₄ cup sugar (optional)
2 tablespoons butter
4 to 6 ears sweet corn, husked

Melted butter and salt and freshly ground black pepper, for accompaniment

In a pot large enough to hold the corn, combine ample salted water, the milk, sugar, and the 2 tablespoons butter. Bring to a boil and add the corn. Cook over medium heat for 5 to 8 minutes, or until as tender as you like. Serve with melted butter, salt, and pepper.

Kent County Corn Pudding

During summer harvest the corn from Kent County is the sweetest imaginable. I enjoy nothing better than eating it lightly cooked and right off the cob, but another way I like it is in this traditional Eastern Shore savory corn pudding.

2 cups fresh corn kernels (4 to 5 ears), coarsely chopped
2 eggs, beaten
1 tablespoon flour
1 tablespoon grated onion

2 tablespoons sugar
2 tablespoons butter, melted
1 1/4 cups milk
1 teaspoon salt
1/4 teaspoon white pepper

Preheat the oven to 325°F. Butter a 1-quart baking dish.

Combine all the ingredients in a bowl and mix well. Pour the mixture into the dish.

Bake for 50 to 60 minutes, or until set. Serve as soon as possible.

Stuffed Tomatoes

For this recipe, it's important to choose tomatoes that are ripe enough to give a full-bodied tomato flavor to the dish, yet are firm enough to hold up during the baking. These tomatoes go nicely with Roast Chicken with Sage Butter and Corn Bread Stuffing (page 134).

Serves 4

4 large firm, ripe tomatoes
2 tablespoons finely chopped onion
2 stalks celery, finely chopped
1 1/2 cups fresh corn kernels (3 ears)

4 tablespoons (1/2 stick) butter
Salt and freshly ground black pepper
Dry bread crumbs
Chopped parsley

Preheat the oven to 375°F. Generously butter a baking dish in which the tomatoes will fit snugly.

Cut about 1/2 inch off the tops of the tomatoes. Scoop out the seeds and pulp and reserve. Turn the tomatoes upside down on a rack to drain while making the stuffing.

Drain off the liquid from the tomato pulp. Combine the pulp, onion, celery, and corn in a mixing bowl. Melt 2 tablespoons of the butter. Add to the bowl with pulp and season with salt and pepper. Stuff the tomatoes with the pulp mixture. Top each tomato with a sprinkling of bread crumbs and parsley. Cut the remaining 2 tablespoons butter into 4 equal pats and place a pat on each tomato. Arrange the tomatoes in the dish.

Bake for about 20 to 25 minutes, or until heated through. Serve right away.

10 ripe tomatoes, peeled and
   cored
2 tablespoons butter
5 tablespoons sugar

Salt and freshly ground black
   pepper, to taste
Pinch of grated nutmeg

Combine the tomatoes and butter in a heavy pot and cook, covered, over low heat for $1^{1}/_{2}$ hours. Mash the tomatoes. Add the sugar, salt, pepper, and nutmeg. Cook for 30 minutes, stirring often. Remove from the heat and serve.

Note: You can make this dish out of season using 2 cans (16 ounces each) of peeled whole tomatoes.

2 large green tomatoes
Milk to cover
1 cup all-purpose flour
2 teaspoons baking powder
$^{1}/_{2}$ teaspoon salt

2 eggs, separated
1 teaspoon sugar
$^{2}/_{3}$ cup milk
Pinch of ground mace
Vegetable oil, for frying

Core the tomatoes and cut into $^{1}/_{4}$-inch-thick slices. Place in a shallow bowl and add milk to cover. Let stand while making the fritter batter.

Sift together the flour, baking powder, and salt in a bowl. Stir in the egg yolks, sugar, $^{2}/_{3}$ cup of milk, and mace. Beat the egg whites until stiff peaks form, then gently fold into the batter.

Pour oil into a skillet to a depth of about 1 inch and heat until very hot, about 375°F. Remove the tomato slices from the milk, dip in batter, and fry, a few at a time, until golden brown on both sides, about 5 minutes. Remove with a slotted utensil to paper towels to drain. Serve hot.

Stewed Tomatoes

When I was down at Tilghman Island visiting, I had lunch with Helen Cummings, a waterman's wife, who served me these old-fashioned stewed tomatoes. I hadn't had them in many a year but suddenly realized then and there that they are as good as tomato cooking gets.

Serves 4

Green Tomato Fritters

Oh my God, what to do with all the tomatoes!" This was Aunt Catherine's yearly cry each summer when she saw her rows of tomato plants hanging low, weighted down with fruit. One of my all-time favorite ways to use up extra tomatoes is this family recipe: a slightly sweet, spiced batter that makes unbelievably good tomato fritters.

Serves 4

Tomato Pie

A fantastic appetizer or, as peculiar as it may sound, dessert. I've seen this pie served both ways. It is perfect as a lunch dish with a tossed salad of dandelion greens mixed with arugula and chopped hard-cooked eggs. You'll like the contrast of the bitter greens with the sweetness of the pie. For dessert, top it with a dollop of whipped cream that has been slightly sweetened with maple syrup. Now how's that for one pie?

Serves 6 to 8

6 ripe tomatoes, peeled and cut into 1/2-inch-thick slices
1/2 cup (firmly packed) brown sugar
Salt and freshly ground black pepper, to taste
Pinch of ground mace
1 cup dry bread crumbs
1 tablespoon fresh lemon juice
4 tablespoons (1/2 stick) butter
Pastry Dough for a Single-Crust Pie (page 247)
1 egg, beaten with 1 tablespoon water, for glaze

Preheat the oven to 350°F. Butter the bottom of a 9-inch pie pan.

Make a layer of tomato slices in the pie pan and sprinkle with some of the sugar, salt, pepper, mace, and bread crumbs. Continue making layers, ending with bread crumbs. Sprinkle with lemon juice and dot with butter.

On a lightly floured surface, roll out the dough to form a top crust, transfer to the pan, and flute the edges. Brush the top with egg glaze.

Bake for 30 to 35 minutes, or until nicely browned. Remove from the oven. The pie is best served warm or at room temperature.

Squash and Tomato Casserole

The vegetable garden at the Dixon family's dairy farm outside of Chestertown, Maryland, produces a bumper crop of zucchini every summer. Here we have a classic summer combination, zucchini and vine-ripened tomatoes, which are lightly spiced and topped with melted cheese.

Serves 4

6 tablespoons (3/4 stick) butter
4 medium zucchini, thinly sliced
1 onion, diced
4 tomatoes, peeled, seeded, and diced
Salt and freshly ground black pepper, to taste
Pinch of Chesapeake seasoning
4 ounces grated mozzarella or sliced provolone cheese

Preheat the oven to 375°F. Butter a 4-cup casserole.

Melt the butter in a skillet. Add the zucchini and onion and sauté for 3 to 5 minutes, or until half-cooked. Remove from the heat and add the tomatoes, salt, pepper, and Chesapeake seasoning.

Pour into the dish and top with cheese.

Bake for 15 minutes, or until the cheese melts and begins to brown. Remove from the oven and let stand 5 minutes before serving.

1 can (20 ounces) hominy,
  broken apart with a fork
2 tablespoons butter
1 small yellow onion, diced
$^1/_2$ medium green bell pepper,
  diced

4 large tomatoes, peeled, cored,
  and chopped
2 tablespoons sugar
1 teaspoon salt
4 strips of bacon

Preheat the oven to 350°F. Butter a 4-cup casserole dish.

Put the hominy in the casserole. Melt the butter in a sauté pan and cook the onion and green pepper until soft, about 3 minutes. Add the tomatoes, sugar, and salt and simmer over low heat for 10 minutes. Pour the mixture over the hominy. Place the bacon strips on top of the mixture.

Bake uncovered for 30 minutes. Remove from the oven and let stand for 5 minutes before serving.

Note: Out of season, substitute 1 can (14$^1/_2$ ounces) diced tomatoes for the fresh tomatoes.

Tomato and Hominy Casserole

In the old days on the Chesapeake, hominy was generally served as a side dish with a fairly simple preparation, as a starch to accompany roast meats or poultry. This casserole recipe was given to me by Miss Ban Deihl of the Lake Packing Company in Lottsburg, Virginia, makers of Manning's Hominy. It is a hearty, satisfying dish that gives this traditional corn product some pizzazz.

Serves 6

Steamed Pattypan Squash

The scallop-rimmed, flying saucer–shape pattypan squash, also known as cymling squash or summer squash, is one of those special treats to be enjoyed only during the summer months. From June to August I feel as though I could live on nothing but these tasty squash and just-picked vine-ripened tomatoes.

8 medium pattypan squash
3 tablespoons butter

Salt, freshly ground black pepper, and fresh lemon juice to taste

Wash the squash and cut into quarters. Barely cover the bottom of a heavy saucepan with salted water. Bring to a boil and drop in the squash. Cover and cook until tender. Drain off the liquid and add butter, salt, pepper, and lemon juice and mash lightly with a fork or potato masher. Serve right away.

Charm on the Chester

Tucked away on the Chester River is the hamlet of Chestertown, Maryland. George Washington made numerous stops here during the Revolution, and became enamored of the area's beauty and bounty, including the oysters and crabs served in the town's homes and taverns. Washington even personally approved the use of his name for the historic Washington College in Chestertown, the nation's tenth oldest college.

The countryside surrounding Chestertown is dotted with dairy farms and with fields of tomatoes, wheat, soybeans, corn, asparagus, potatoes, and the area's famous peaches. The landscape of marshes and fields is rich with waterfowl and deer, making the area a sportsman's paradise.

Modern-day Chestertown is perhaps most famous as home to the annual Chestertown Tea Party, a full-costume reenactment of the town's 1774 protest against British taxes, held each Memorial Day weekend amidst parades and parties.

1 large onion, chopped
1/2 pound country ham, cut into
    1-inch pieces
2 pounds green beans, trimmed

Salt and freshly ground black
    pepper, to taste
Dash of red wine vinegar

Fill a pot with enough water to cover the beans. Add the onion and ham and bring to a boil. Add the beans and cook very slowly until tender, about 1 hour, or to taste. Remove from the heat and pour off all but one quarter of the water. Season the beans with salt, pepper, and vinegar. Place in a serving bowl and serve with a slotted spoon.

2 pounds green beans
8 tablespoons (1 stick) plus 6
    tablespoons (3/4 stick) butter
Juice of 2 lemons
2 tablespoons Dijon mustard

Salt and freshly ground black
    pepper
2 cups julienned Smithfield ham
1 1/2 cups peanuts, coarsely
    chopped

Using scissors, snip off the ends of the beans on the diagonal, leaving the beans whole. Bring a saucepan filled with salted water to a boil. Add the beans and cook, checking constantly, until done but still crisp, about 5 to 8 minutes. Drain immediately and place in a large deep bowl. Cut the stick of butter in chunks over the beans. Add the lemon juice and mustard. Season with salt and pepper. Add the ham and stir gently to mix all ingredients.

Sauté the peanuts in the remaining 6 tablespoons butter for just a few minutes, stirring constantly. Place peanuts in a strainer to drain off any excess butter. Arrange the beans on an oval platter and spoon a long line of sautéed peanuts down the center. Serve immediately.

While I'm a fan of tender young green beans that have been steamed or slightly blanched and dressed with nothing more than a squeeze of fresh lemon, I actually prefer Southern-style green beans. For those of us who grew up on the Southern style, just sitting down to a goodly helping of these beans can bring tears of joy to our eyes.

Serves 8

Green Beans with Country Ham and Sautéed Peanuts

William Taylor likes to cook up a platterful of crisp green beans, which are generously coated with a tart and pungent Dijon butter sauce, then tossed with Smithfield ham and sautéed peanuts.

Serves 10 to 12

Cooking Country Greens Serves 6

The Chesapeake isn't exactly in Dixie, but it is, to be sure, on the south side of the Mason-Dixon Line. Ham-flavored greens slide down easy and can pack a wallop, depending on the wrist action when adding the black pepper and hot pepper flakes. Those not disposed to giving greens a try—mustard, collard, turnip, or beet—are missing out on one of life's great pleasures. Mother always told us to eat our greens, and now, according to recent nutritional research, we're finding out she was right. This recipe technique is a Southern-style classic: A potful of fresh greens is slowly cooked, absorbing the smoky aroma of the country ham. Don't give me any stuff about overcooked greens! Loosen up and try them the good old-fashioned country way.

1 to 1½ pounds smoked ham hocks
2 pounds collard or mustard greens

Salt, freshly ground black pepper, crushed red pepper, and cider vinegar, to taste

Bring 4 cups water and the ham hocks to a boil in a large pot. Cook over medium heat for about 1 hour. Remove and discard any wilted leaves and the large stems from the greens and add the greens to the pot. Simmer a long time, at least 2 hours. Strain off most of the liquid, leaving a little to keep the greens moist. Take out the ham hocks and pick off the meat. Season the greens with salt, black pepper, red pepper, and vinegar. Add the ham pieces back to the greens and stir well. Place greens in a serving bowl and serve hot.

Vegetables and Other Side Dishes

4 bunches (6 to 8 ounces each)
watercress, large stems
removed
6 tablespoons olive oil

1 teaspoon chopped garlic
Juice of 1 lemon
Salt and freshly ground black
pepper, to taste

Bring a pot of water to a boil. Blanch the watercress for 1 minute. Drain, rinse with cold water, and drain again.

Heat the olive oil in a skillet. Add the watercress and garlic and cook briefly over high heat. Season with lemon juice, salt, and pepper. Serve hot or, as in the Italian tradition, at room temperature.

Fried Watercress

Watercress grows wild along the streams and smaller tributaries of the Chesapeake Bay. According to Chesapeake culinary lore, cress cleanses the blood. Serve this garlicky treat with Roast Wild Goose with Apple-Chestnut Stuffing (page 148) or Chicken Breasts with Crabmeat and Mozzarella (page 140).

Serves 6

Kale and Country Ham Serves 4

With the cold winds blowing on the waters of Tangier Island in the fall and winter, the locals there need to eat their greens to stay afloat. Alva Crockett tells us just how he makes his kale taste so fine.

Salt, to taste
1/2 pound country ham
1 1/2 pounds kale

Freshly ground black pepper, to taste
White or red wine vinegar, to taste
(optional)

"In a pot just big enough for your kale, fill it up about half way with cold water. Pour in a little salt and some smoky country ham cut up into inch squares.

"Bring all that to the boil and add the kale. Don't forget to wash your kale first, or it'll be gritty as the devil. Cook on a medium heat about 45 minutes to an hour.

"Pour off some of the water and season with salt and pepper. You might want to sprinkle on a little vinegar for some bite."

Maple-Glazed Sweet Potatoes

Sweet potatoes play a major role in the kitchens of the Bay, and I play the role of chief cook at family holiday gatherings. I would be in the doghouse if I did not prepare this traditional dish, in which the cooked sweet potatoes are glazed with an orange-scented maple syrup and topped with black walnuts. Be careful about eating the sweet potatoes piping hot: They tend to stick to the lips.

Serves 4 to 6

6 large sweet potatoes
$^3/_4$ cup (firmly packed) brown sugar
4 tablespoons ($^1/_2$ stick) butter
$^1/_4$ cup maple syrup
Grated zest of 1 orange
Juice of 1 orange
$^1/_2$ cup chopped black walnuts

Preheat the oven to 375°F. Generously butter a 13 × 9 × 2-inch baking dish.

Bring a large pot of salted water to a boil. Add the sweet potatoes and boil until just tender, about 30 to 35 minutes. Drain and peel the sweet potatoes. Cut them into quarters and spread in the baking dish.

Combine the brown sugar, $^1/_2$ cup water, butter, maple syrup, orange zest, and orange juice in a heavy-bottomed pan. Stir to dissolve the sugar, bring to a boil, and cook until the mixture forms a syrup, about 5 minutes. Pour the syrup over the yams and sprinkle with the chopped nuts. Cover the baking dish tightly with foil.

Bake for 30 minutes. Remove the foil and continue to bake for 10 minutes more. Remove from the oven and let stand 5 minutes before serving.

1 pumpkin (5 to 6 pounds)
Softened butter, for brushing
Salt, to taste

4 to 6 tablespoons butter,
melted

Preheat the oven to 350°F.

Cut the pumpkin into large bite-size pieces. Remove all the seeds and strings, but leave the rind on. Arrange the pieces on a lightly greased baking pan. Brush each piece with softened butter and sprinkle lightly with salt. Cover with foil.

Bake for 30 to 45 minutes, or until tender. Pour melted butter to taste over the pumpkin and serve.

Baked Pumpkin

Colonial cooking expert Marjorie Steen says pumpkin, which was introduced to the colonists by local Indian tribes, is native to the Chesapeake area. Gigantic pumpkins are fine for carving, but for eating, small and firm ones are best.

Serves 4

1 pound elbow macaroni
6 tablespoons (³/₄ stick) butter
6 tablespoons all-purpose flour
3 cups milk
1¹/₂ teaspoons salt
¹/₂ teaspoon cayenne

2 teaspoons dry mustard
Few dashes of Tabasco Sauce
2 cups grated sharp cheddar
  cheese
2 eggs, beaten
Dry bread crumbs, for topping

Preheat the oven to 375°F. Butter a 8 × 8 × 2-inch baking dish.

Bring a large pot filled with salted water to a boil. Add the macaroni and cook until just tender. Drain and set aside.

Melt the butter in a saucepan and whisk in the flour. Cook, stirring, for 1 to 2 minutes, taking care not to brown the flour. Remove from the heat and stir in the milk, 1¹/₂ teaspoons salt, the cayenne, mustard, and Tabasco. Return to the heat and bring to a boil, stirring constantly. Lower the heat and simmer, stirring from time to time, until the sauce thickens, about 3 minutes. Remove from the heat and stir in the cheese. When the sauce has cooled slightly, add the eggs and mix well.

Layer half of the macaroni in the baking dish. Top with half of the sauce. Repeat the layers. Sprinkle the top with bread crumbs and bake for 30 minutes, or until the top is brown and the sauce is hot. Remove from the oven and let stand 5 minutes before serving.

Macaroni and Cheese

When the ladies at Saint Ann's church in Baltimore prepare this dish for their church hall fish fry dinners, they cook 15 to 20 pounds of macaroni at a time, so for us they've scaled the recipe back for home use.

Serves 8 to 10

A City and Its Kraut. Sauerkraut, That Is.

Many folks know the role New York's Ellis Island played during the great immigration of the nineteenth century, but often unknown is that Baltimore was the second largest port-of-entry for the waves of humanity making their way to the New World. While many of the new arrivals transferred from ship to railroad, making their way to prearranged destinations, many thousands chose to stay in either Baltimore or the surrounding Chesapeake countryside. One of the largest ethnic groups to settle here was the Germans, and over the years the cooking of their homeland has become ingrained in the culinary heritage of the Chesapeake.

Of all the German dishes introduced here, sauerkraut is without a doubt the one that Baltimore has embraced most heartily. As recently as one generation ago, most city homes kept huge earthenware crocks in a cool corner of the cellar as the yearly supply of brined fall cabbage fermented. Nowadays, most locals purchase their kraut from one of the numerous small producers of homestyle sauerkraut, generally preferring fresh kraut to canned kraut. Fresh is available in plastic bags or jars and sometimes can be found in specialty shops, sold in bulk from old-fashioned barrels. As would be expected, sauerkraut is primarily served with pork dishes as well as used as a braising ingredient with smoked sausages and roasts. The one sauerkraut phenomenon that distinguishes Baltimore is the almost sacred tradition of serving roast turkey with kraut. The absence of sauerkraut when turkey is present, Thanksgiving included, is unthinkable, comparable to potatoes without gravy or crisp french fries without ketchup. Around here in Baltimore it is just not done. This tradition over time has spilled over to chicken as well. Many homes serve a steaming bowl of kraut that has been simmered with apples, onions, bacon, and sometimes a touch of caraway to accompany roast chicken.

6 tablespoons (³/₄ stick) butter

4 slices of bacon, cut into ¹/₂-inch pieces

1 small onion, thinly sliced

3 tart apples, such as Stayman or Pippin, peeled, cored, and thinly sliced

2 pounds sauerkraut, drained and lightly rinsed

1 bottle (12 ounces) flat beer (see page 27)

Salt and freshly ground black pepper, to taste

¹/₂ teaspoon caraway seeds

Melt the butter in a heavy pot and render the bacon for a few minutes. Add the onion and apples and sauté for 3 to 4 minutes. Put the sauerkraut in the pot. Pour in the beer and add salt, pepper, and caraway. Toss together, then bring to a boil. Cover tightly, reduce the heat, and simmer for 45 minutes. Or bake in an oven preheated to 350°F. for 1 hour. Remove from the oven, stir, and serve hot.

Sauerkraut and Apples

Baltimore is one of the sauerkraut capitals of the world. Any time of the day or night, particularly in the east Baltimore homes of European ancestry, pots are simmering with this zesty fermented cabbage. This recipe calls for flat beer as the braising liquid, which is quite common, but I have used apple cider with excellent results.

Serves 8

6 tablespoons (³/₄ stick) butter

1 teaspoon ground cinnamon

¹/₄ teaspoon ground nutmeg

¹/₄ teaspoon ground mace

¹/₈ teaspoon ground cloves

8 apples, such as Jonathan, York, or Pippin, peeled, cored, and sliced

Apple cider, as needed

Melt the butter in a deep skillet. Add the cinnamon, nutmeg, mace, and cloves and mix well. Add the apples and cook over medium heat, turning often, about 3 to 5 minutes. Cover the apples with cider and bring barely to a boil. Reduce the heat and simmer until the apples are tender, 10 to 12 minutes. Serve hot or cold.

Fried Apples

This dish, from an Early American–style Chesapeake recipe, is much like spiced apple sauce, but here the apple pieces hold their form. The Chesapeake region is blessed with a variety of apples, including Stayman, Jonathan, and York, as well as Red and Golden Delicious apples.

Serves 6

Volunteer Fire Department
of Millington, Maryland

As opposed to giving standard directions, such as "two miles east on state route 291 off 301," townsfolk in Millington, Maryland, give their community's location as "Head of the Chester." Typical of Eastern Shore residents, they gauge their location by their proximity to the water. I did find my way there, nonetheless, and pulled into the parking lot of the Millington Community Fire Hall wondering if I had the right day of the event: It was very quiet and all seemed tranquil outside the building.

Upon entering, I was immediately relieved by the sight of Miss Alice and her card-table display for a Christmas tree raffle. Of course, one quick look also revealed a flurry of activity inside the massive hall, lined with banquet tables covered in white tablecloths, as volunteers methodically put down place settings and coffee cups. On the far side of the hall was a 30-foot stretch of tables, every inch covered with homemade desserts.

On the other side of the hall a large door opened to the kitchen, and as I walked toward it, a billowy white cloud of flour came wafting into the dining hall. The kitchen crew was in high gear with a slippery dumpling production line in full swing. The supervisor of this gargantuan production was Edie Morales. Thousands of dumplings were cut from large squares of thinly rolled dough, as Edie kept an eye open for dumplings that failed to meet her high standards. Volunteer cooks then carefully transferred these uncooked dumplings to the stove area and slipped them into caldrons of boiling water where they cooked for several minutes. Later the dumplings were drained, sauced with chicken gravy, and whisked away to the hundreds of hungry diners. (Slipperies cannot be cooked too far ahead of time.)

It was not easy for me to follow all the dishes being simultaneously prepared in this kitchen. Pots of steamed potatoes were being buttered and put into large pans to be served. Several volunteers were laughing and carrying on with each other as they sliced a row of freshly baked country hams. Green beans, scented with ham trimmings, emerged from yet another gigantic pot. All the workers seemed to be having the time of their lives in the kitchen while working together as if they did this every day. For these seasoned volunteer cooks, it was just another fire hall supper for six hundred hungry folks.

A Fire Hall Supper in Millington

Baked Maryland Ham (page 153)

Millington Chicken Salad (page 178)

Slippery Dumplings and Gravy

Southern Green Beans (page 195)

2 cups all-purpose flour, plus
    extra as needed for dusting
    and gravy
1 teaspoon salt
$^1/_4$ cup vegetable shortening

$^1/_2$ cup cold water
8 cups Chicken Stock (page
    127) or turkey stock or ham
    broth, if preferred

Sift the flour and salt together in a large bowl. Work the shortening into the flour with your fingertips or a pastry blender until the mixture is the consistency of coarse meal. Add the water, 1 tablespoon at a time, mixing with a fork after each addition. The dough should be just moist enough to hold together, not wet. Form dough into a ball and turn out onto a lightly floured surface. Gently knead for 1 minute. Cover the dough with a towel or plastic wrap and let it rest for at least 30 minutes.

Divide the dough in half and roll each piece out very, very thin, about $^1/_{16}$ inch. Cut the dough into $1^1/_2 \times 3$-inch rectangles.

Heat the stock in a large pot just until it comes to a boil. (If the stock is unsalted, add salt.) Reduce the heat to medium and add the dumplings. Gently stir from time to time with a spoon. Cook for 5 to 7 minutes, or until the dumplings float to the top of the pot. With a slotted spoon transfer the dumplings to a bowl or platter. Cover with foil to keep warm.

To make the gravy, strain the cooking stock through a coarse strainer. Pour the liquid back into the pot, return to the heat, and bring to a boil. Reduce heat and cook, stirring often. If the cooking broth seems too thin for a gravy consistency, thin 3 or 4 tablespoons of flour with enough cold water to make a loose paste. Slowly whisk into the hot liquid. Simmer over medium heat for 5 minutes. Season with salt and pepper. Remove from the heat and place the cooked dumplings into the gravy. Serve immediately.

Slippery Dumplings and Gravy

Not just any dumpling measures up to the quality of a firehouse supper dumpling, but these slippery dumplings sure do. This recipe is from Edie Morales of the Millington Volunteer Fire Department. Her slippery dumplings always make an appearance at the volunteers' semi-annual fundraising suppers. Noodle-ish in consistency, slipperies also make a perfect side dish with braised chicken, turkey, or even boiled ham. The trick in making these dumplings is to roll out the dough very thin. After the dumplings are formed they can be stored, uncooked in the refrigerator for up to twenty-four hours. Before cooking they should be brought back to room temperature and once cooked should be served immediately.

Serves 6 to 8

Lena's Spicy Rice

Lena Crayman grew up along the Potomac River, where she had her fill of the bounty of the Chesapeake. Her father would bring home freshly caught fish, local poultry, and wild game from his weekly hunting expeditions in the nearby woods. She recalls that her mother was a good cook but that she had an inordinate fear of spices. She thought of them as "smelly old weeds." Consequently Lena said most meals were "kind of bland and tasteless." Lena had been to neighbors' homes and tasted food that had been well spiced, so she made a vow that when she got married and had a kitchen of her own, those spices would be flowing! And she lived true to her word. This is Lena's rendition of an herbed spicy rice that goes well with most any Chesapeake meal.

Serves 4

2 cups Chicken Stock (page 127) or water
1/2 cup minced green onion
1/2 cup minced parsley
4 tablespoons (1/2 stick) butter
1 cup long grain rice
1/2 teaspoon Chesapeake seasoning
1/2 teaspoon salt
1 small clove garlic, minced
1/8 teaspoon cayenne
1/8 teaspoon freshly ground black pepper
1 bay leaf

Pour the stock into a blender and add the green onion and parsley. Process at a high setting until well blended. Set aside.

Melt the butter in a heavy saucepan and stir in the rice. Cook for 1 minute over low heat, stirring to coat the rice. Stir in the Chesapeake seasoning, salt, garlic, cayenne, black pepper, chicken stock mixture, and bay leaf. Bring to a boil, stir the rice, and tightly cover the pot. Reduce the heat to very low and continue to cook for 15 minutes. Remove the rice from the heat, fluff with a fork, and re-cover the pot. Let stand for 5 minutes before serving.

Breakfast Dishes

No other meal conjures up so many warm memories of hearth and home as does breakfast, and hearty, in a word, sums up the Chesapeake's breakfast philosophy. Breakfasts in this region have always been filling because, while Chesapeake living may be aesthetically beautiful, the work is hard. Long days of labor on the water and in the fields called for well-fed laborers, so Chesapeakans developed recipes to fit the bill.

Two major influences on Chesapeake-style breakfasts are country cooking, a perceived rural style of cooking, and oompah-pah cooking, a style that can be traced to the large populations of people of German and East European descent who live in communities around the Bay. Country-style breakfasts are composed of dishes such as country ham and fried green tomatoes; fish and bacon cakes; and smoked pork sausages, hominy, and pan gravy simmering in cast-iron skillets. These meals are traditionally served with hot-from-the-oven biscuits or skillet-baked corn bread. Dishes from the central European cooking tradition were normally served with pots of strong coffee to wash them down: buckwheat waffles with sweet butter and maple syrup; egg-rich, baked soufflé-like pancakes; and ham-scented flannel hash topped with poached eggs.

The two breakfast styles are not as separate as they once were. Today both have incorporated the seafood, smoked meats, and produce unique to the Chesapeake. That's the beauty of living in a melting pot: Traditions come together and, over time, adapt themselves to the region of which they have become a part.

Gertie's Crab Cakes (page 33)
Vegetable oil, for frying
4 English muffins, split, lightly
toasted, and buttered

8 eggs, poached
Chesapeake Hollandaise Sauce
(page 48)

Prepare the crab cakes mixture and gently form 8 crab cakes to fit on the muffin halves. They will be flatter and thinner than regular crab cakes. Fry the crab cakes in a little oil in a skillet until golden brown on both sides. Or slip them under a preheated broiler and cook until browned, turning once. Place the cakes on the buttered muffin halves and top with eggs. Spoon warm hollandaise sauce over the top. Serve immediately.

A Baltimore variation on the eggs benedict theme, with lightly fried crab cakes replacing grilled Canadian bacon. Chesapeake Hollandaise Sauce, which is easily made in a blender, is the perfect topping for Charm City's number-one Sunday brunch choice.

Serves 4

Charm City

Have you ever been to Baltimore, aka Charm City, the Monumental City, "Hairdo Capitol of the World," and my hometown? Baltimore is a city of neighborhoods, white marble steps, screen paintings, farmers' markets, crab houses, and beehive coifs.

Baltimore is also nationally recognized as a "renaissance city." A victim of urban blight several decades ago, it has now blossomed into what *Life* magazine deemed "the most livable city in America." And in 1996 Baltimore placed 12th on *Fortune* magazine's "Best Cities to Live in America" list. Now, one must keep in mind the criteria for placement on that distinguished list included essentials such as the average price of a martini, the Pope having visited the city within the last two years, and the home of professional sports clubs, among others. Indeed, Baltimore does have good martini prices, the Pope was just here, and the Orioles and Ravens are packing the stadiums. But many others have thought of Baltimore as a pretty nice place to hang their hats before the stadiums were built. Home to Edgar Allan Poe, Babe Ruth, Billie Holiday, H. L. Mencken, and Wallace Simpson, to name just a few, Baltimore is a city proud of its cultural heritage.

Eggs Edie

Two of the things I miss most in Baltimore are streetcars and the late Edie Massey. Edie is better known to some people as the Egg Lady in John Waters's film, **Pink Flamingos**. *A beloved fixture on the Baltimore scene, Edie was really crazy about eggs. She came over one morning for breakfast and all I had in the Frigidaire was a bunch of hard-cooked eggs. What I came up with was this dish, which Edie loved. Now, when friends come by early in the day, they always ask me if I'll fix those eggs Edie liked. And here they are, with love.*

Serves 4

4 slices of bacon
$^1/_2$ cup chopped mushrooms
$^1/_4$ cup chopped onion
2 tablespoons butter
2 tablespoons flour
2$^1/_2$ cups milk
1 tablespoon dry mustard
Juice of 1 lemon
1 whole clove
Salt and freshly ground black pepper, to taste
6 hard-cooked eggs, coarsely chopped
4 English muffins, split, toasted, and buttered

Cook the bacon in a heavy-bottomed saucepan. Remove the bacon, reserving the drippings in the saucepan, and chop into small pieces. Set aside. Add the mushrooms and onion to the drippings, and sauté until soft. Remove the mushrooms and onion with a slotted spoon.

Add the butter to the same saucepan and heat until bubbly. Whisk in the flour and cook, stirring, for 1 to 2 minutes. Remove from the heat and gradually whisk in the milk. Stir in the mustard, lemon juice, clove, salt, and pepper. Return to the heat and bring to a boil, stirring constantly. Lower the heat and add the bacon, mushrooms, and onion. Fold in the eggs. Remove the clove and serve on buttered muffin halves.

6 tablespoons ($^3/_4$ stick) butter
1 tablespoon minced shallot
1 cup sliced fresh mushrooms
2 tablespoons dry sherry
3 tablespoons flour
1 cup Fish Stock (page 109) or
    bottled clam juice
1$^1/_4$ cups heavy (whipping)
    cream

$^1/_2$ cup grated swiss cheese
Salt, freshly ground black
    pepper, and freshly grated
    nutmeg, to taste
$^1/_2$ pound backfin crabmeat,
    picked over
2 tablespoons minced parsley or
    chives

Crabmeat Omelet Filling

A good seafood omelet is always a sure crowd-pleaser at breakfast or brunch. In this dish sweet lumps of crabmeat are bathed in a cheese-laden mornay sauce that has just the slightest hint of sherry. For a slight variation in the recipe, I sometimes use gruyère cheese with its wonderfully rich and nutty flavor in place of the swiss cheese.

Makes filling for 4 omelets

Melt 3 tablespoons of the butter in a heavy-bottomed saucepan. Add the shallot and cook over medium heat for 1 to 2 minutes. Add the mushrooms and continue to cook until they are soft. Increase the heat and add the sherry. Deglaze the pan, scraping up any bits on the pan bottom. Turn off the heat and remove the mushrooms with a slotted spoon. Set aside.

Return the saucepan to the stove and melt the remaining 3 tablespoons butter. Stir in the flour and cook for 1 to 2 minutes, stirring constantly. Remove from the heat and whisk in the stock, stirring until completely smooth. Add the cream, return to the heat, and stir well until the mixture comes to a boil. Reduce the heat to low and simmer for 5 minutes, stirring often. Remove from the heat and stir in the cheese. Season with salt, pepper, and nutmeg. Gently fold in the crabmeat and stir in the parsley or chives. Remove from the heat.

If omelets are going to be made right away, keep the mixture warm; otherwise, the filling can be made ahead of time, cooled, and then refrigerated until ready to use. Gently reheat filling before the omelets are prepared.

Tilghman Island Inn's Eggs Choptank

*A*fford*ing gorgeous views of the Bay, the surrounding marshland, and its waterfowl, the Tilghman Island Inn is a perfect spot for a break from hectic city life and a destination for sampling culinary delights. With Chesapeake oyster harvests on the rise, Tilghman Island Inn Chef Randolph Sprinkle and the inn's exuberant co-owner David McCallum have created this brunch dish that is composed of oysters teamed with corn bread rounds and tomatoes, bathed in a fragrant basil-scented* beurre blanc *sauce.*

Serves 6

1 recipe Old-fashioned Skillet
    Corn Bread (page 227)
1 cup all-purpose flour
1 cup dry bread crumbs
1 tablespoon garlic powder
1 tablespoon salt
1 tablespoon Tilghman Island
    Seasoning (recipe follows)

Vegetable oil, for frying
24 shucked oysters
12 slices fresh tomato
12 poached eggs
Herbed Beurre Blanc (recipe
    follows)
Chopped parsley, for garnish

With a biscuit cutter cut 6 standard-size biscuit rounds from the corn bread. Cut each round in half lengthwise. Lightly toast the corn bread rounds in a preheated oven or broiler. Set aside.

Mix together the flour, bread crumbs, garlic powder, salt, and Tilghman Island Seasoning in a bowl. Coat each oyster lightly in the mixture and place on a sheet pan. Pour oil into a skillet to a depth of $1^1/2$ inches and heat until very hot, about 375°F. Fry the oysters on both sides until golden brown, about 2 minutes per side. Remove from the pan and drain on paper towels.

Place the corn bread slices on 6 plates, topping each with a slice of tomato and 2 oysters. Carefully place a poached egg on top of each round, spooning the Herbed Beurre Blanc over the top. Garnish with chopped parsley and serve at once.

Tilghman Island Seasoning   Makes $^1/_4$ cup

1 tablespoon paprika
1 teaspoon cayenne pepper
1 teaspoon garlic powder
1 teaspoon salt
$^1/_2$ teaspoon freshly ground
    white pepper

$^1/_2$ teaspoon dried thyme
$^1/_2$ teaspoon dried oregano
$^1/_2$ teaspoon celery salt

Thoroughly mix together all the ingredients in a bowl. Store in a container with a tight-fitting lid. The leftover seasoning mix is an excellent spice for preparing grilled or sautéed seafood or poultry.

Herbed Beurre Blanc Makes $3/4$ to 1 cup

1 cup dry white wine
Pinch of salt
$1/4$ cup heavy (whipping) cream
$1/2$ pound (2 sticks) butter,
   softened

$1/4$ cup minced parsley
$1/4$ cup minced basil

Place the wine, salt, and heavy whipping cream in a saucepan, and cook over medium heat until the volume is reduced by half. Remove from the heat and whisk in the softened butter, 1 tablespoon at a time, until the sauce is thickened. Add the herbs and stir well. Hold at room temperature until ready to use.

Milk Toast for Aunt Minnie Serves 2

Aunt Catherine added this dish to our family's culinary archives during her sister Minnie's medical crisis. It seems Minnie, who had come to the Eastern Shore for a rest, had a spell while she was lounging on the screened porch. The family thought it a case of the vapors caused by the summer humidity, and the doctor was summoned. The diagnosis: "an upside-down stomach." After ten days on Aunt Catherine's milk toast, Minnie was declared cured.

1½ tablespoons flour
2¼ cups milk
2 tablespoons butter
2 tablespoons sugar

Pinch of salt
Pinch of ground nutmeg
4 slices of bread, toasted

Mix together the flour and ¼ cup water in a small bowl until smooth. Pour the milk into a saucepan, add the flour mixture, and bring to a boil, stirring constantly. Remove from the heat and stir in the butter, sugar, salt, and nutmeg. Place 2 toast slices in each bowl and cover with hot milk. Serve hot.

Breakfast Dishes

1 1/2 cups all-purpose flour
1/2 cup buckwheat flour
1 tablespoon baking powder
1 tablespoon sugar
1/2 teaspoon salt
1/2 cup ground gingersnaps
3 eggs, separated

5 tablespoons butter, melted and
  cooled
2 cups milk
1 teaspoon vanilla extract
Warm maple syrup or
  sweetened whipped cream
  and fruit, for accompaniment

Aunt Catherine's Buckwheat-Ginger Waffles

The ground gingersnaps give these waffles exactly that—a ginger snap. Aunt Catherine came up with this recipe as a treat for all us children who came to visit her shore home on Tilghman during the summer.

Makes 8 waffles

Preheat the waffle iron.

Sift together the all-purpose and buckwheat flours, baking powder, sugar, and salt in a bowl. Mix in the gingersnaps. Beat together the egg yolks, butter, milk, and vanilla in a mixing bowl. Stir in the dry ingredients. Do not overbeat. Beat the egg whites until stiff peaks form. Fold into the batter. Do not overmix.

Cook in the waffle iron, according to manufacturer's instructions, until golden brown. Serve with warm maple syrup or with sweetened whipped cream and fruit.

8 tablespoons (1 stick) butter,
  melted and cooled
6 eggs, beaten
1 1/2 cups all-purpose flour
1/2 teaspoon salt

1 tablespoon granulated sugar
1 1/2 cups milk
Softened butter, confectioners'
  sugar, and maple syrup, for
  accompaniment

Dutch Babies

Julie McGowan, a former crab house waitress who lives just outside Chestertown, Maryland, grew up eating these breakfast treats. She believes her mother got this recipe from the surrounding Amish community. With an egg-enriched batter that bakes up light and fluffy, these babies give you a perfect excuse to haul out the maple syrup.

Serves 4

Preheat the oven to 425°F. Grease and flour a 9-inch square baking pan.

Beat together the butter and eggs in a mixing bowl. Sift together the flour, salt, and sugar. Mix the flour mixture into the butter mixture. Beat in the milk. Pour the mixture into the pan. Bake for 15 to 20 minutes, or until firm yet still somewhat moist. Top with butter and confectioners' sugar. Serve with maple syrup.

Sausages and Hominy with Pan Gravy

Hominy has its own unique texture and flavor that go well with meats and fowl. But hominy is not just for dinner, as this recipe will attest. Here, breakfast sausage is cooked in a skillet, and a pan gravy is made from its drippings; then the gravy is spooned over the sausage and the simmered hominy. This is a real hearty and down-home country breakfast dish. Serve it with Buttermilk Biscuits (page 223).

Serves 4

8 breakfast-sausage patties
3 tablespoons flour
1¼ cups milk
Salt and freshly ground black pepper, to taste

1 can (20 ounces) hominy, broken apart with a fork
1 teaspoon sugar
4 tablespoons (½ stick) butter

Cook the sausage patties in a skillet until well browned. Remove the patties, reserving 3 tablespoons of the fat in the skillet, and keep warm.

For the pan gravy, heat the fat and stir in the flour. Cook, stirring constantly, for 1 to 2 minutes. Remove from the heat and gradually whisk in 1 cup of the milk. Return to the heat and bring to a boil, stirring constantly. Reduce the heat and simmer for 5 minutes, stirring often. Season with salt and pepper.

Combine the hominy, the remaining ¼ cup milk, sugar, ½ teaspoon salt, ½ teaspoon pepper, and butter in a saucepan. Heat to serving temperature. Arrange the sausage patties and hominy on individual plates. Spoon the gravy over the top. Serve at once.

4 slices of bread, broken in
    pieces
1 pound sausage meat, cooked
    and drained
1 cup grated sharp cheddar
    cheese

6 eggs, beaten
2 cups milk
Salt and freshly ground black
    pepper, to taste

Preheat the oven to 350°F. Generously butter a 8 × 8 × 1¹/₂-inch baking dish.

Place the bread in the baking dish. Top with the sausage meat and cheese. Beat together the eggs and milk in a bowl. Pour over all. Season with salt and pepper.

Bake for 1 hour. Remove from the oven and let stand 5 minutes before serving.

Cranky Hank's Breakfast Sausage Pudding

Hank Farbo hates mornings. Even a potful of coffee doesn't help. During the summer he always has a house full of guests who have made their way to the Eastern Shore for a bit of R&R and like to start their day with a hearty breakfast. This dish, which can be assembled the night before, has made mornings a breeze for Hank and is a breakfast favorite of his regulars. If desired, country ham or cooked bacon can be substituted for the sausage.

Serves 6

Country Ham and Fried Green Tomatoes with Cream Gravy

This St. Mary's County breakfast features some of the best eating country life has to offer. After cooking the ham and tomatoes, don't clean out the skillet before making the gravy: The cooking residue gives the gravy lots of flavor. I always serve this combo with eggs any-which-way and a batch of hot Buttermilk Biscuits (page 223).

Serves 4

4 to 6 tablespoons ($^1/_2$ to $^3/_4$ stick) butter or oil, for frying
4 slices of country ham, about $^1/_2$ inch thick
2 to 3 green tomatoes, cored, sliced $^1/_2$ inch thick, and soaked in milk
All-purpose flour seasoned with salt and freshly ground black pepper
Pinch of sugar
Cream Gravy (recipe follows)

Melt 4 tablespoons of the butter in a heavy skillet and sauté the ham slices about 3 minutes on each side. Remove the ham to a heated platter and keep warm.

Drain the tomatoes and dust them with the seasoned flour. Add more butter to the pan if necessary and fry the tomatoes 3 minutes on each side or until tender, sprinkling each side with a little sugar. Remove and drain on paper towels, then arrange on the platter with the ham.

While the tomatoes are cooking, make the gravy. Pour the gravy over the ham and tomatoes and serve immediately.

Cream Gravy Makes about 1$^3/_4$ cups

4 tablespoons ($^1/_2$ stick) butter
$^1/_4$ cup all-purpose flour
2 cups milk or half-and-half
Salt and freshly ground black pepper, to taste

Melt the butter in the same skillet used for cooking the ham and tomatoes. Whisk in the flour. Cook, stirring, 2 to 3 minutes. Gradually stir in the milk and bring to a boil. Reduce the heat and cook, stirring constantly, until thickened, about 2 minutes. Reduce the heat to low and simmer for 5 minutes. Remove from the heat and season with salt and pepper.

Fried Green Tomatoes and Beyond

Due to the success of Fanny Flagg's novel *Fried Green Tomatoes at the Whistlestop Café*, and the motion picture based on it, fried green tomatoes, once a little known culinary treasure, have become a household name. Well before the book was written, or for that matter well before Ms. Flagg was born, Chesapeake cooks were frying, frittering, and pickling green tomatoes, and turning them into vegetarian mincemeat.

The Chesapeake region's rich and somewhat sandy soil provides the perfect growing environment for outstanding tomatoes. One problem of having a garden with a lot of tomato vines, though, is that when they come to fruition, there are more tomatoes than a family can possibly eat, sauce, stew, or can. Generations ago it was discovered that green tomatoes with their firm and nonacidic flesh are perfect for frying. A platter full of fried green tomatoes accompanied with country ham or scrambled or fried eggs and hot buttermilk biscuits makes for a memorable homestyle Chesapeake breakfast.

Scrapple

Some of the best scrapple in the country is made around the Chesapeake, coming from its numerous pork producers. Scrapple is exactly what it sounds like: scrap. But these are scraps of pork stewed together with spices, ground up, and bound together with cornmeal. When locals whip up a batch of scrapple, they usually make an enormous amount and freeze it in 1-pound packages that will—hopefully—last throughout the year. This recipe is for a smaller quantity, but there will still be plenty to freeze for later.

Serve the scrapple with fried or scrambled eggs, covered with maple syrup, or teamed with scrambled eggs and ketchup in a toasted sandwich. And don't laugh until you've tried it.

Makes about 5 pounds

2 pounds pork shoulder
$1/2$ pound pork liver
1 pound pork scraps, such as feet, jowls, knuckles, and so on
Yellow cornmeal, to thicken

Salt, freshly ground black pepper, and dried sage, to taste
All-purpose flour, for dusting
Bacon drippings or butter, for frying

Cut the pork shoulder into chunks. Wash the shoulder, liver, and scraps with cold water. Put all the meats in a heavy pot and add just enough water to cover them. Cook until the meat is quite tender, about 2 to 3 hours. Remove the meats from the pot with a slotted utensil. Grind them in a meat grinder or food processor.

Return the ground meat to the pot with the cooking juices and continue cooking. Add just enough cornmeal for the mixture to become mushlike. Season well with salt, pepper, and sage. Pour the mixture into loaf pans, cover, and refrigerate. If the scrapple is to be frozen, remove it from the loaf pan after it has chilled and cut it into blocks large enough for a breakfast. Double wrap each block in plastic and place in freezer bags.

To serve, cut scrapple in $1/4$- to $1/2$-inch-thick slices, according to taste. Dust the slices with flour and fry in bacon drippings for 2 to 3 minutes on each side, or until heated through, browning well. Serve at once.

2 cups diced cooked potatoes
2 cups flaked cooked fish
¼ pound smoked rockfish, bluefish, salmon, or trout, chopped into small pieces
8 ounces (1 stick) butter
1 small yellow onion, diced
2 green onions, minced
1 tablespoon chopped garlic
1 teaspoon Tabasco Sauce
Salt and freshly ground black pepper, to taste
2 tablespoons chopped parsley
1 tablespoon chopped dill or basil
3 tablespoons bacon drippings or vegetable oil, for frying

Combine the potatoes and fish in a mixing bowl and mix well. Melt the butter in a skillet and sauté the yellow and green onions and garlic until soft. Add to the potato-fish mixture. Add the Tabasco, salt, pepper, parsley, and dill and mix well. Heat the bacon drippings in a skillet and fry the fish mixture until browned on the underside. Flip and brown the second side. Serve immediately.

Seafood Hash

One night a week in the family kitchen we would have "hish-hash," my mother's name for a leftover concoction. She would pull containers from the refrigerator and empty their contents to mix a little of this and a little of that. As in every good Chesapeake kitchen, among the leftovers were usually cold potatoes—either mashed or boiled, sometimes both—that would bind together the cold cooked meats and vegetables.

This version is a novel approach that my aunt Minnie developed for all the surplus fish she had in the freezer from Uncle Rob's fishing expeditions. According to Aunt Minnie, "Fry it up in a cast-iron skillet with some bacon drippings and you'll have the cats howling and your guests grinning from ear to ear." Serve the hash as is, or with poached eggs on top.

Serves 4 or 5

Go 'Way Salt Fish with Boiled Potatoes

Working on the waters of the Chesapeake can be a bone-chilling job. Since the day on a workboat starts well before sunrise, a good hot breakfast for the crew is a must. This is a traditional breakfast dish that galley cooks have been frying up on the Chesapeake for generations. Salting fish is an ancient method of preservation that was very common before adequate methods of refrigeration were developed.

Around these parts, the folks who work the water call this dish "Go 'Way," a name believed to have been derived from a similar dish prepared around Galway Bay, Ireland.

Serves 6 to 8

$^1/_2$ pound salt herring, salt hake, or salt cod
$^1/_2$ pound bacon
2 yellow onions, chopped
6 large potatoes, boiled, peeled, and cut into $^1/_2$-inch pieces
Salt and freshly ground black pepper, to taste
Tabasco Sauce, to taste (optional)

Soak the salt fish in water for 4 to 6 hours, to remove saltiness. Change the water at least twice during the soaking. Drain and remove any skin and bones. Place the fish in a pot of fresh, boiling water. Reduce the heat and simmer for about 5 minutes, or until tender. Drain and flake with a fork.

Cook the bacon in a large heavy skillet until fairly crisp. Remove from the pan and drain on paper towels. After bacon has cooled, coarsely chop, and set aside.

Pour off all but 4 tablespoons of the bacon drippings and reserve the rest. Heat the skillet and add the onions. Cook over medium heat, stirring often, until the onions begin to brown. Stir in the cooked potatoes and flaked fish and mix well. Continue to cook over medium heat, stirring often, for about 5 minutes, or until heated through. Season with salt, pepper, and Tabasco, if desired. Serve at once with the reserved bacon drippings on the side.

Bread

One of the tragedies of the late twenti-eth century is the demise of honest-to-goodness bread baked from scratch. Home cooks of yesteryear fashioned their own loaves of bread, but as life became more hurried the populace began to rely on high-quality Old World neighborhood bakeries. Eventually, large bakery conglomerates bought and assimilated, or put out of business, these smaller bakeries. Thus began the unfortunate homogenization of American bread. Today some Chesapeake cooks still realize the joy of crafting risen dough into crusty loaves, but authentic Chesapeake-style breads consist primarily of biscuits, rolls, and corn breads.

The reputations of Chesapeake country cooks are built on their biscuit making expertise. Recipes and techniques vary—and until quite recently were almost never written down. The method was verbally handed down with "a handful of this, and a wineglass of that, until it feels like this." Buttermilk biscuits with their slightly tangy flavor are a favorite, but the most famous of Chesapeake biscuits are Maryland beaten biscuits. These crusty little rounds are literally beaten to tenderness by pounding the dough with a mallet or, as was done in the old days, the flat side of an axe. Beaten biscuits are often served with platters of thinly sliced country ham (and sometimes tender cress, too) to make small sandwiches.

Yeast dough, blended with potatoes, sweet potatoes, or hominy, is formed into a variety of dinner rolls. They are perfect for sopping up gravies or the pan juices of roasted and braised meats and poultry. Corn bread batter, made from stoneground yellow cornmeal, is baked in muffin tins, loaf pans, and heated cast-iron skillets to produce a multitude of corn breads, which are eaten hot from the oven or used as the basis for a savory stuffing with fowl and pork.

2 cups all-purpose flour
2 teaspoons baking powder
$^1/_2$ teaspoon baking soda
$^1/_2$ teaspoon salt

6 tablespoons lard or vegetable
  shortening
$^3/_4$ cup buttermilk

Preheat the oven to 450°F.

Sift together the flour, baking powder, baking soda, and salt into a large bowl. Work in the lard with your fingertips or a pastry blender until the mixture is the consistency of coarse meal. Beat in the buttermilk until a stiff (not wet) dough is formed. Turn the dough out onto a lightly floured surface and knead gently for 1 minute. Roll out the dough on a lightly floured surface $^1/_2$ inch thick. With a biscuit cutter, cut out 12 to 14 rounds. Place the biscuits on an ungreased baking sheet.

Bake for 12 to 15 minutes, or until nicely browned. Serve hot.

Buttermilk
Biscuits

A sound biscuit recipe is a must for every self-respecting Bay household. It is the cornerstone of many meals and an invaluable tool for dipping into gravy. Biscuits made with buttermilk have that characteristic tanginess and a light, tender texture.

Makes 12 to 14 biscuits

3 cups all-purpose flour, or
  more as needed
4 teaspoons baking powder
1 teaspoon salt
1 teaspoon sugar

$^1/_4$ teaspoon cream of tartar
$^1/_2$ cup vegetable shortening or
  lard
$^1/_2$ cup milk

Preheat the oven to 450°F.

Sift together 3 cups of flour, the baking powder, salt, sugar, and cream of tartar in a mixing bowl. Cut in the shortening with your fingertips or a pastry blender until the mixture has the consistency of coarse meal. Mix together the milk and add to the flour mixture, stirring until a stiff batter forms. If it is too sticky, add a little more flour. Wrap and chill the dough for at least 30 minutes.

On a lightly floured surface roll out the dough $^1/_2$ inch thick. Cut the dough into about 24 rounds and arrange on a baking sheet.

Bake for 10 to 12 minutes, or until nicely browned.

Bayside
Biscuits

This recipe, with plain milk, sugar, and a touch of cream of tartar, makes lighter, fluffier biscuits than the buttermilk style. They are great with country-style dinners and as an accompaniment to egg dishes and fried green tomatoes at breakfast.

Makes about 2 dozen biscuits

Maryland Beaten Biscuits   Makes about 3 dozen biscuits

The oldest and most famous biscuit recipe of the Chesapeake Bay region originated on the plantations of southern Maryland. The traditional preparation can be termed, at the very least, a culinary cardiovascular-aerobic exercise.

Its execution is best described by Joanne Pritchett, whose great-great-grandmother was a cook on a St. Mary's plantation: "Honey, every time I know I'm going to make these biscuits, I get myself good and mad. Normally I think about my sister-in-law, Darlene, who ran off with my husband right after Granny Pritchett's funeral. That was years ago, but it still galls me into making some of the tenderest biscuits around."

4 cups all-purpose flour	1³/₄ to 2 cups water
1 teaspoon salt	
1¹/₂ tablespoons lard or vegetable shortening	

"It's very simple. I just sift the flour and salt together in a bowl. Some people, nowadays, like to use Crisco or something like that. But I believe in lard. It gives it that certain taste.

"So then, I cut the lard into the flour with the tips of my fingers, working it real quick. During this step I make believe I'm putting out Darlene's eyes.

"Then, little by little, I pour in the cold water, until I get a good stiff dough. Put it on a real solid table with flour. Now if your table is weak, honey, the legs will fall right off. I've seen it happen!

"Depending on my mood, I use an axe or a big old mallet. I make a ball out of the dough to look like Darlene's head and, baby, I let her have it. Use the flat side of the axe or mallet, and beat the hell out of the dough till it blisters good. Takes about half an hour, but honey, it makes them tender as butter.

"Form the dough into balls, the size of little eggs, and flatten them a bit on the board. Put a few pokes in the center with a fork, then bake in a hot 425°F. oven for about 20 to 25 minutes. Serve hot and put some liniment on your arm, or it'll be acting up the next day."

2 cups all-purpose flour
2¹/₂ teaspoons baking powder
¹/₂ teaspoon salt
2 tablespoons lard or vegetable
   shortening

²/₃ cup milk
²/₃ cup grated sharp cheddar
   cheese

Preheat the oven to 450°F.

Sift together the flour, baking powder, and salt. Work in the lard with your fingertips or a pastry blender until the mixture is the consistency of coarse meal. Mix in the milk and cheese. Turn the dough out onto a floured surface and knead for about 1 minute. Roll out the dough ¹/₂ inch thick, cut out 8 to 10 rounds with a biscuit cutter, and arrange on a baking sheet.

Bake for about 12 to 15 minutes, or until golden. Serve hot or at room temperature.

*C*heese biscuits made with a good-quality sharp cheddar are the perfect partner to hearty stews and soups or thin slices of St. Mary's County Stuffed Ham (page 155). In biscuit making it is important to mix the dough only just enough to incorporate all the ingredients, to ensure tender biscuits.

Makes 12 to 15 biscuits

I Believe in Lard

As Joanne Pritchett has testified, lard, or rendered pork fat, is superb for making biscuits, as well as for making pastry dough and frying poultry. There are two kinds of lard. Leaf lard is made from the fat surrounding the pork kidneys. The other, more readily available type, is commercial or processed lard, which is made from pork fat and stabilized, resulting in a product similar in texture to vegetable shortening. Chesapeake country cooks, who always have a good supply of pork and pork by-products at hand, render their own leaf lard. It is somewhat softer than commercial lard and has a superior taste.

To render the fat, pull or cut off the fat surrounding the pork kidneys, and place it in a deep baking dish or ovenproof pot. Cook in a slow (300°F.) oven, checking frequently so the fat does not burn. From time to time, as the fat renders, pour off the already melted fat through a strainer into a bowl. Continue until all the fat is melted, and all that remains is crunchy bits of residue. Country cooks always save these browned bits, known as cracklings, for use in corn breads, stuffings, and even potato salads.

Two O'Clock Club Corn Bread

Years ago Trixie Shine, a Baltimore gal-about-town and dancer at the Two O'Clock Club, was determined to head for New York to become a Broadway dancer. She had gotten a taste of the spotlight during a high school production of South Pacific. Trixie found New York "too highfalutin" and returned to the Baltimore stage, making the rounds of Baltimore Street's more prestigious dance clubs. She also got a taste for corn bread from her grandmother, who had come up from the Deep South before World War II. This is Trixie's rendition of Grandma Shine's recipe.

Corn bread is a mainstay of Chesapeake cooking, traditionally served with soups, stews, poultry, pork and hams, and fried fish; it is enjoyed at breakfast, lunch, and dinner.

Serves 4 to 6

1 cup yellow cornmeal, preferably stoneground
1 cup all-purpose flour
1/4 cup sugar
3 teaspoons baking powder
1/2 teaspoon salt
2 eggs, lightly beaten
1 1/4 cups milk
2 tablespoons butter, melted and cooled

Preheat the oven to 425°F. Grease and flour an 8-inch square pan.

Mix together the cornmeal, flour, sugar, baking powder, and salt in a bowl. In another bowl, combine the eggs, milk, and butter. Add to the dry ingredients and mix thoroughly without overbeating. Pour into the pan.

Bake for 30 minutes, or until a toothpick inserted in the center comes out clean. Let corn bread rest for a few minutes before cutting. Cut into 2-inch squares and serve.

2 cups yellow cornmeal, stoneground
2 cups all-purpose flour
3 tablespoons sugar
5 teaspoons baking powder
1 teaspoon baking soda
1 teaspoon salt
2 eggs
$^{1}/_{3}$ cup plus 2 tablespoons bacon drippings or vegetable oil
2$^{1}/_{2}$ cups milk

Preheat the oven to 450°F.

Sift together the cornmeal, flour, sugar, baking powder, baking soda, and salt in a large mixing bowl. In another mixing bowl, beat together the eggs, $^{1}/_{3}$ cup bacon drippings, and milk, add to the cornmeal mixture, and mix thoroughly without overbeating.

Place a large cast-iron skillet on the stovetop over high heat. When the pan is very hot, pour in the remaining 2 tablespoons bacon drippings and tilt to coat the bottom of the skillet evenly. Remove from the heat and pour in the batter. Immediately place the skillet in the oven.

Bake for 20 minutes, or until a toothpick inserted in center comes out clean. Serve hot, cut into wedges.

Old-fashioned Skillet Corn Bread

Hickory-smoked bacon drippings and a sizzling-hot cast-iron skillet are the keys to creating this, the finest country-style corn bread I've ever had the pleasure of eating. This skillet method, in which the pan is seasoned with bacon grease, makes for an unbelievable crust and flavor—the corn bread has a fantastic aroma with a moist, yet somewhat crumbly texture. A word to the wise: After heating the cast-iron skillet, make sure you use a hot pad to grab the handle when slipping the skillet into the oven. That handle gets hot.

Serves 8 to 10

Chesapeake Schmaltz?

My grandmother Gertie always kept leftover bacon drippings—she referred to them as "bacon grease"—in the freezer, as do many good cooks around the Chesapeake. Bacon is used in many Chesapeake dishes and is often served with Bay breakfasts. The resulting leftover drippings are superb to add to soups or stews or to use as a substitute for oil or butter when sautéing onions and vegetables.

Johnnycake

This is an Early American dish that I don't see made often these days, but at one time it was regularly found in the kitchens of Chesapeake cooks. Food historians believe the name comes from "journey cakes," which would keep and travel well. In New England they are known as jonnycakes and are made like a pancake. Farther down in the South they call it a hoecake.

For years my grandmother had me believing that she baked these cakes for me, and that's how they got their Chesapeake name of Johnnycake. If you can't believe your own grandmother, who can you believe?

Serves 6 to 8

1 egg
1 tablespoon sugar
1^1/$_2$ cups milk
^{1}/$_2$ teaspoon salt
^{3}/$_4$ cup yellow cornmeal, stoneground

^{1}/$_4$ cup all-purpose flour
2 tablespoons butter, melted
4 tablespoons bacon drippings, melted

Preheat the oven to 400°F.

Beat the egg and sugar together in a bowl. Stir in the milk and salt. Beat in the cornmeal and flour. Mix in the butter and 2 tablespoons of the bacon drippings. Generously grease an 8-inch cast-iron skillet with the remaining 2 tablespoons bacon drippings. Put in the hot oven for about 5 minutes. Wearing mitts, remove from the oven and pour in the batter.

Return to the oven and bake for 30 to 40 minutes, or until well browned. Serve hot, cut into wedges.

1 cup white cornmeal
³/₄ teaspoon baking powder
¹/₂ teaspoon salt
3 tablespoons grated onion
1 egg, beaten

2 tablespoons lard or vegetable
   shortening, melted and
   cooled
¹/₂ cup milk
Vegetable oil, for frying

Mix together the cornmeal, baking powder, and salt in a large bowl. In a small bowl, mix together the onion, egg, lard, and milk. Beat the wet ingredients into the dry ingredients. Pour oil into a skillet to a depth of about 1¹/₂ inches. Heat the oil until very hot, about 375°F. and fry batter, dropping into the hot oil by the tablespoonful, a few at a time, until golden brown on all sides. Remove with a slotted utensil to paper towels to drain. Serve hot.

1 cup milk
1 can (8¹/₂ ounces) hominy,
   broken apart with a fork
4 tablespoons (¹/₂ stick) butter,
   melted
¹/₄ cup sugar

1 teaspoon salt
2 tablespoons grated orange zest
¹/₂ package active dry yeast
¹/₄ cup lukewarm (105° to
   115°F.) water
3¹/₂ cups all-purpose flour

Pour the milk into a saucepan and bring just to a boil, then pour into a bowl. Add the hominy, butter, sugar, salt, and orange zest and mix well. Stir until lukewarm. Sprinkle the yeast in the lukewarm water and let stand until foamy, about 5 minutes. Mix the yeast mixture into the milk mixture. Beat in the flour, 1 cup at a time. Cover the bowl with a tea towel and let stand in a warm place overnight.

In the morning, punch down the dough and divide it among about 24 buttered muffin cups, filling each about two thirds full. Cover and let rise in a warm place for 1 hour.

Preheat the oven to 400°F.

Bake the muffins for 15 to 20 minutes, or until golden. Serve hot.

Hush Puppies

As soon as you cross the Mason-Dixon Line into the South, you meet hush puppies. Margie Clark, who hails from outside St. Michaels, gave me her family recipe. They are a kind of corn bread, the difference being a thicker batter that is fried by the spoonfuls in hot oil.

Serves 4

Hominy Muffins

Here is another recipe that comes from the Amish communities of the Eastern Shore. These yeasted country muffins have the mellow flavor of pearl hominy. You can put together the dough, let it rise overnight, and bake the muffins in time for breakfast in the morning. Serve them fresh from the oven with fruit preserves and sweet butter.

Makes about 2 dozen muffins

South Baltimore Frigidaire Rolls

When I was growing up in Baltimore in the 1950s, ice boxes were a thing of the past, yet no one had a refrigerator. We kept things cold in our "Frigidaires." Of course in "Bawlamer" we "warshed" our hands in the "zink," so it's no surprise that in my neighborhood these classic American ice box rolls were referred to as Frigidaire rolls. They are perfect for the host or hostess on the go. You can make the dough several days ahead and bake the rolls just before your meal.

Makes about 4 dozen rolls

1 package active dry yeast
¹/₄ cup lukewarm (105° to 115°F.) water
1 cup warm mashed potatoes
¹/₂ cup potato water, reserved from cooking potatoes
1 cup milk

8 tablespoons (1 stick) butter, melted
¹/₂ cup sugar
2 eggs, beaten
1¹/₂ teaspoons salt
4 to 5 cups all-purpose flour
Melted butter, for brushing rolls

Dissolve the yeast in lukewarm water and let stand until foamy, about 5 minutes. Combine the mashed potatoes, potato water, milk, butter, sugar, eggs, salt, and the yeast mixture in a bowl and mix well. Beat 4 cups of the flour, 1 cup at a time, adding as much of the remaining cup as needed to form a stiff dough. Turn the dough out onto a floured surface and knead for 8 to 10 minutes, or until smooth, adding flour as necessary to eliminate stickiness. Place in an oiled bowl, cover with a towel, and let rise in a warm place until doubled in bulk, about 1 hour.

Punch down the dough, put in a bowl, and cover tightly. Refrigerate until ready to use, up to 3 days. Check now and then to make sure dough isn't rising. If it is, punch it back down.

When ready to use, preheat the oven to 375°F.

Take out as much dough as needed and form into rolls. Arrange the rolls on a baking sheet and brush with melted butter. Let rise for 30 minutes.

Bake for about 15 minutes, or until golden brown. Serve hot.

A Baltimore Tale in the Bawlamer Language

Bawlamer, Merlin, has its own language to boot! Wanna hear? Well hon, come on down, meet ya over to the table to eat some crab, and I'll tell yous a story:

Some time ago Mom-Mom (my mother) called to tell me about her day.

"Oh my Gawd, you have no idear what happened to me over to Hustler's today! Oh it was awful turble! I went over there to buy a nice cammer for Pat's birfday so she can take pictures when she's downey ayshin, and I lost my pockeybook! I got the pohleez but when I was talking to them I kept calling my pockeybook a ring-a-ding and then that pohleez osifer said if I didn't calm down he was gonna have to get me an amblanz! But I got my act together and I kept my nice lunch appointment with Ann Egan in Litlitlee and I'm feelin' much better.

"So hon, how is your day?"

amblanz—ambulance
birfday—birthday
cammer—camera
downey ayshin—down to the ocean
Hustler's—Hutzler's department store
hon—hon
idear—idea
Litlitlee—Little Italy
osifer—officer
over to—at
pockeybook—pocketbook
pohleez—police
ring-a-ding—whatcha-ma-call-it
turble—terrible

Sweet Potato Rolls

At Chesapeake farmers' markets I have found two varieties of sweet potatoes: white ones and dark, amber ones, which are sometimes mistakenly called yams. For a sweeter roll use the amber variety.

Makes about 3 dozen rolls

6 tablespoons lard or vegetable shortening
1 cup warm mashed sweet potatoes
1 package active dry yeast
1¼ cups lukewarm (105° to 115°F.) water

2 tablespoons sugar
1 tablespoon salt
1 egg, beaten
⅛ teaspoon ground allspice
⅛ teaspoon ground nutmeg
4 to 4½ cups all-purpose flour

Work the lard into the sweet potatoes in a mixing bowl.

Dissolve the yeast in the lukewarm water in a large bowl and let stand until foamy, about 5 minutes. Stir in the sugar and salt. Beat in the egg. Mix in the sweet potato mixture, allspice, and nutmeg. Beat in the flour, 1 cup at a time, just until the dough pulls away from the sides of the bowl. Turn out onto a lightly floured surface and knead for about 10 minutes. Form into a ball and put into a well-oiled bowl, turning to coat all sides of the ball. Cover the bowl with a tea towel and let rise in a warm place until doubled in bulk, about 1 hour.

Preheat the oven to 400°F. Grease a baking sheet.

Punch down the dough and divide into thirds, cutting each portion into 12 pieces. Roll each piece into a ball with the palms of your hands and place on the baking sheet. Cover with a towel and let rise for 30 minutes.

Bake for 15 to 20 minutes, or until nicely browned. Serve hot.

2 packages active dry yeast
$^1/_2$ cup sugar
1 cup lukewarm water (105° to 115°F.)
$^3/_4$ cup milk
1 teaspoon salt
8 tablespoons (1 stick) butter, melted

2 eggs, beaten
5 to 6 cups all-purpose flour
Filling for Sticky Buns (recipe follows)
Topping for Sticky Buns (recipe follows)
Melted butter, for brushing on dough

Sticky Buns

These Sticky Buns have roots in the Amish communities on the Chesapeake's Eastern Shore. They are so good that I can't imagine how some people have lived a lifetime never having known the joy of biting into one of these fresh-from-the-oven, caramel-coated buns.

Makes about 24 buns

Dissolve the yeast and 1 teaspoon of the sugar in the lukewarm water and let stand until foamy, about 5 minutes. Combine the remaining sugar, milk, and salt in a saucepan and bring just to a boil, stirring to dissolve the sugar. Remove from the heat, add the melted butter, and cool to lukewarm. Add the yeast mixture and eggs to the milk mixture and beat well. Mix in 5 cups of the flour, 1 cup at a time, adding as much of the remaining cup as needed to form a soft dough. Turn the dough out onto a lightly floured surface. Cover with a towel and let rest 10 minutes. Knead the dough for 10 minutes, using more flour as needed to prevent stickiness.

Place in a well-oiled bowl, turning the dough to coat all sides. Cover with a tea towel and let stand in a warm place to rise until doubled in bulk, about 1$^1/_2$ hours.

Prepare the filling and topping and set aside. Butter four 8-inch cake pans.

Turn the dough out onto a floured board and divide in half. Knead each half for 1 to 2 minutes, then roll each out into a rectangle 12 × 8 × $^1/_2$ inch. Brush the dough with melted butter, leaving $^1/_2$-inch borders around all 4 sides. Sprinkle the rectangles with the filling mixture. Roll each up from a long side, jelly-roll fashion. With a sharp knife, cut into slices about 1$^1/_2$ inches thick. Divide the topping among the four pans, spreading evenly to cover the bottom of the pan. Arrange the slices in the prepared pans. Cover with towels and let rise again, until doubled in bulk, 30 to 45 minutes.

Preheat the oven to 350°F.

Bake the buns for about 30 minutes, or until brown. Remove from the oven and let sit for 5 minutes. Invert onto a plate or platter and let the topping run over the sides. Serve warm or cool.

Filling for Sticky Buns Makes 2 cups

½ cup granulated sugar
½ cup (firmly packed) dark
   brown sugar
½ cup raisins, plumped in hot
   water

½ cup chopped walnuts
2 teaspoons ground cinnamon
6 tablespoons (¾ stick) butter,
   melted

Mix together the granulated and brown sugar, raisins, walnuts, and cinnamon in a bowl. Add the butter and toss well.

Topping for Sticky Buns Makes 2½ cups

8 ounces (2 sticks) butter,
   softened
2 cups (firmly packed) dark
   brown sugar

5 tablespoons dark cane syrup
¾ cup raisins, plumped in hot
   water
¾ cup walnut pieces

Combine the butter, brown sugar, and cane syrup in a bowl and mix together until very well blended. Sprinkle the raisins and nuts evenly over the sugar mixture.

Desserts

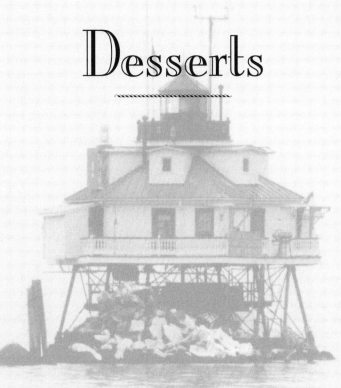

In their daily lives, Chesapeake folk eat with an elementary philosophy: Be moderate while enjoying the incredible bounty of the Chesapeake table so you may be able to enjoy the other gifts life has to offer. Simply put, leave room for dessert! Next to crab, there is *nothing* that so greatly occupies the minds and recipe collections of Chesapeake cooks. Cakes, pies, cobblers, crisps, and puddings head the roster of kitchen favorites, demonstrated by the width and breadth of our index card files, the file boxes stuffed to bursting with the dessert recipes of our mothers, grandmothers, and aunts, all fastidiously recorded on yellowed scraps of papers—painstakingly taped to sturdy file cards, of course.

A classic American dessert, which was all the rage at afternoon teas in the early twentieth century, is the Lady Baltimore Cake. Its origin is not known for sure, as several bakers in Baltimore and farther south have laid claim to being the creator of this multilayered cake with its rich filling of raisins, nuts, and figs.

Shortcakes and cobblers showcase the spring and summer harvests of strawberries, wild berries, and peaches. These fruits—as well as apples—are often tucked under a flaky pie or cobbler crust. Custard pies are also held in equally high regard in these parts, as are sweet potato pies and the classic colonial chess pie. And molasses, an Early American sweetener, gives the prominent flavor to the Chesapeake's Amish community's recipe for Shoofly Pie.

The early English presence is reflected in the puddings of the Chesapeake Bay region, in such dishes as a rich hominy custard, and in an apple and walnut pudding served warm with a touch of heavy cream.

2 cups all-purpose flour
1 tablespoon baking powder
$^1/_4$ teaspoon salt
8 ounces (2 sticks) butter
$1^1/_2$ cups granulated sugar
1 teaspoon vanilla extract
3 eggs, separated

$^3/_4$ cup milk
$1^1/_2$ cups ground black walnuts
Confectioners' sugar, for dusting
Vanilla ice cream and/or fresh
   strawberry sauce, for
   accompaniment (optional)

Maryland Black Walnut Cake

This is a Chesapeake-style cake with a flavor uniquely its own, coming from the remarkable fragrance of black walnuts, which grow in abundance around the Bay. It is one of those cakes that cry out for ice cream, but it can also be served simply dusted with confectioners' sugar and with sliced strawberries or other berries on the side.

Serves 12 to 16

Preheat the oven to 350°F. Grease and flour a 10-inch tube pan.

Sift together the flour, baking powder, and salt. Cream together the butter and sugar in a large bowl until light and fluffy. Add the vanilla and egg yolks. Beat the mixture well. Alternately add the dry ingredients and the milk in small portions to the batter, mixing well after each addition. Beat the egg whites until stiff but not dry. Gently fold them into the batter, one third at a time. Fold in the walnuts. Pour the mixture into the pan.

Bake for 30 minutes. Cool on a wire rack.

Dust with confectioners' sugar, and serve with vanilla ice cream or surround with a fresh strawberry sauce. Or if you feel like pulling out all the stops, try all three.

Lady Baltimore Cake

Famous throughout the South, this cake is said to have originated as a centerpiece for afternoon teas in the late 1800s. The ladies I've spoken to lately don't hold many teas, but they swear by this cake for first communions, bridal showers, and your more "upper crust" Tupperware parties.

Trudy Paskowski, the undisputed Lady Baltimore of the Tupperware circuit, suggests doubling the Cognac in the filling and throwing a "touch" of it into the icing to increase sales.

Serves 12 to 16

8 tablespoons (1 stick) butter, softened
2 cups sugar
3 1/2 cups cake flour
1 tablespoon baking powder
1/4 teaspoon salt

1 teaspoon almond or vanilla extract
1 1/4 cups milk
6 egg whites
Lady Baltimore Filling and Frosting (recipe follows)

Preheat the oven to 350°F. Grease and flour two 9-inch round cake pans.

Beat together the butter and sugar in a mixing bowl until pale and creamy. In another bowl, sift together the flour, baking powder, and salt. Add the almond extract to the milk. Add a little of the dry ingredients to the butter-sugar mixture and mix in. Then stir in a little of the milk. Alternately add the remaining dry and wet ingredients in small amounts until both are completely incorporated. Beat until a smooth batter is formed. Beat the egg whites until stiff but not dry. Fold the whites into the batter, a third at a time. Pour into the cake pans.

Bake for 20 to 25 minutes, or until a toothpick inserted in middle of cake comes out clean. Let cool for 5 minutes in the pans, then turn out onto a rack and cool completely.

Prepare the filling and frosting while the cake layers are cooling, then fill and frost.

Lady Baltimore Filling and Frosting
Makes enough for one 9-inch cake

4 egg whites
1 1/2 cups sugar
1/4 teaspoon salt
1 teaspoon cream of tartar
2 teaspoons vanilla extract

1/2 cup chopped raisins
3/4 cup chopped walnuts or pecans
8 figs, finely chopped
2 tablespoons Cognac

Combine the egg whites, sugar, salt, cream of tartar, and 2/3 cup water in the top pan of a double boiler. Beat with an electric beater over simmering water until soft peaks form, about 7 minutes. Remove from the water and beat in the vanilla. Continue beating until the frosting is stiff. Put aside half of the frosting.

238   **Desserts**

Beat the raisins, nuts, figs, and Cognac into the remaining half of the frosting. Use this mixture as a filling between the 2 layers of the cake. Ice the entire cake with the reserved frosting.

Lord Baltimore Cake: The Untold Story

Lady Baltimore was not the only one in her family to have a cake named after her. Her husband loaned his name to one after an infamous episode. After sampling his wife's egg white–laden cake, Maryland's first governor, Lord Baltimore, noticed the large amount of egg yolks her ladyship was letting go to waste. After giving her a sound tongue-lashing, the governor snatched the yolks from his wife and dashed off to the kitchen looking for the mansion's head cook, Miss Florene.

Putting their heads together, Lord Baltimore and Florene worked into the wee hours of the morning, sipping sherry and perfecting a yolk-rich cake. As the sun was rising, and with the sherry nearly gone, Lord Baltimore and Miss Florene, in a fit of culinary ecstasy, began to grab anything within reach to make a filling for their masterpiece. They combined walnuts, almonds, macaroon crumbs, and a smattering of maraschino cherries, binding it all together with a marshmallow-like boiled frosting. And when the cake was finished, they decorated it with more frosting and bits of candied cherries and nuts.

During my research I was unable to confirm the complete accuracy of the details of this historic occasion. But since my grandfather recounted this tale at every Fourth of July cookout, I am sure it is very close to what actually happened.

Hot Milk Cake

This old-fashioned cake is from the sponge cake family and is a favorite of Chesapeake cooks. It is a little heavier and more moist than a normal sponge cake. Serve plain, with ice cream, or sweetened sliced strawberries.

Serves 8 to 10

2 cups granulated sugar
4 eggs, beaten
2 cups all-purpose flour
2^1/$_2$ teaspoons baking powder
^{1}/$_2$ teaspoon salt

4 tablespoons (^{1}/$_2$ stick) butter
1 cup milk
1^1/$_2$ teaspoons vanilla or almond extract
Confectioners' sugar, for dusting

Preheat the oven to 325°F. Grease and flour a 10-inch tube pan.

Beat together the granulated sugar and eggs in a large bowl until fluffy. Sift together the flour, baking powder, and salt, then beat it into the sugar mixture. Combine the butter and milk in a saucepan and bring to a boil. Slowly pour the hot milk mixture into the batter, mixing well. Mix in the vanilla. Pour the batter into the pan.

Bake for 45 minutes to 1 hour, or until a toothpick inserted in cake comes out clean. Cool on a wire rack.

Dust the top with confectioners' sugar.

1 cup milk
8 tablespoons (1 stick) butter, softened
4 eggs, beaten
2 1/2 cups sugar

2 cups all-purpose flour
2 teaspoons baking powder
1/2 teaspoon salt
1 tablespoon plus 1/2 teaspoon ground mace

Mrs. Morrison's Mace Cake

Preheat the oven to 350°F. Grease and flour a 9 × 13-inch baking pan.

Combine the milk and butter in a saucepan, bring to a boil, and remove from the heat. Beat together the eggs and 2 cups of the sugar in a mixing bowl. Sift together the flour, baking powder, salt, and 1 tablespoon mace. Mix the dry ingredients into the egg mixture. Add the milk and butter while still hot and mix well. (Mrs. Morrison always insisted on 300 strokes to blend the mixture well, but you may choose to use an electric mixer.) Pour into the pan. Mix the remaining 1/2 cup sugar and 1/2 teaspoon mace together and sprinkle the mixture over the top.

Bake for 25 to 35 minutes, or until a toothpick inserted in the middle comes out clean. Cool on a wire rack. Serve warm or at room temperature.

Note: The cake may also be baked in a 10-inch tube pan at 325°F. for 1 hour.

Mrs. Morrison was the housekeeper at Saint Luke's Episcopal Church in Baltimore for at least two to three generations, and this cake was appreciated by each succeeding congregation. I was given this recipe by Catherine LeVeque, who wrote down Mrs. Morrison's oral instructions for posterity. Catherine, the wife of an Episcopal priest, says she makes this cake often, not only because it is an unusual dessert, but because it's also great for funerals. As she says, sometimes you need to prepare something for a large number of people very fast. The cake needs no frosting, but for important occasions I have served mine topped with sliced strawberries and a dollop of sweetened whipped cream.

Serves 8 to 10

Mudd Cake

Versions of this outstanding, dense chocolate cake of Southern heritage have been found in the recipe files of many a Chesapeake family. I like mine topped with a bit of lightly whipped cream or placed on a bed of Sweet Cream (page 261).

When you prepare the cake, the batter will be quite thin, but not to worry. It is baked very slowly at a low temperature, giving it an extraordinary texture. And be sure to use coffee that has been brewed: I was once served a piece of this cake prepared by a hostess (no names here) who had misunderstood the recipe, and used ground coffee instead. Unfortunately for all, the cake lived up to its name.

Serves 10

1³/₄ cups brewed coffee
¹/₄ cup bourbon whiskey
5 ounces unsweetened chocolate
¹/₂ pound (2 sticks) butter, cut into pieces
2 cups sugar

2 cups all-purpose flour
1¹/₂ teaspoons baking soda
¹/₈ teaspoon salt
2 eggs, lightly beaten
1 teaspoon vanilla extract
Confectioners' sugar, for dusting

Preheat the oven to 275°F. Grease and flour a 9 × 2-inch round cake pan.

Combine the coffee, bourbon, and chocolate in the top of a double boiler. Place over simmering water and stir until the chocolate melts. Whisk in the butter, a little at a time, until all of it is melted. Remove from the heat, transfer to a large bowl, and beat in the sugar.

Sift together the flour, soda, and salt into a bowl. Add the sifted ingredients to the coffee mixture. Beat well for about 1 minute. Add the eggs and vanilla and beat until the batter is smooth. Pour the batter into the pan.

Bake for 1¹/₂ hours, or until a toothpick inserted in the center comes out clean. Let the cake cool in the pan for 30 minutes, then turn out onto a rack. When ready to serve, dust the top of the cake with confectioners' sugar.

8 tablespoons (1 stick) butter, softened
1 cup (firmly packed) brown sugar
2 eggs
1 cup milk
3 cups all-purpose flour
$^1/_2$ teaspoon salt
2 teaspoons baking soda

$^1/_4$ cup hot water
1 cup dark molasses
1 teaspoon ground cinnamon
$^1/_2$ teaspoon ground ginger
$^1/_2$ teaspoon ground nutmeg
Grated zest and juice of 1 orange
Confectioners' sugar, for dusting

Preheat the oven to 325°F. Butter and flour a 10-inch tube pan.

Cream together the butter and brown sugar in a large bowl until smooth. Add the eggs and beat until fluffy. Add the milk and mix well. Beat in the flour and salt. Dissolve the baking soda in hot water and add to the batter. Mix in the molasses, cinnamon, ginger, nutmeg, and orange zest and juice. Mix well, but do not overbeat. Pour into the pan. Bake for 45 to 50 minutes, or until a toothpick inserted in the center of the cake comes out clean. Let the cake cool in the pan for 5 minutes, then turn out onto cake racks.

Dust with confectioners' sugar.

Molasses Cake

This rich, moist cake is a good example of the Early American use of molasses and brown sugar as a sweetener in desserts. I prefer to use dark molasses, as opposed to the blackstrap variety. Blackstrap is the darker, more intensely flavored type of molasses, and I find it somewhat overpowering in this recipe.

This cake needs no frosting. Just lightly dust with confectioners' sugar and, if desired, top with a bit of lightly whipped cream.

Serves 8 to 10

Peach Pie

Peaches are a remarkable fruit from start to finish. Around the Chesapeake in the springtime when the peach trees blossom, their fragrance fills the air. When picked and left to stand in the kitchen for a day or two for their final ripening, the bouquet scents the entire house. And when sliced and mounded into a flaky pie crust, the aroma of this pie as it bakes is absolutely intoxicating.

If the peaches are extremely juicy, add a tablespoon more of flour to the mixture to keep the pie from being loose and runny.

Serves 8

Pastry Dough for a Double-
    Crust Pie (recipe follows)
1/4 cup granulated sugar
1/4 cup (firmly packed) brown
    sugar
4 to 5 tablespoons all-purpose
    flour
1 teaspoon ground cinnamon
1/2 teaspoon ground nutmeg
1/4 teaspoon salt
6 cups peeled and sliced peaches
    (see Note)
1/4 cup heavy (whipping) cream
1 egg, beaten with 1 tablespoon
    water (optional)

Preheat the oven to 450°F. Prepare the pastry dough. Divide the dough in 2 parts, one slightly larger than the other. Roll out the larger piece and line a 9-inch pie pan.

Mix together the granulated and brown sugar, flour, cinnamon, nutmeg, and salt in a large bowl. Add the peaches and mix gently. Sprinkle in the cream and toss. Pour the peaches into the pie shell. Roll out the remaining pastry on a lightly floured surface to form a top crust, transfer to the pan, and flute the edges. Make a few vents in the top for steam to escape. If desired, brush the top with the egg-water wash.

Bake for 10 minutes, then reduce the heat to 375°F. and continue baking for 40 to 45 minutes until the crust is well browned. Place the pie on a rack and let cool before serving.

Note: An easy way to peel peaches is to drop them into a pot of boiling water for 1 minute, remove, and place them in very cold water until cool enough to handle. The skins should slide right off.

Pastry Dough for a Double-Crust Pie

Makes pastry for 1 double-crust 9-inch pie

2 1/4 cups all-purpose flour
1 teaspoon salt
3/4 cup vegetable shortening
5 to 7 tablespoons cold water

Sift together the flour and salt into a mixing bowl. Work the shortening into the flour with your fingertips or a pastry blender until the mixture is the consistency of coarse meal. Add the water, 1 tablespoon at a time, mixing with a fork after each addition. Dough should not be wet, but just moist enough to hold together. Form the dough into a ball. Wrap and refrigerate for at least 15 to 30 minutes before rolling. Divide dough into 2 pieces, one slightly larger than the other. Roll out the larger piece on a lightly floured board to $1/8$ inch thick and line the bottom of the pie pan. Roll the second piece to the same thickness and use to top the pie.

Colonial Gingerbread

Chesapeake gingerbread recipes date back to the early colonial days. Most of the baking done in the 1700s did not use white sugar, since it was a precious commodity. Instead, folks used molasses, a by-product of sugar processing that was within the means of most cooks, as a sweetener. Many traditional recipes for pies, cakes, and confections call for molasses.

Serves 8

8 tablespoons (1 stick) butter	$1^1/_2$ teaspoons baking soda
$1/2$ cup sugar	$1/2$ teaspoon salt
2 eggs	$1/2$ tablespoon ground ginger
1 cup dark molasses	1 teaspoon ground cinnamon
1 cup boiling water	$1/4$ teaspoon ground cloves
$2^1/_2$ cups all-purpose flour	Whipped cream, for topping

Preheat the oven to 350°F. Grease and flour an 8-inch square baking pan.

Cream together the butter and sugar in a mixing bowl until light. Add the eggs and beat until fluffy. Mix together the molasses and water. Stir into the creamed mixture. Sift together the flour, baking soda, salt, ginger, cinnamon, and cloves. Add to the batter and beat until smooth. Pour the batter into the pan.

Bake for 40 to 45 minutes, or until a toothpick inserted in the center comes out clean. Let cool in pan for 5 minutes, then turn out onto a rack. Serve warm or at room temperature with whipped cream.

Strawberry-Rhubarb Pie

Strawberry-rhubarb pie is an old-time Chesapeake dessert that is at its best in the late spring when the Bay's fields are alive with cherry red stalks of rhubarb and rows of plump ripe strawberries. Rhubarb is a misunderstood fruit—or is it a misunderstood vegetable? Actually, rhubarb, with its celery-like stalks and toxic leaves, is a member of the buckwheat family, thus making it a vegetable. The bright red stalks of rhubarb are the only part of the plant that is used (the leaves are toxic). The pinkish-red flesh tastes extremely tart when cooked, so it is usually cooked with sugar to create a sweet-and-sour taste.

Serves 8

Pastry Dough for a Single-Crust Pie (page 247)
1 1/2 pints strawberries, stemmed
2 cups diced rhubarb (see Note)
1 cup sugar
3 tablespoons cornstarch
1/2 cup water
1 tablespoon fresh lemon juice
1/4 teaspoon salt
Sweetened whipped cream, for accompaniment

Preheat the oven to 425°F.

Prepare the pastry dough and roll it out to line a 9-inch pie pan. Flute the edge of the shell. Prick the bottom of the shell with a fork. Press aluminum foil into the bottom and sides of the shell and cover foil with pie weights or raw rice or dried beans to weight the pastry and prevent the crust from swelling during baking.

Bake for 8 minutes. Remove the foil and weights and continue to bake for 8 to 10 minutes, or until the crust is lightly browned. Cool before filling.

Place half of the strawberries in a pot. Mash with a fork or potato masher. Add the rhubarb and 1 cup sugar. Combine the cornstarch, 1/2 cup water, lemon juice, and salt in a small bowl and stir to dissolve the cornstarch. Add to the strawberry-rhubarb mixture. Cook over medium heat until the mixture is thick and rhubarb is tender, stirring often.

Halve the remaining strawberries and arrange them in the baked pie shell. Pour the rhubarb-strawberry mixture over the berries, cover, and chill.

Serve topped with whipped cream.

Note: If the rhubarb is tough, peel it just as you would peel celery.

Pastry Dough for a Single-Crust
   Pie (recipe follows)
2 eggs, beaten
$1/2$ cup granulated sugar
$1/2$ cup (firmly packed) brown
   sugar
2 cups mashed cooked sweet
   potato
1 cup milk or light cream

2 tablespoons butter, melted and
   cooled
1 teaspoon ground cinnamon
$1/2$ teaspoon ground ginger
$1/2$ teaspoon ground mace
$1/2$ cup coarsely chopped pecans
   (optional)

Sweet Potato Pie

This is just one of the desserts served at the Saint Ann's Church Hall Fish Fry. It reflects the rich Southern heritage of the Chesapeake region. Although similar in texture and seasoning to a pumpkin pie, this custard-style pie derives a more rustic, full-bodied flavor from the sweet potatoes.

Serves 8

Prepare the pastry dough and roll it out to line a 9-inch pie pan. Flute the edge of the shell. Set aside.

Preheat the oven to 425°F.

Mix the eggs, granulated sugar, and brown sugar together in a large bowl. Beat well until smooth and creamy. Add the sweet potato and mix thoroughly. Beat in all the milk, butter, and spices. Pour into the pie shell. If desired, sprinkle pecans on top of the filling.

Bake for 10 minutes. Reduce the heat to 350°F. and bake for 35 to 40 minutes more, or until a thin knife inserted into the pie comes out clean. Remove the pie from the oven and place on a rack to cool. Serve at room temperature or cold.

Pastry Dough for a Single-Crust Pie
Makes pastry for 1 single-crust 9-inch pie

$1^1/2$ cups all-purpose flour
$3/4$ teaspoon salt

$1/2$ cup vegetable shortening
3 to 4 tablespoons cold water

Sift together the flour and salt into a mixing bowl. Work the shortening into the flour with your fingertips or a pastry blender, until the mixture is the consistency of coarse meal. Add the water, 1 tablespoon at a time, and mix with a fork after each addition. Dough should not be wet, but just moist enough to hold together. Form the dough into a ball. Wrap and refrigerate for at least 15 to 30 minutes before rolling.

Saint Ann's Church in East Baltimore

A s I walk in the front door of the old rectory of Saint Ann's Church on Greenmount Avenue in east Baltimore, beehivelike buzzing sounds rise from the dark hallway ahead. Moving closer, my nostrils are greeted by the smells of fresh trout frying and pots of ham-scented greens steaming—undoubtedly smells of a church hall fish fry.

Reaching the kitchen, the only appropriate words that come to mind are Fats Waller's rambunctious lyrics, "this joint is jumping!" The women, bedecked in their colorful cooking aprons, are flying around the narrow kitchen, dipping trout in seasoned flour and laying the fish side by side in time-worn cast-iron skillets filled with bubbling hot oil. Plates, passed from one church hall volunteer to another, are being piled high with mounds of spicy macaroni and cheese, potato salad, country green beans, and those melt-in-your-mouth greens—all of which the girls say are "surefire preventatives against pernicious anemia."

Peeking around the corner into the dining hall, I see lines forming to stake out choice seats for this mildly spiritual culinary repast. These habitual fish-fry goers know from experience to come early in the day before the greens and beans run out; they go fast. Lips are smacking on the fine array of edibles. Jaws are flapping out all the latest gossip on who's running with whom, and the physical deterioration and or improvement of grandmothers, fathers, nieces, nephews, aunts, and uncles. For what more could one ask? A friendly place to sit down and get a bellyful, plus the 411 on neighbors and friends.

In the far corner of the room, on a round, dark oak table topped with lace, are plates of all shapes and sizes bearing sweets: cakes, big and little, coconut topped and strawberry laden; sweet potato pies; nut pies. Parishioners and friends make their way to these sweet treats, deciding on which of their favorites to choose. "Honey, I know I really shouldn't, but I'll just throw caution to the wind and maybe just loosen up my girdle a bit." That is the philosophy of the day.

Everyone is here to raise money for the church and the Lord—and perhaps to raise a few pounds on the scale. A small price to pay to be part of a good old-fashioned, fundraising fish fry, the likes of which have been adding to the tills of churches and community organizations along the Bay for generations.

A Church Hall Fish Fry

Panfried Lake Trout (page 106)

Father Joe's Favorite Potato Salad (page 176)

Macaroni and Cheese (page 199)

Country Greens (page 196)

Sweet Potato Pie

Pastry Dough for a Single-Crust
    Pie (page 247)
3 tablespoons butter, softened
1 cup sugar
4 eggs, beaten
2 tablespoons flour
$\frac{1}{8}$ teaspoon salt
1 cup dark corn syrup
1 teaspoon vanilla extract
1 cup black walnut pieces
Sweetened whipped cream, for
    accompaniment

Prepare the pastry dough and roll it out to line a 9-inch pie pan. Flute the edge of the shell. Set aside.

Preheat the oven to 425°F.

Cream together the butter and sugar in a mixing bowl. Add the eggs, flour, salt, corn syrup, and vanilla. Mix well. Stir in the black walnut pieces. Pour into the pie shell.

Bake for 10 minutes. Reduce the heat to 350°F. and bake for 40 to 45 minutes more, or until set. Remove the pie from the oven and place on a rack to cool.

Serve warm or cold, topped with whipped cream.

Black Walnut Pie

The mildly bitter flavor of black walnut is a favorite with nut connoisseurs. This variety, which differs from the more common English walnut that has a slightly bitter flavor, is the most prevalent nut tree growing in the Chesapeake region. The pie is similar to a Southern-style pecan pie.

Serves 8

Old-fashioned Chess Pie

*C*hess pie is considered a classic Southern dessert, and it is a very popular pie throughout the Chesapeake region. It was originally made in England as small tartlettes, rather than a whole pie, that were served with afternoon tea. The filling is thickened slightly with cornmeal and baked in a flaky pastry. Lemon juice gives the pie a zesty spark. Local cooks sometimes add black walnuts for a little extra flavor.

Serves 8

Pastry Dough for a Single-Crust Pie (page 247)
8 tablespoons (1 stick) butter, softened
1/2 cup granulated sugar
1/2 cup (firmly packed) dark brown sugar
3 eggs
1 tablespoon yellow cornmeal
2 tablespoons fresh lemon juice
1 teaspoon vanilla extract
1/2 cup chopped black walnuts (optional)

Preheat the oven to 425°F.

Prepare the pastry dough and roll it out to line a 9-inch pie pan. Flute the edge of the shell. Prick the bottom of the shell with a fork. Press aluminum foil into the bottom and sides of the shell and cover the foil with pie weights or raw rice or dried beans to weight the pastry and prevent the crust from swelling during baking. Bake for 8 minutes. Remove the foil and continue to bake for another 5 minutes. Let cool before filling.

Preheat the oven to 350°F.

Cream together the butter and granulated and brown sugar in a bowl. Beat in the eggs, cornmeal, lemon juice, and vanilla. Mix well. Pour into the pie shell, and add walnuts, if desired.

Bake for 45 minutes, or until browned and set. Remove the pie from the oven and place on a rack to cool. Serve pie warm or at room temperature.

Pastry Dough for a Single-Crust Pie (page 247)
1 teaspoon baking soda
1 cup boiling water
1 cup dark molasses
1 cup all-purpose flour
1 cup (firmly packed) brown sugar
$^1/_4$ teaspoon salt
4 tablespoons vegetable shortening or butter
Molasses, for brushing on crust
Sweetened whipped cream and ground cinnamon, for garnish

Prepare the pastry dough and roll it out to line a 9-inch pie pan. Flute the edge of the shell. Set aside.

Preheat the oven to 350°F.

Dissolve the baking soda in boiling water and add to the molasses. Mix together the flour, sugar, and salt in a bowl. Work in the shortening with your fingertips or a pastry blender until the mixture has the consistency of coarse meal. Brush the bottom of the pie crust with a little undiluted molasses. Pour in the molasses mixture and sprinkle the flour mixture on top.

Bake for 40 to 45 minutes, or until set. Remove the pie from the oven and place on a rack to cool.

Serve warm or cold, topping each slice with whipped cream and a dash of cinnamon.

Shoofly Pie

This recipe is molasses cookery at its finest. The Amish communities around Chestertown, Maryland, produce an outstanding molasses-rich shoofly pie. It has a crumbly top with a caramel-like filling underneath, and it is a breeze to make. Be sure the screen windows are in place or the flies will be lighting on your pie.

Serves 8

Grandma's Apple Dumplings

Although these dessert dumplings do bring back memories of Grandma in her kitchen, you don't have to be a grandmother to make them. They are round, mini fruit pies that are baked and basted with a light syrup. Serve them warm, with the pan syrup poured on top and a scoop of vanilla ice cream.

Serves 6

1 cup (firmly packed) brown sugar
1 cup plus 6 teaspoons granulated sugar
Ground cinnamon
Ground nutmeg
12 tablespoons (1½ sticks) butter
3 cups all-purpose flour
1 teaspoon salt
1 tablespoon baking powder
1 cup vegetable shortening
¾ cup milk
6 tart apples, such as Stayman or Jonathan, peeled and cored
Vanilla ice cream or sweetened whipped cream, for accompaniment

Bring the brown sugar, 1 cup granulated sugar, 2 cups water, ½ teaspoon cinnamon, ¼ teaspoon nutmeg, and 6 tablespoons of the butter to a boil in a saucepan, stirring to dissolve the sugar. Cook until the mixture turns into a light syrup, about 10 minutes. Remove from the heat and set aside.

Sift together the flour, salt, and baking powder in a bowl. Work in the shortening with your fingertips or a pastry blender until the mixture is the consistency of coarse meal. Stir in the milk and beat until a fairly stiff dough forms.

Preheat the oven to 375°F. Butter a baking dish large enough to hold the apples comfortably.

Roll out the dough about ¼ inch thick on a lightly floured surface. Cut the dough into six 5-inch squares. Place an apple on each square. Sprinkle each apple with 1 teaspoon granulated sugar and cinnamon and nutmeg to taste. Dot each apple with 1 tablespoon butter. Bring the dough together at the top of the apple and twist to seal. Put the dumplings in the baking dish 1 inch apart. Pour the reserved syrup over the dumplings.

Bake for 35 to 45 minutes, basting often with the syrup until tender when pierced with a knife. Serve warm with vanilla ice cream or sweetened whipped cream.

8 to 10 tart apples, such as York or Stayman, peeled, cored, and sliced
$^1/_2$ cup granulated sugar
Grated zest of 2 lemons
Ground nutmeg and butter, as needed
A bottle of good bourbon whiskey, fitted with a pouring spout
1 cup all-purpose flour
1 teaspoon baking powder
$^1/_4$ teaspoon salt
1 cup rolled oats
1 cup (firmly packed) brown sugar
8 tablespoons (1 stick) butter, softened
1 teaspoon ground nutmeg
1 teaspoon ground cinnamon
Heavy (whipping) cream and vanilla ice cream, for accompaniment

Preheat the oven to 400°F. Butter a 13 × 9 × 2-inch baking pan.

Fill the baking pan with apples. Sprinkle with the granulated sugar, lemon zest, and a little nutmeg. Dot with butter. Drizzle some bourbon over all. Combine the flour, baking powder, salt, rolled oats, brown sugar, 8 tablespoons butter, 1 teaspoon nutmeg, and the cinnamon in a bowl. Mix with your fingertips until crumbly. Pat down on top of apples. Cover with aluminum foil.

Bake for 30 minutes. Uncover and bake for 20 minutes more to brown the top.

Remove from the oven and cut into squares while still warm. Slip into dessert dishes and pour a little heavy cream around, not over, each square. Top each square with a scoop of ice cream, and, if desired, drizzle more bourbon over each portion. Serve immediately.

Bourbon-Apple Crisp

Fruit is not in short supply around the Chesapeake, and all kinds find their way into homemade crisps. Crisps are no-crust crumb pies: a crumbly topping of flour, oats, and brown sugar blankets lightly sweetened fresh fruit. Mr. William Taylor of Hollywood in southern Maryland gives his warm crisps an added punch by drizzling a little Rebel Yell bourbon whiskey over each serving for a true Southern taste.

Serves 12

Peach Cobbler

Cobblers are deep-dish fruit pies with rich biscuit-dough crusts. There are various kinds—apple, cherry, pear, and berry, for example—but the all-time Chesapeake favorite is peach. I don't believe a better summertime dessert can be found than a bowl full of warm peach cobbler topped with a scoop of creamy vanilla ice cream.

Serves 6

3 cups peeled and sliced ripe
    peaches (see page 244)
1 cup plus 3 tablespoons sugar
1¼ cups plus 1½ tablespoons
    all-purpose flour
Salt
2 teaspoons baking powder
1 egg
¾ cup milk
4 tablespoons (½ stick) butter,
    melted
Vanilla ice cream, for
    accompaniment

Preheat the oven to 375°F. Butter an 8-inch square baking dish.

Toss the peaches with 3 tablespoons sugar, 1½ tablespoons flour, and a pinch of salt in a bowl. Pour into the baking dish. Sift together 1¼ cups flour, 1 teaspoon salt, and the baking powder in a bowl. Mix with 1 cup sugar. Beat together the egg, milk, and butter in a large bowl. Stir into the dry ingredients and mix well. Pour over the peaches.

Bake for 40 minutes.

Serve the cobbler warm, topped with vanilla ice cream.

At least 2 pints ripe
    strawberries, hulled
Granulated sugar
2 cups all-purpose flour
1 tablespoon baking powder
$^1/_2$ teaspoon salt
$^1/_8$ teaspoon ground mace
6 tablespoons ($^3/_4$ stick) butter,
    cut into pieces

$^3/_4$ cup milk
1 egg, beaten
Softened butter, for spreading
    on shortcake
Confectioners' sugar, for
    topping
Sweetened lightly whipped
    cream, for accompaniment

Strawberry Shortcake

It's sure not summertime without strawberry shortcake. The sweetened biscuitlike shortcake, enriched with bits of butter rubbed into the flour, is a favorite on Chesapeake dessert plates. There are two types of shortcake. One favors butter over liquid, creating a thick mixture which is rolled out like biscuit dough, cut into small rounds, and baked. The other type, this style, favors milk over butter, making a more cakelike product that still has a soft biscuit texture. This shortcake may be served as a single decorated cake, or it can be cut into individual serving pieces and topped with strawberries and whipped cream.

Serves 8

Preheat the oven to 400°F. Grease and flour a 9-inch cake pan.

Slice most of the strawberries in half, leaving some whole for the top, into a bowl and sprinkle lightly with granulated sugar. Let them sit while making the shortcake.

Sift together the flour, baking powder, salt, 3 tablespoons granulated sugar, and mace in a mixing bowl. Work the butter in with your fingertips until the mixture is the consistency of coarse meal. Mix the milk with the beaten egg. Stir the milk mixture into the dry ingredients to form a smooth dough that pulls away from the sides of the bowl. Roll out the dough on a floured surface into a round to fit the pan and transfer it to the pan.

Bake for 25 to 30 minutes, or until a toothpick inserted in the center comes out clean.

Remove from the oven and cool on a rack.

Turn the cake out of the pan and cut into 2 layers. Butter the layers. Arrange the sweetened strawberries between the layers and on top. Sprinkle the top with confectioners' sugar and serve with whipped cream.

Paca House Snickerdoodles

The Paca House in Annapolis, Maryland, is what remains of the estate of William Paca, a governor of Maryland and signer of the Declaration of Independence. The magnificent house has been restored to its former grandeur, complete with period furniture and formal gardens, and is open for tours. After finishing my Christmastime tour of the historic home, I fell in love with these cookies, and the warm spiced punch, offered in the restored colonial kitchen.

Makes about 5 dozen cookies

8 tablespoons (1 stick) margarine or butter, softened
$^1/_2$ cup vegetable shortening
$1^1/_2$ cups plus 2 tablespoons sugar

2 eggs
1 teaspoon vanilla extract
$2^2/_3$ cups sifted all-purpose flour
2 teaspoons cream of tartar
1 teaspoon baking soda
1 teaspoon ground cinnamon

Preheat the oven to 400°F.

Cream together the margarine and shortening in a large bowl until light. Add the $1^1/_2$ cups sugar and beat until fluffy. Beat in the eggs and vanilla. Sift together the flour, cream of tartar, and baking soda. Add to the margarine mixture. Mix well. Combine the cinnamon and the 2 tablespoons sugar.

With your palms, roll the dough into 1-inch balls. Roll the balls in the cinnamon mixture and arrange 2 inches apart on an ungreased baking sheet.

Bake for 8 to 10 minutes. Remove and cool on racks.

Paca House Christmas Punch   Serves 30 to 40

A warming punch for your holiday entertaining.

4 quarts cranberry juice
4 quarts apple juice
1 quart ginger ale

1 cup fresh lemon juice
1 cup Spiced Tea Concentrate (recipe follows)

Combine all the ingredients in a large saucepan and heat. Serve warm.

¹/₂ pound (2 sticks) butter,
   softened
3 eggs, lightly beaten
1¹/₂ cups maple syrup
3 cups all-purpose flour
1 teaspoon baking powder

¹/₄ teaspoon salt
1 teaspoon baking soda
¹/₂ cup hot water
1 cup chopped black walnuts
1¹/₂ cups dried figs, cut into
   small pieces

Preheat the oven to 350°F.

Cream the butter in a medium bowl and add the eggs and maple syrup. Mix well. Mix the flour, baking powder, and salt in a small bowl. Add the dry ingredients to the butter-egg mixture and mix thoroughly. Put the baking soda in a large cup and slowly add the hot water, stirring all the while. Add to the batter and mix well. Fold in the walnuts and figs. Drop by the teaspoonful onto a lightly greased cookie sheet.

Bake for 10 minutes, or until lightly browned. Transfer to a rack to cool.

Maple-Fig Cookies

To the west of the Chesapeake are the Allegheny Mountains, the source of several Chesapeake tributaries, including the mighty Potomac River. This region is known for high-quality maple syrup. This is a traditional Maryland cookie, richly flavored with the sweet amber syrup. These fruit and nut cookies are perfect for the holiday season. The recipe makes ample numbers, and the cookies store well in an airtight container.

Makes about 5 dozen cookies

Spiced Tea Concentrate Makes 1 cup

1¹/₄ cups boiling water
2 tea bags
2 cinnamon sticks

1 tablespoon allspice berries
1 tablespoon whole cloves

Combine all the ingredients in a saucepan and simmer for 15 minutes. Strain.

Senator Barbara Mikulski's Favorite Krusciki

These cookies are all the rage at Maryland Senator Barbara Mikulski's Inner Harbor office. The senator hails from a long line of Baltimore bakers, and this family recipe for Polish bow-tie cookies is legendary throughout the senator's east Baltimore neighborhood.

Makes about 3 dozen cookies

6 egg yolks
3 tablespoons grated orange zest
1/2 teaspoon salt
1 cup sour cream
3 cups all-purpose flour

1 cup confectioners' sugar, sifted
Vegetable oil, for deep-frying
Confectioners' sugar, for dusting cookies

Beat the egg yolks well in a mixing bowl until pale in color. Add the orange zest, salt, and sour cream. Mix well. Add 2 1/2 cups of the flour and 1 cup confectioners' sugar to the egg mixture. Mix well. Place dough on a floured surface and knead in the remaining 1/2 cup of flour. Divide the dough into quarters. Taking 1 piece at a time, roll it out until fairly thin. Cut the dough into small rectangles and twist in the center to form a bow tie.

Pour oil to a depth of 1 inch in a deep skillet or deep-fryer and heat until very hot, about 375°F. Deep-fry until golden brown. Remove with a slotted utensil to paper towels to drain. Let cool, then sift confectioners' sugar lightly over cookies. Repeat with the remaining dough.

Hominy Custard

The Indians who discovered how to make hominy wouldn't recognize their food staple in this incarnation. This is some good eating—real old-fashioned comfort food.

Serves 6 to 8

1 can (20 ounces) hominy, broken apart with a fork
2 eggs
1/3 cup sugar
2 cups milk

1/3 cup raisins
1 teaspoon vanilla extract
1/4 teaspoon cinnamon
Pinch of salt
Freshly grated nutmeg

Preheat the oven to 350°F. Lightly butter a 2-quart casserole dish.

With a fork, break the hominy apart in a mixing bowl. Beat the eggs with the sugar in a separate bowl until pale in color. Mix in the milk, raisins, vanilla, cinnamon, and salt. Pour into the hominy and mix well. Pour into the dish and dust top with a little grated nutmeg.

Bake for 30 minutes, or until set. Remove from the oven and allow to cool at least 30 minutes. Serve warm or cold.

4 cups half-and-half
4 cups milk
$^2/_3$ cup long-grain white rice
$^1/_2$ teaspoon salt
1 cup raisins
$^1/_2$ cup sugar

3 eggs
2 teaspoons vanilla extract
Ground cinnamon, for topping
Half-and-half or heavy
   (whipping) cream, for
   accompaniment

Bring the half-and-half, milk, rice, and salt to a boil in a saucepan. Reduce the heat and simmer for 30 minutes, stirring frequently. Add the raisins and continue to cook for 15 minutes. Beat together the sugar, eggs, and vanilla in a small bowl. Add to the rice mixture. Bring back to a boil and cook for 1 minute, stirring constantly. Pour into a buttered 3-quart casserole and sprinkle with cinnamon on top. Cool to room temperature. Pudding will thicken as it cools. Serve with half-and-half or cream.

4 tablespoons ($^1/_2$ stick) butter,
   softened
1 cup sugar
1 egg, beaten
4 tart apples, such as York,
   Jonathan, or Granny Smith,
   peeled, cored, and coarsely
   chopped

$^1/_2$ cup walnut pieces
1 teaspoon vanilla extract
1 cup all-purpose flour
1 teaspoon baking soda
1 teaspoon ground cinnamon
Heavy (whipping) cream, for
   accompaniment

Preheat the oven to 350°F. Butter an 8-inch square baking dish.

Cream together the butter and sugar in a large bowl. Add the egg and mix. Stir in the apples, walnuts, and vanilla. Sift together the flour, baking soda, and cinnamon. Add to the apple mixture and stir to combine. Pour into the dish.

Bake for 35 minutes, or until set. Remove from the oven and let stand for at least 20 minutes before serving. Serve warm with a little cream.

Jana's Rice Pudding

Jana Leisenring of east Baltimore and her best girlfriend Rosie worked over at the Domino sugar factory for years. Rice pudding is a must on every Chesapeake tavern menu, and the girls tried out many different versions. They put on a few pounds along the way, but said it was worth it because Jana came up with the perfect recipe.

Serves 6 to 8

Apple and Walnut Pudding

Judy Curtis of Towson, Maryland, serves this pudding as dessert for her Christmas dinner, and finds that her family always comes back for more. When preparing the mixture, don't be surprised to find a thick, un-pudding-like batter; it bakes up into a finely textured custard.

Serves 6

Baked
Apples

Baked apples are often overlooked as a dessert choice. Yet, there's no finer sensation than coming in out of the crisp fall air, hands still chilly from a southwesterly blowing off the Bay, and breathing in the aroma of baking apples touched with spice. They are usually served warm with a touch of cream or ice cream.

Serves 4

4 baking apples, such as York or Rome
3 tablespoons granulated sugar
2 tablespoons brown sugar
4 tablespoons ($^1/_2$ stick) butter, softened
4 teaspoons raisins
$^1/_2$ teaspoon ground cinnamon
Pinch of ground nutmeg
Boiling water
Heavy (whipping) cream or vanilla ice cream, for accompaniment

Preheat the oven to 375°F.

Core each apple, hollowing out the center to form a cavity about $^3/_4$ inch in diameter. In a small bowl mix together the granulated and brown sugar, butter, raisins, cinnamon, and nutmeg. Evenly divide the mixture among the apple cavities. Pour a little boiling water into the bottom of a baking dish large enough to hold the apples snugly. Put the apples in the dish.

Bake, basting the apples several times with the pan juices, for 40 to 45 minutes, or until soft. Serve warm with cream or ice cream.

4 cups dry white wine
1½ cups sugar
1 cinnamon stick
1 teaspoon ground cinnamon
2 teaspoons whole cloves
1 teaspoon vanilla extract

1 lemon, sliced
1 bay leaf
8 firm ripe peaches
Sweet Cream (recipe follows)
Fresh berries or sprigs of mint, for garnish

Combine the wine, sugar, cinnamon stick, ground cinnamon, cloves, vanilla, lemon, and bay leaf in a large pot and bring to a boil. Boil for about 3 minutes. Add the peaches and cover the pot with a light towel or cloth. Reduce the heat and simmer until the peaches are tender, 15 to 20 minutes. Remove the peaches from the liquid with a slotted utensil and set aside in a bowl. Chill the poaching liquid. When it is cold, pour it over the peaches. Cover the bowl holding the peaches with a towel and refrigerate until well chilled.

Before serving, prepare the Sweet Cream and let it cool. Remove the peaches from the liquid and slide off the skins. Pour some of the Sweet Cream onto each of 8 plates or large saucers. Place a peach in the center of each plate. Garnish with berries. Serve with a knife, fork, and spoon.

Sweet Cream Makes about 4 cups

6 egg yolks
1 cup sugar
3 cups half-and-half

½ vanilla bean, split, or 1 teaspoon vanilla extract

Beat together the yolks and sugar in a stainless-steel or enameled pot until the mixture is pale and makes a ribbon. Combine the half-and-half and vanilla in another pot and bring almost to a boil. Whisk the hot milk into the yolk mixture. Cook over low heat, stirring constantly with a wooden spoon. Continue cooking until the mixture becomes heavy, creamlike, and thoroughly coats the back of the spoon. Remove from the heat. If a vanilla bean was used, remove it and scrape the seeds from the bean into the cream.

Cool at room temperature, stirring occasionally. Refrigerate until ready to use.

Poached Peaches on Sweet Cream

This is an elegant dessert of fresh peaches that are poached in spiced wine and served on a bed of slightly thickened sweet cream. As the peaches simmer, take care not to overcook: They should be tender, yet still somewhat firm on serving. The recipe calls for white wine, but a cabernet or zinfandel would also make for a good poaching liquid.

Serves 8

Stewed Fresh Figs in a Warm Marsala Zabaglione

Mealy Sartori, of Little Italy in Baltimore, has grown just about everything in her yard from collard greens to figs. Right next to her backdoor she has a large fig tree growing, and she picks the figs when they are perfectly ripe and plump. In this dish, she briefly stews the figs in a simple sugar syrup and serves them between layers of warm zabaglione, a frothy Italian egg custard that is quickly prepared on the stove top.

Serves 8

¹/₂ cup sugar
¹/₂ cinnamon stick

1¹/₂ pounds ripe figs, stemmed
Zabaglione (recipe follows)

Combine the sugar, 1 cup water, and cinnamon stick in a heavy-bottomed pot, stirring to dissolve the sugar. Bring to a boil. Add the figs, cover, reduce the heat, and simmer slowly until tender, 15 to 20 minutes. With a slotted spoon remove the figs to a bowl. Return the sugar water to high heat and boil until the syrup thickens slightly, about 5 minutes. Slice the figs into quarters lengthwise and return to the bowl, covering with the hot syrup. Allow the figs to cool in the syrup.

Spoon a little of the Zabaglione into 8 wineglasses. Divide the figs among the glasses and top with the remaining sauce.

Zabaglione   Makes about 2 cups

8 egg yolks (save an eggshell
   half for measuring)
¹/₂ cup sugar

8 eggshell halves dry Marsala
   (1 cup)

Select a pot large enough to accommodate a mixing bowl resting in the top. Fill with water and bring to a boil. Reduce the heat to a simmer.

Put the egg yolks and sugar in a large stainless-steel mixing bowl and beat with a wire whisk until pale and creamy. Whisk in the Marsala.

Rest the bowl on top of pot above simmering water. Whisk the mixture vigorously and constantly until it becomes frothy and thickened, about 3 to 5 minutes. Do not overcook or the eggs in the sauce will scramble.

Preserves

and

Pickles

A Chesapeake cook's pantry—well stocked with mason jars of preserves, jams, chutneys and relishes—bears witness to the abundance of fruits and produce from this region. Chesapeake Bay natives learn early in life that in order to enjoy the winter and spring, they must haul out the canning jars, paraffin, and pectin in the summer and fall. This yearly ritual of putting-up has become a rite of passage for Bay homesteaders. Communities come together and pool their efforts, often entering the yield of cooperative gardens in local competitions. Children boast of their grandma's pickles, mother's chow-chow, or father's fig preserves. Often these pickles and preserves are traded back and forth between homes and extended families and find their way into holiday gift packages.

English traditions have heavily influenced the canning recipes of the Bay, resulting in chutney, marmalade, and fruit butters. A colonial technique that packed a punch was to preserve ripe fruit in spiced brandy. In late summer, vines in the Chesapeake are heavy with tomatoes, which are turned into jars of whole tomatoes, batches of homemade ketchup, pickled green tomatoes, and green tomato mincemeat.

Many Chesapeake locals use the process of pickling to create signature relishes to accompany meat and poultry dishes. Pickling transforms simple cabbage into crocks of pungent sauerkraut, grated horseradish root into jars of fiery prepared horseradish, and firm cucumbers into crisp pickles.

Preserving Tips

Various methods are employed in the canning of preserves, jellies, relishes, and the like. When referring to "standard canning procedures," I suggest using a reference cookbook such as *The Fannie Farmer Cookbook* for clear, detailed, and safe instructions. Here are some general guidelines for canning and preserving:

Jars and lids must be clean and sterilized for preserving. Wash the jars in hot suds and rinse in scalding water. Place the hot jars on a jelly-roll pan and place in a preheated 225°F. oven for at least twenty minutes before filling. Or keep them in a saucepan of simmering water and dry them with a clean towel before using. Separate the metal rings from the lids, place the lids in a shallow bowl, and cover with boiling water to soften the rubber seal. Soak for three minutes before using.

Tightly pack ingredients into the hot jars. If adding a liquid, pour to within $1/2$ inch of the top of the jar to allow for expansion of the food when processed. Run a knife between the food and the jar to release air bubbles.

To seal the jars, wipe the rim of each jar with a clean, damp towel and fit with a hot lid. Tightly screw on a metal ring.

Hot-Water Bath Procedure

A hot-water bath destroys microorganisms that cause spoilage. Place the jars, without touching, on a rack or folded dish towels in a deep pot. Add water to cover by 1 inch. Cover the kettle and boil as indicated in the recipe. Taking care not to burn yourself, remove the jars to a cooling rack, and allow to cool completely. When the jars have cooled, check the seal. The lid should be slightly concave in the middle.

A pop or a ping may be heard, but not necessarily. When the jars are completely cool, label them and store in a cool, dry place. You may remove the metal rings.

For more product information and assistance with home canning questions, you may contact:

Alltrista Consumer Products Company
P.O. Box 2729
Muncie, IN 47307-2729
(800) 240-3340

Apple Butter

It may come as some surprise that there is actually no butter in apple butter. The name refers to the smooth consistency of the finished product. A spicy spread made by slowly simmering apples with spices and apple cider, apple butter has been a staple in Chesapeake kitchens for generations. It is a perfect companion to breakfast rolls or warm, buttered toast.

Makes about 5 pint jars

5 pounds tart apples (about 16 medium apples), such as Granny Smith or Stayman
2 cups apple cider
2 cups sugar
2 teaspoons ground cinnamon
1 teaspoon ground cloves
1 teaspoon ground allspice
1/4 cup apple cider vinegar

Cut the apples into quarters. It is not necessary to peel or core them. Place the apples in a heavy-bottomed pot. Pour in the apple cider and enough water to come about halfway up the apples. Cook until the apples are very soft. Press the mixture through a sieve or food mill and return to the pot.

Add the sugar, cinnamon, cloves, allspice, and vinegar. Cook over medium heat, stirring frequently, until thick and smooth, about 10 minutes.

Transfer to pint or half-pint containers and fill to 1/2 inch of the top. Immediately seal the lids according to Preserving Tips (see page 265), and process for 10 minutes according to Hot-Water Bath Procedure (see page 265).

Brandied Peaches

The preserving process used here is called pickling because of the use of vinegar in the cooking solution, but the result is a wonderful peach compote, which will quickly turn a plain bowl of ice cream into a special treat.

Makes about 4 pint jars

5 pounds firm ripe peaches
Boiling water
6 cups sugar
3/4 cup cider vinegar
1 cinnamon stick
1 teaspoon whole cloves
1 cup brandy

Place the peaches in a large pot of boiling water. Let stand for 2 to 3 minutes. Drain and remove the skins and pits. Cut into quarters.

Combine the sugar, vinegar, and 4 cups water in a large heavy pot. Tie the cinnamon stick and cloves in a square of cheesecloth. Add to the pot and bring to a boil. Add the peaches, reduce heat, and cook until just tender, 6 to 8 minutes.

Remove the peaches with a slotted spoon and pack tightly in hot sterilized jars. Add the brandy to the liquid and boil until syrupy, 10 to 15 minutes. Discard the cheesecloth bag. Pour the hot liquid over the peaches to within 1/2 inch of top. Immediately seal the lids according to Preserving Tips (see page 265), and process for 10 minutes according to Hot-Water Bath Procedure (see page 265).

2 tablespoons pickling spices
4 cinnamon sticks
10 cups sugar
2 quarts apple cider vinegar

1 gallon water
8 quarts firm, ripe figs (about
   60 medium figs), washed
   and drained

Place the pickling spices and cinnamon in a piece of cheesecloth and tie into a bag. Dissolve the sugar in the vinegar and 1 gallon of water in a heavy pot and bring to a boil. Add the spice bag to syrup. Continue to cook to form a light syrup, about 20 minutes. Drop the figs into the boiling syrup, reduce the heat, and cook slowly for 20 to 30 minutes, or until easily pierced with a toothpick.

Carefully place the figs in hot sterilized jars, filling about two thirds full. Pour boiling syrup into the jars to within 1/2 inch of the top. Immediately seal the lids according to Preserving Tips (see page 265), and process for 15 minutes according to Hot-Water Bath Procedure (see page 265).

1 gallon prepared watermelon
   rind (see Note)
7 cups sugar

2 cups white vinegar
1/2 teaspoon oil of cinnamon
1/2 teaspoon oil of cloves

Cover the watermelon rind with boiling water and parboil until easily pierced. Drain.

Combine the sugar, vinegar, oil of cinnamon, oil of cloves, and 12 cups water in a heavy saucepan and mix well. Bring to a boil and cook until a light syrup is formed, about 15 to 20 minutes. Pour over rind, but do not place in jars. Cover and leave overnight in a cool spot.

The next day, strain the syrup back into a pot and bring to a boil. Pour the syrup over the rind. Again, do not place in jars. Cover and leave overnight in a cool spot.

The following day, put the rind and syrup in a saucepan and bring to a rolling boil. Remove from the heat and pour into hot sterilized jars to within 1/2 inch of the top. Immediately seal the lids according to Preserving Tips (see page 265), and process for 10 minutes according to Hot-Water Bath Procedure (see page 265).

Note: To prepare the rind, cut off the skin and pink pulp. Cut the rind into whatever size pieces you like.

Sweet Pickled Figs

Outside the Biddlecomb waterside home in Reedville, Virginia, there are two massive fig trees that produce enough plump, juicy figs to keep the entire family supplied. The figs are cooked in a sweet pickling solution and packed in the syrup. Makes about 8 quarts or 16 pint jars

Pickled Watermelon Rind

Beverley Biddlecomb of Reedville, Virginia, prepares jars and jars of these preserved watermelon rinds every year. It's a good thing, too, for I have watched members of her family snack on these sweet treats, and the jars empty fast. Oil of cinnamon and oil of cloves are available at drugstores and specialty food stores.

Makes about 6 pint jars

Green Tomato Mincemeat

*O*riginally prepared with small bits of beef, most mincemeat today is made solely with fruit and spices. This recipe includes beef suet, which is a traditional flavoring in mincemeat and gives it its amazing richness.

To make a 9-inch pie, use one pint of mincemeat mixed with two cups of diced apples, and bake in a flaky pastry crust.

Makes about 6 pint jars

4 quarts green tomatoes (about 30 medium tomatoes), cut into chunks
3 cups granulated sugar
2 cups (firmly packed) brown sugar
3 cups raisins
2 teaspoons salt
1 cup cider vinegar

$^{1}/_{2}$ cup chopped beef suet (optional)
2 teaspoons ground cloves
$^{1}/_{2}$ teaspoon ground ginger
$1^{1}/_{2}$ tablespoons ground cinnamon
1 teaspoon ground nutmeg
$^{1}/_{2}$ teaspoon ground mace

Put the tomatoes in a large heavy enameled or stainless-steel pot and add water to cover. Bring to a boil and drain. Repeat. Add the granulated and brown sugar, raisins, salt, vinegar, and suet, if using. Bring to a boil, stirring frequently. Reduce the heat and simmer, stirring often, until mixture becomes as thick as commercial mincemeat, about 15 minutes. When almost finished cooking, add all the remaining ingredients.

Pack in hot sterilized jars to within 1 inch of the top. Immediately seal the lids according to Preserving Tips (see page 265), and process for 25 minutes according to Hot-Water Bath Procedure (see page 265).

Green Tomato and Apple Chutney

*T*his spicy condiment pairs two of the Chesapeake's star ingredients: apples and green tomatoes. Green tomatoes, a unique ingredient in chutney, add a pleasant flavor and texture. It is delicious on breads, biscuits, or rolls with cheese.

Makes about 6 pint jars

4 cups chopped green tomatoes (about 8 medium tomatoes)
Salt
3 cups cider vinegar
1 cup fresh lemon juice
$2^{1}/_{2}$ cups granulated sugar
$2^{1}/_{2}$ cups (firmly packed) dark brown sugar
8 cups chopped peeled and cored tart apples (about 10 medium apples)

$^{1}/_{2}$ cup chopped fresh ginger or 3 tablespoons ground ginger
1 pound raisins
1 teaspoon cayenne
2 onions, chopped
1 green bell pepper, seeded and chopped
1 red bell pepper, seeded and chopped

Place the tomatoes in a colander and sprinkle with 2 tablespoons salt. Let stand overnight. Combine the vinegar, lemon juice, and granulated and brown sugar in a large heavy enameled or stainless-steel pot and bring to a boil. Add the tomatoes, 2 teaspoons salt, and all the remaining ingredients. Bring to a boil, reduce the heat, and simmer until thick, about $1^{1}/_{2}$ hours.

Pack in hot sterilized jars to within $^1/_2$ inch of the top. Immediately seal the lids according to Preserving Tips (see page 265), and process for 10 minutes according to Hot-Water Bath Procedure (see page 265).

El's Tomato Ketchup

4 quarts ripe tomatoes (about 24 large tomatoes), peeled, cored, and chopped
1 cup chopped onion
$^1/_2$ cup chopped red bell pepper
$1^1/_2$ teaspoons celery seed
1 teaspoon dry mustard
1 teaspoon ground allspice
1 cinnamon stick
1 cup sugar
1 tablespoon salt
$1^1/_2$ cups white vinegar
1 tablespoon paprika

Combine the tomatoes, onion, and pepper in a large heavy enameled or stainless-steel pot and cook over medium heat until soft. Press through a food mill or sieve. Return the mixture to the pot, add the remaining ingredients, and bring to a boil, stirring often. Reduce the heat and cook slowly, stirring frequently, until thickened, about 30 minutes. Remove the cinnamon stick and discard.

Ladle hot ketchup into hot sterilized jars to within $^1/_2$ inch of the top. Immediately seal the lids according to Preserving Tips (see page 265), and process for 10 minutes according to Hot-Water Bath Procedure (see page 265).

El Farace of Parkville, Maryland, is a spectacular cook, one not disposed to the run-of-the-mill. And that's how she feels about ordinary mass-produced ketchup. Here is her recipe for homemade ketchup, a welcome change with a fresh tomato flavor accented with cinnamon and sweet red bell peppers. It's so good, you'll want to eat it right out of the jar.

Makes about 4 pint jars

Bread and Butter Pickles

These sliced pickles are an old-fashioned treat that still grace tables and pantries around the Chesapeake. Simple to prepare, the pickles have a pleasant sweet-and-sour flavor.

Makes about 7 pint jars

4 pounds cucumbers (4 to 6 inches)
7 small onions
Salted ice water
3 cups white or cider vinegar
2½ cups sugar
½ cup salt
2 teaspoons celery seed
2 teaspoons mustard seed
½ teaspoon ground turmeric
½ teaspoon whole cloves
1 teaspoon ground ginger

Thinly slice the cucumbers and onions. Place in a bowl with salted ice water to cover and let stand for 3 to 4 hours.

Bring all the remaining ingredients and 2½ cups of water to a boil in a large heavy enameled or stainless-steel pot. Drain the cucumbers and onions, add to the pot, and bring back to a boil. Reduce the heat and simmer for 10 minutes.

Spoon the hot mixture into hot sterilized jars to within ½ inch of the top. Immediately seal the lids according to Preserving Tips (see page 265), and process for 10 minutes according to Hot-Water Bath Procedure (see page 265).

The Smell of Money

Around the bend of the Virginia Northern Neck of the Potomac River you'll find one of the most delightful small towns on the Chesapeake Bay: Reedville, Virginia. Now a quiet fishing village, in its heyday in the mid-1800s it was quite the boomtown as a major Chesapeake seafood processing center. During those heady times, Reedville boasted the highest per-capita income in the United States. All that prosperity accounts for the lovely Victorian homes that line Main Street, which runs down the center of town and ends at the water's edge. Walt Disney could have filmed a Hayley Mills–type picture there—it is *that* cute. I've met some outstanding cooks from the Reedville area and their kitchen skills make their fabulously fresh seafood, game, and local produce shine.

Reedville is not only a destination for tourists seeking relaxation in the beautifully restored bed and breakfast homes, but it is still a major seafood center as home to menhaden processing plants (menhaden is a small, bony fish that is not eaten, but used for oil products and as a fertilizer). These processing plants sometimes produce a fishy odor that wafts across the town, but the locals don't seem to mind—they refer to the distinctive fragrance that arises from processing the highly profitable menhaden as "the smell of money."

12 ears of corn
6 red bell peppers
6 green bell peppers
1 bunch of celery
4 onions
1 medium head cabbage

1 quart cider vinegar
3 cups sugar
2 tablespoons salt
2 teaspoons mustard seed
2 teaspoons celery seed

Cut the kernels from the corn cobs. Chop the peppers, celery, onions, and cabbage into $1/8$-inch pieces. Place all the vegetables in a pot, cover with water, and bring to a boil. Drain and return the vegetables to the pot. Add all the remaining ingredients and bring to a boil. Reduce the heat and simmer for 30 minutes, stirring occasionally. Remove from the heat and cool.

Spoon into hot sterilized jars to within $1/2$ inch of the top. Immediately seal the lids according to Preserving Tips (see page 265), and process for 15 minutes according to Hot-Water Bath Procedure (see page 265).

Corn and Pepper Relish

This simple-to-prepare condiment is a perfect accompaniment to chicken or seafood fritters, oysters on the half shell, and sliced roasts and country hams.

Makes about 8 pint jars

Horseradish, Bay Style

Freshly grated horseradish root is used as a pungent condiment with sliced pork, beef, and ham. It can be added to sour cream to make a bold sauce that sets the eyes to tearing.

More common is the processed variety in which the grated root is preserved in vinegar. Baltimore, Maryland, is known as the horseradish-processing capital of the East Coast, with its local brands enjoying a reputation as the very best. Prepared horseradish is widely used with seafood and beef, and it adds zest to composed sauces or corned beef sandwiches.

Peel 1 to 2 pounds of horseradish root and cover with cold water. Squeeze a lemon into the water and let the horseradish soak for about 30 minutes. This will keep it from turning brown.

Drain off the water and chop the horseradish very fine in a food processor. Spoon the horseradish into half-pint glass jars two-thirds full and top each with 1 teaspoon of salt. Pour distilled white vinegar, or half white and half cider vinegar, into the jars to cover the horseradish completely. Screw on caps, let cool at room temperature, and refrigerate.

A Chesapeake Bay
Resource Guide

Environmental

Listed below are two of the many organizations that exist to preserve and protect the Chesapeake Bay. Get involved with one of these, or contact them to find out what other possibilities there may be. A web site address is listed if the organization has information available on the World Wide Web.

Alliance for the Chesapeake Bay
P.O. Box 1981
Richmond, VA 23218
(800) 662-CRIS
http://www.gmu.edu/bios/Bay/acb

"The Alliance for the Chesapeake Bay strives to build, to maintain, and to serve the partnership among the general public, the private sector, and government that is essential for establishing and sustaining policy, programs and the political will to preserve and restore the resources of the Chesapeake Bay." If you are able, be sure to visit their web site. It is full of interesting and essential information.

Chesapeake Bay Foundation
162 Prince George St.
Annapolis, MD 21401
(410) 268-8816
http://www.savethebay.cbf.org

An excellent grassroots-type organization with which I'm personally involved. The Chesapeake Bay Foundation endeavors not only to reverse the damage already inflicted on the Bay, but also to initiate ecological guidelines to preserve the Chesapeake for future generations.

Food

⌒⌒⌒⌒

Below are some places where you can order Chesapeake foods for shipment—this list is not exhaustive by any means. If ordering over the World Wide Web is a possibility, the web site address of the company is also listed.

Basse's Choice
Smithfield, VA
(800) 292-2773
http://www.smithfieldham.com

Purveyors of the world-famous Gwaltney Genuine Smithfield Ham, Basse's Choice offers many other gourmet food products that can be ordered and shipped. Their web address is misleading, but the site is a pleasure to visit: a veritable grocery store on your computer and easy to navigate.

Café Metropol
1713 N. Charles St.
Baltimore, MD 21201
(410) 385-3018

The women at Café Metropol will house-smoke and ship just about anything for you, including their specialty, Chesapeake rockfish.

Faidley's Seafood
Lexington Market
200 N. Paca St.
Baltimore, MD 21202
(410) 727-4898

Faidley's is well known in Baltimore for its excellent selection of seafood. Faidley's will air-freight crabmeat, crab cakes, steamed crabs, and seafood soups and gumbos, plus an array of fresh, in-season Chesapeake seafood. If you're shopping there in person, take some time to explore the rest of the lively historic market where its located.

John T. Handy Company
P.O. Box 309
Crisfield, MD 21817
(800) 426-3977
(410) 968-1772

The largest producer of soft-shell crabs in the world, the Handy Company will air-freight them in all shapes and sizes. If you get a busy signal on their tollfree phone line, it's probably because you're calling in the summer. Try the other number—the experience of Handy's soft-shells are well worth the cost of a phone call.

J. O. Seasoning
J. O. Spice Company
3721-25 Old Georgetown Rd.
Baltimore, MD 21227
(800) 537-5714

J. O. Spice has an excellent line of Chesapeake products ranging from traditional blends of seafood seasoning to mixes for crabcakes, shrimp seasoning, and assorted Chesapeake-style sauces.

Manning's Hominy
Lake Packing Co.
Box 200
Lottsburg, VA 22511
(804) 529-6101

Call these folks when you need your fix of hominy. They are the producers of Manning's Hominy, a canned pearl hominy.

Nick's Inner Harbor Seafood
Cross Street Market
265 Cross St.
Baltimore, MD 21230
(410) 685-2020

You can't go wrong ordering from Nick's. Staffed by congenial and extremely seafood-knowledgeable employees, Nick's will air-freight their steamed crabs, crab cakes, and soft-shells, plus a tremendous assortment of locally caught shellfish and fish. Be sure to stop by if you're in town and sit with a crowd of Baltimore locals at the bar, where you can enjoy freshly shucked oysters or hot steamed crabs washed down with a cold beer.

Old Bay Seasoning
P.O. Box 1802
Baltimore, MD 21203
(800) 632-5847

Yes, the seemingly ubiquitous Chesapeake seasoning may be ordered direct if you can't find it on your local supermarket shelves.

Smithfield Farms
1801 S. Church St.
P.O. Box 639
Smithfield, VA 23430
(804) 357-2145
http://www.itribe.net/smithfield1

Smithfield Farms of Virginia will ship any item from their selection of Smithfield hams, cured hams, smoked turkeys, and sausages. The employees are charming, very polite, accommodating, and eager to answer your questions, as only Southern folks can be.

Tourism

Maryland and Virginia both have excellent resources available for the prospective visitor and residents. They also keep updated listings of current events and activities that take place around the Chesapeake Bay. Below are first stops on the road of travel—be sure to visit their web sites if you can.

Maryland Travel & Tourism
Maryland Office of Tourism
217 E. Redwood St.
Baltimore, MD 21202
Out of state: (800) MD-IS-FUN (634-7386)
In state: (410) 767-3400
http://www.mdisfun.org

Virginia Travel & Tourism
Virginia Division of Tourism
901 E. Byrd St.
Richmond, VA 23219
Attractions & Points of Interest: (800) VISIT-VA (847-4882)
State Parks & Camping Info: (800) 933-PARK (933-7275)
http://www.virginia.org

Tastes of the Chesapeake Festivals

~~~~~

Throughout the year the folks of the Chesapeake are getting together, enjoying each other's company, and celebrating their community's heritage and the bounties of the Bay. In case you didn't know, Chesapeakans love to party. There are so many yearly events taking place that to enjoy them all, I'd have to sell my home, rent a Winnebago, and hit the road traveling nonstop from one to the next. Though that's not a bad idea, for now I've included a number of typical Chesapeake Bay events to whet your appetite. Maybe I'll see you at a few. Dates and locations of festivals often change from year to year. For updated specifics on events of interest, call:

Maryland Office of Tourism: 800-MD-IS-FUN (634-7386) or
Virginia Division of Tourism: 800-VISIT-VA (847-4882)

April

Nanticoke River Shad Festival is held in late April along the shore of the Nanticoke River in the town park of Vienna, Maryland. Shad planking, exhibits, folk music, and a canoe race take place, with proceeds funding shad restoration on the Nanticoke River.

International Azalea Festival in Norfolk, Virginia, is a week-long celebration acknowledging Norfolk's role as headquarters for the North Atlantic Treaty Organization (NATO). It's the oldest festival in the region, and a favorite of the military community that it honors.

May

Preakness Week Celebration and Race is *the* party of Baltimore, Maryland. A week-long celebration precedes the second jewel in horse racing's Triple Crown. Events include crab races, music, food, a parade, neighborhood parties, and even a frog hop in historic Fell's Point.

Chestertown Tea Party Festival is a reenactment of the Chestertown Tea Party, which took place May 23, 1774, one year after the one in Boston. It takes place in the historic district of Chestertown, Maryland, with food, a parade, and entertainment.

Crisfield Soft-Shell Spring Fair happens in late May in Crisfield, Maryland, at the town dock. A soft-shell crab cooking contest, entertainment, crafts, food, games, and tours are all part of the event.

June

Harborfest in Norfolk, Virginia, is a three-day whirlwind of activity, with more than 250,000 people attending this annual waterfront celebration, which began in 1976. The star of the annual East Coast waterfront spectaculars, Harborfest is a nonstop flurry of live entertainment, sailing ships, water and air shows, more food than you could possibly sample in a weekend, and the most singular display of fireworks you'll witness all year.

Delmarva Chicken Festival, almost a half century old, is held each spring on the strip of land that separates the Chesapeake Bay from the Atlantic Ocean, the Delmarva peninsula. Poultry is king on the Delmarva, which is one of the largest poultry-producing regions in the country. Events include carnival rides, an egg toss, a spoon race, and a chicken cook-off in the festival's very own giant frying pan that can cook eight hundred chicken quarters at one time. Date and location change each year so call ahead to the Maryland Office of Tourism.

July

Country Festival at Sailwinds Park, held in early July in Cambridge, Maryland, is an old-time country fair with a carnival, parade, Princess Neptune pageant, live bands, cooking and lumberjack contests, water sport demos, and traditional Eastern Shore food.

J. Millard Tawes Crab and Clam Bake is going full steam in mid-July at Somers Cove Marina, in Crisfield, Maryland, with all-you-can-eat steamed crabs, clams, fish, corn, and watermelon.

Chincoteague Pony Penning and Auction, a world-famous event, takes place in late July on Chincoteague Island, Virginia, where wild ponies from Assateague Island are rounded up by local firemen and herded across a narrow channel to Chincoteague, where they are auctioned. A gigantic carnival, entertainment, and local seafood are all part of the event.

August

Cheseapeake Bay Maritime Museum Crabfest is held in early August in St. Michaels, Maryland. It features crabbing demonstrations, crabs to eat, kids' activities, live music, skipjack rides, and more.

September

River Rib Fest in Norfolk, Virginia, is a fierce barbecue cook-off, accompanied by foot-tapping music all weekend long. The festival is fun for the entire family, especially the ever-popular Spam carving contest. And don't miss the Town Point Clogging Classic that is held at the same time, same place.

National Hard Crab Derby and Fair, one of the Chesapeake's best known festivals, takes place on Labor Day weekend at Somers Cove Marina in Crisfield, Maryland. Highlights include the National Hard Crab Derby crab race, the Miss Crustacean Beauty pageant, a parade, Governor's Cup crab race, crab cooking, crab picking contests, and entertainment.

Skipjack Race and Festival, also held on Labor Day weekend, happens on and around Deal Island, Maryland, not very far from the Crab Derby in Crisfield. The skipjack race is quite a spectacular sight to behold, featuring the impressive sail-powered workboats of the Chesapeake Bay.

October

Chesapeake Appreciation Day at Sandy Point State Park in Maryland, held each October, celebrates the Bay on the waterfront in the shadow of the Chesapeake Bay Bridge. Along with lots of food and entertainment, there is the Crab Soup Cook-Off, which attracts the top restaurants in the area and benefits the Chesapeake Bay Foundation.

St. Mary's County Oyster Festival, the premier oyster celebration in Maryland, takes place in mid-October. It is home of the National Oyster Shucking Championship and the National Oyster Cook-Off. Bushels and bushels to eat with continuous entertainment.

Chincoteague Oyster Festival, held in mid-October in Chincoteague, Virginia, celebrates the world-famous oyster of the same name, with oysters served stewed, fried, frittered, and on the half shell.

St. Mary's Annual Turkey and Ham Dinner has been going on for over half a century at St. Mary's Church in Barnesville, Maryland. It features country hams, roast turkey, crafts, baked goods, canned goods, cider, and old-fashioned hayrides.

November

The first-class *Urbana Oyster Festival,* held in the beginning of November in Urbana, Virginia, brings oyster lovers from all across the country. Highlights are an oyster cook-off, shucking competitions, food stands, and entertainment.

Chesapeake Bay Maritime Oysterfest in St. Michaels, Maryland, is the maritime museum's fall food fest, celebrating the Chesapeake oyster. There are oystering demonstrations, raw and cooked oysters, kids' activities, and live music.

Waterfowl Festival, held at the beginning of November in Easton, Maryland, is the premier wildlife art show and sale of the Chesapeake region. It boasts five hundred exhibitors, auction, demonstrations, seminars, and calling contests.

Food and Feasts in Seventeenth-Century Virginia, held at the end of November, takes place in the restored Jamestown settlement, as well as in the authentic colonial setting of Williamsburg, Virginia. It is a food extravaganza featuring the colonial cuisine of Tidewater Virginia.

December

Christmas at the William Paca House and Gardens in Annapolis, Maryland, showcases the meticulously restored eighteenth-century home of William Paca, signer of the Declaration of Independence. The home is impressively festive, adorned with the decorations of colonial times. Guided tours, as well as special events, are offered throughout the holiday season.

Candlelight Pub Crawl in Annapolis, Maryland, is a seasonal feast of food and revelry. It combines a festive atmosphere with candlelight walks through the historic streets of Annapolis, and group tours may be scheduled during the entire Christmas season. Call the Maryland Office of Tourism for details.

World Wide Web

The following is a very small sample of the many resources pertaining to the Chesapeake Bay that are available on the Internet. Some of the web sites are fun, and some are boring, but they all provide useful information. Use this list as a springboard toward your own discovery of the Bay.

Chesapeake Bay Cooking with John Shields
http://www.johnshields.com

This is my web site, of course. Keep abreast of my current projects, see if I'll be cooking in your local area soon, or discover some more exciting recipes of mine, which I couldn't squeeze into this book. I have even included links to other web sites to help you find lots of essential Chesapeake information.

The "Complete" Chesapeake Bay Information Link List
http://www.cbl.cees.edu/~gottlieb/Chesapeake.html

The title doesn't lie: This site is a very comprehensive source of Chesapeake Bay information available on the Internet. The extensive list is simply and clearly organized into logical categories to aid your search.

Chesapeake Bay Maritime Museum
http://www.cbmm.org

This site will tell you everything you ever wanted to know about the museum in St. Michaels, Maryland. Unfortunately for non-Chesapeake folks, it cannot substitute for an actual visit to this fascinating museum.

Capt'n W on the Chesapeake Bay
http://www.captnw.com

Want a taste of the Chesapeake? This site lets you sample the flavor of the Bay by way of local personalities. There's a slight leaning toward nautical subjects, naturally, but it's fun, not at all pretentious, and covers subjects ranging from crabs and beer to the weather. Discover for yourself the local color of the Chesapeake.

Baltimore on the WWW
http://www.baltimore.com

Yes, hon, there really is a Baltimore on the WWW. The creators claim, "Your one source for WWW information related to, from, or about Baltimore. If it has anything to do with Baltimore, and it's on the WWW, you'll find it here!" This is my personal favorite, but then I'm from Baltimore. Visit and learn more about Charm City.

Maryland's Eastern Shore and Chesapeake Bay Home Page
http://www.covesoft.com/Eastern

An excellent web site full of information about places to visit and stay around the Bay, with an emphasis on the beautiful and tranquil Eastern Shore.

Virginia's Chesapeake Bay
http://www.insiders.com/chesapeake-va/index.htm

A valuable, if not exhaustive, resource for parts of the Chesapeake Bay, including Virginia Beach, Norfolk, Portsmouth, Chesapeake, Suffolk, and the Eastern Shore. Visit here to research a wide range of topics, from restaurants and hospitals, to real estate and annual events.

Maryland's Mid-Atlantic Coast Region
http://www.atbeach.com/beachmd.html

This site covers territory from Ocean City to Salisbury, Maryland, with lots of tourism information.

Bibliography

The American Heritage Cookbook. American Heritage Publishing Co., 1964.

Andrews, Mrs. Lewis R., and Mrs. J. Reany. *Maryland's Way.* Annapolis: Hammond-Harwood House Association, 1978.

Beard, James. *James Beard's American Cookery.* Boston: Little, Brown & Co., 1972.

————. *James Beard's New Fish Cookery.* Boston: Little, Brown & Co., 1976.

Cameron, Angus, and Judith Jones. *The L.L. Bean Game and Fish Cookbook.* New York: Random House, 1983.

Cunningham, Marion. *The Fannie Farmer Baking Book.* New York: Alfred A. Knopf, 1984.

Dubroff, Rich. *How Was the Game?* Baltimore: Diamond Publishing Co., 1994.

Farmer, Fannie Merritt. *The Boston Cooking School Cookbook.* Boston: Little, Brown & Co., 1928.

Foley, Joan, and Joe Foley. *The Chesapeake Bay Fish and Fowl Cookbook.* New York: Macmillan, 1981.

From a Lighthouse Window. St. Michaels: Chesapeake Bay Maritime Museum, 1989.

Glenn, Camille. *The Heritage of Southern Cooking.* New York: Workman Publishing Co., 1986.

Herbst, Sharon Tyler. *Food Lover's Companion.* New York: Barron's Educational Series, 1995.

Hopkins, John Root. *Muskrat Cookin'.* Cambridge, Maryland: Lee Creek Enterprises, 1996.

Humphrey, Theodore, and Lin Humphrey. *We Gather Together.* Ann Arbor: UMI Research Press, 1988.

Kitching, Frances, and Susan Stiles Dowell. *Mrs. Kitching's Smith Island Cookbook.* Centerville, Maryland: Tidewater Press, 1981.

Michener, James A. *Chesapeake.* New York: Random House, 1978.

Riely, Elizabeth. *The Chef's Companion.* New York: Van Nostrand Reinhold, 1986.

Sokolov, Raymond. *Fading Feast.* New York: Farrar, Straus, Giroux, 1979.

Stieff, Frederick Philips. *Eat, Drink and Be Merry in Maryland.* New York: G. P. Putnam's Sons, 1932.

Warner, William. *Beautiful Swimmers.* Boston: Little, Brown & Co., 1976.

Index